Object-oriented Matrix Programming using Ox

Jurgen A. Doornik

INTERNATIONAL THOMSON BUSINESS PRESS
I ⓣ P An International Thomson Publishing Company

London • Bonn • Boston • Johannesburg • Madrid • Melbourne • Mexico City • New York • Paris
Singapore • Tokyo • Toronto • Albany, NY • Belmont, CA • Cincinnati, OH • Detroit, MI

Object-oriented Matrix Programming using Ox

Copyright © 1996 Jurgen A. Doornik
First published 1996 by International Thomson Business Press

I ⓣ P   A division of International Thomson Publishing Inc.
        The ITP logo is a trademark under licence

British Library Cataloguing-in-Publication Data
A catalogue record for this book is available from the British Library

Library of Congress Cataloging-in-Publication Data
A catalog record for this book is available from the Library of Congress

First edition 1996

Printed in the UK by Clays Ltd, St Ives plc

ISBN 1-86152-056-5

International Thomson Business Press   International Thomson Business Press
Berkshire House   20 Park Plaza
High Holborn   14th Floor
London WCIV 7AA   Boston MA 02116
UK   USA

http://www.itbp.com

Object-oriented Matrix Programming using Ox

Contents

Figures

Tables

Listings

Preface

My interest in computer languages was awakened by reading a short book on compiler building written by Niklaus Wirth (see Wirth, 1987). The first opportunity to dabble in this field was the design and implementation of the algebra language in PcGive 7 (also used in later versions). The result was a tiny vector language, not very efficient, but it worked. My ambition was to write a more powerful language, to leverage the growing body of computational code. The next attempt took a few weeks at the end of 1992. It did not lead to a useful program, but the experience helped in the third and serious attempt: Ox. That project was started in April 1994, just after completing version 8 of PcGive. The aim was to use it for the simulations required for my doctoral thesis. Having done most of my programming of recent years in C, I was not pleased with the syntax of the matrix languages I tried. By November I had a preliminary version. It had a database and PcFiml class, and I could use it for my simulations. The Ox library gradually expanded, but my thesis had a higher priority. In the summer of 1995, there was a veritable explosion in the number of users: both Neil Shephard and Richard Spady started to use Ox. That helped push Ox towards its current form: two enthousiastic and demanding users. Now Ox runs under Linux and on the Alpha, and yes: you can call all the underlying C functions, or create extension DLL's with e.g. the QuadPack integration routines. And there are beta random numbers and QQ-plots, etc.

The origin of the name Ox is a bit vague. It is the first and last letter of Object-oriented matrix. I compared the program to an ox: a solid work animal but quite slow. In the mean time, however, Ox became a lot faster, to the point where it is even beating native C and Fortran programs. There is a also resemblance to the city where I work. Finally, the combination of Ox and the C language gives a powerful result.

Of course, there is still much to be added to Ox, and development will continue. The main entries on the to do list are 3D graphics and an integrated environment for development and debugging. These have to wait a little, while other activities get priorites. Please don't stop sending suggestions for improvements and entries for the How To chapter. Contact me if you need Ox on a platform which is currently not supported. My work page at http://www.nuff.ox.ac.uk/Users/Doornik/ will be regularly updated with pointers to relevant Ox information.

Clearly, I wish to thank Neil Shephard and Richard Spady for adopting Ox early on, and their many comments and suggestions. Also to their students, who were encouraged to use Ox and gave feedback. By now, many more people have downloaded Ox, and

and given it a try, among these Francisco Cribari-Neto deserves special thanks. Please keep sending comments. I thank David Hendry for continuing support for this project, and also wish to thank Maureen Baker, Mark Lawton, Aurora Manrique and Nuffield College.

As the proverbial last but not least, I thank Kate Dewhurst, whom I must have bored at times with Ox statements.

Nuffield College, June 1996

We wish you enjoyable and productive use of

Ox

Chapter 1

Prologue

1.1 Which Ox version?

Under Windows there are three options for running your Ox source code:

- oxlw.exe: 32-bit Windows command line,
- oxl.exe: MS-DOS command line,
- oxrun.exe: Windows dialog.

These programs run on the following platforms:

- oxlw.exe: Win95/WinNT, in an MS-DOS window,
- oxl.exe: Win 3.1/Win95/WinNT, in an MS-DOS window,
- oxrun.exe: Win 3.1/Win95/WinNT.

Oxlw.exe is the fastest and can handle long file names. Output appears on the console. The simplest way to get the produced results into a file is to redirect the output (e.g. oxlw test.ox > t). Oxlw can create and save graphs (but cannot display them).

OxRun interacts with *GiveWin*: text output and graphics appear in *GiveWin* windows (where you can edit graphs, e.g. draw lines or add text, move legends, add regression lines, etc.; graphs can also be cut and pasted into other applications).

The windows versions (oxlw and oxrun) can be extended using DLL libraries.

Oxl.exe is the MS-DOS console version (32-bit, using a DOS-extender). It can display graphs (but not very well, it might be required to switch back to text mode using the mode CO80 command). It does not support long file names nor DLLs. It is somewhat slower than oxlw.

The Windows version is the preferred version, but is only available for a fee. The MS-DOS and Unix versions are available free of charge for educational and research purposes, see availability below.

1

1.2 Availability

The MS-DOS and Unix version of Ox can be downloaded from:

http://www.nuff.ox.ac.uk/Users/Doornik/

Please see the readme.ox file before installation. The Windows version is available, together with *GiveWin*, from International Thomson Business Press. The address is on the copyright page of this book.

1.3 Other platforms

Ox is currently available on Windows, MS-DOS, Linux for PC, and for HP, SGI and Sun workstations. If you need Ox on other platforms, contact the author.

1.4 Ox is fast

Ox is faster than most other matrix programming languages; some benchmarks are in:
http://www.nuff.ox.ac.uk/Users/Doornik/bench.html.

1.5 Ox supported data formats

Ox can read (and write) the following data files directly into a matrix:

- .mat (ASCII matrix file),
- .dat (ASCII data file with load information),
- .in7 (PcGive 7 data file, with data in .bn7 file),
- .xls (Excel version 4 spread sheet file),
- .wks/.wk1 (Lotus spread sheet file),
- .dht (Gauss data file, with data in .dat file),
- .fmt (Gauss matrix file).

In addition, there are text and binary functions for reading and writing.

1.6 Ox for windows

Under Windows, Ox can be extended. The documentation provides examples of what you can do:

- Make extensions to Ox in e.g. C/C++ or Fortran, and put that in a DLL; such functions are then callable from Ox code.

- Use Ox as a mathematics library (e.g. if you are programming in C/C++ but do not want to program in Ox; or to call functions such as Choleski decomposition or a random number generator in your Ox extension DLL).
- Write an interface wrapper around Ox code.

Using *OxRun*, Ox can use *GiveWin* as a front-end, which holds databases, and receives text and graphical output from Ox (and also other modules such as PcGive, and soon STAMP and PcFiml).

1.7 World Wide Web

Check `http://www.nuff.ox.ac.uk/Users/Doornik/` for information on bugs, bug fixes, new features, benchmarks and other information relevant to Ox.

1.8 Online documentation

The Ox help system is implemented as a set of HTML pages which can be read with an internet browser. The file `\ox\docs\ox.html` has a link to the original documentation. If you have a slow link, or are not connected to the internet, you can put a copy of the HTML documentation on your machine, and read it that way.

1.9 Ox version

This documentation refers to version 1.10. It is likely that functions and packages will be added. Check the WWW address given above. For the Windows version, intermediate upgrades will involve replacing `oxwin.dll` and perhaps `oxstd.h`.

Chapter 2

Installation

2.1 Basic installation

All versions of Ox require files which are in the basic installation. To install the basic version:

- copy `oxbas110.zip` and `unzip.exe` to the directory from which you wish to install Ox. Normally that is the root directory of the C or D drive.
- type[1] `unzip oxbas110.zip` which will unzip the archive, creating a subdirectory called `ox` and relevant subdirectories in which the files are put.[2]
- Delete `oxbas110.zip` and `unzip.exe` if you wish.

2.2 Ox for Windows

The Windows components of Ox are included with GiveWin. When GiveWin is set up with the menu driven installation program, these components will be installed automatically.

Note that the basic installation is still required. Make sure that the basic and Windows installation use the same `ox\bin` directory.

2.3 Ox for other platforms

For other versions, manual installation is required: Ox is packaged in various zip files, which can be unzipped using the provided *unzip* program (or with `pkunzip`). The files for downloading are (the 110 in the name is the version number, which could be higher):

---

[1]If you use `pkunzip`, type `pkunzip -d oxbas110.zip` to unpack the directory structure.

[2]Ox is packaged using Info-ZIP's compression utility. The installation uses UnZip to read the zip files. Info-ZIP's software (Zip, UnZip and related utilities) is free and can be obtained as source code or executables from various bulletin board services and anonymous-ftp sites, including CompuServe's IBMPRO forum and `ftp.uu.net:/pub/archiving/zip/*`.

oxbas110.zip	–	Ox headers, source and samples, HTML documentation, MS-DOS executable. This file is required by all installations.
oxlnx110.zip	–	Linux (i386) executables and libraries,
oxsun110.zip	–	SunOS executables and libraries,
oxsol110.zip	–	Sularis executables and libraries,
oxhp110.zip	–	HP-UX executables and libraries,
oxsgi110.zip	–	SGI (Irix) executables and libraries.

The files mentioned here can be downloaded, see §1.7. The readme.ox file has installation instructions. When unzipping these files, make sure you extract with the directories (e.g. use pkunzip -d oxbas110.zip); when using ftp for downloading, use binary transfer.

NO WARRANTY WHATSOEVER IS GIVEN FOR THESE PROGRAMS. YOU USE THEM AT YOUR OWN RISK!

All company and product names referred to in this book are either trademarks or registered trademarks of their associated companies.

2.4 Basic installation

To run Ox from other directories (assuming you installed on the C drive), add:

```
c:\ox\bin
```

to your PATH statement in the autoexec.bat file (or use the system icon in the control panel), and add the line:

```
set INCLUDE=c:\ox\include
```

This enables the Ox interpreter to find the standard header files.

The basic installation creates the following directories:

ox/bin	– executables and DLLs
ox/doc	– documentation (HTML files)
ox/include	– Ox header files
ox/packages	– Ox extension packages
ox/samples	– Ox samples directory with code for Ch. 3
ox/src	– Ox code for .oxo files in ox/include

`ox/samples/bench`	– benchmark samples
`ox/samples/callback`	– call an Ox function from C code*
`ox/samples/classes`	– Line and Angle classes from §12.5.6
`ox/samples/database`	– database class examples
`ox/samples/fortran`	– link Fortran code to Ox*
`ox/samples/graphics`	– graphics examples
`ox/samples/inout`	– input/output examples
`ox/samples/maximize`	– function maximization and differentiation
`ox/samples/pcfiml`	– PcFiml examples
`ox/samples/ranapp`	– C++ wrapper around Ox code*
`ox/samples/simula`	– Simulation class examples
`ox/samples/threes`	– Simple C-code extension to Ox
`../threes/bc45`	– Borland implementation (Win32)*
`../threes/linux`	– Linux implementation (gcc 2.5.8)
`../threes/msvc20`	– for Microsoft Visual C++(Win32)*
`../threes/watcom10`	– Watcom implementation (Win32)*
`../virtual`	– virtual class member functions

The entries labelled with * need the Windows version to run. The main files are:
`ox/`

`readme.ox`	– read me file with latest changes

`ox/bin/`

`oxl.exe`	– Ox executable for MS-DOS

`ox/include/`

`database.h`	– Database class header file
`database.oxo`	– Database class compiled source code
`maximize.h`	– maximization header file
`maximize.oxo`	– maximization compiled source code
`nortest.h`	– normality test header file
`nortest.oxo`	– normality test compiled source code
`oxstd.h`	– standard Ox header file
`oxdraw.h`	– Ox header file for graphics
`oxfloat.h`	– Ox header file for floating point constants
`pcfiml.h`	– PcFiml class header file
`pcfiml.oxo`	– PcFiml class compiled source code
`pcnaive.h`	– PcNaiveDgp class header file
`pcnaive.oxo`	– PcNaiveDgp class compiled source code
`quadpack.h`	– Ox header file for QuadPack*
`simula.h`	– Simulation class header file
`simula.oxo`	– Simulation class compiled source code

```
ox/src/
    database.ox         – Database class source code
    maximize.ox         – maximization source code
    nortest.ox          – normality test source code
    pcfiml.ox           – PcFiml class source code
    pcnaive.ox          – PcNaiveDgp class source code
    simula.ox           – Simulation class source code
```

2.5 Windows

The Windows installation adds executables and DLL files for Windows, a graphical front end for graphs and text created using Ox.

The main files added are:

```
ox/bin/
    oxlw.exe            – Ox console executable for Windows NT/Windows 95
    oxrun.exe           – Windows NT/95/3.1 front end, uses *GiveWin*
    oxwin.dll           – Ox DLL for Windows NT/95/3.1 (for oxlw, oxrun)
    oxgwin.dll          – Ox DLL, enables *OxRun* to use *GiveWin*
    quadpk.dll          – QuadPack DLL for Ox DLL (Windows)
```

The oxlw.exe version of Ox will not run under Windows 3.1. It works under Windows NT and 95 without any additional DLL files. *OxRun* will need *GiveWin* to run properly.

2.6 Linux, SunOS, HP-UX, SGI

Installation for these platforms is on a PC, from where you can transfer the files to a PC running Linux, or a Sun, Hewlett Packard or SGI workstation.

(1) First do the basic installation.
(2) Add the relevant Unix installation.

Alternatively, if you have a *zip* compatible unzipper, you can unpack oxbas110 and the Unix zip file directly on the target platform.

The relevant executable is added:

```
ox/bin/
    oxlinux             – Ox executable for Linux (Intel based Linux)
    oxsun               – Ox executable for Sun (SunOS 4.1)
    oxhp                – Ox executable for HP (HP-UX)
    oxsgi               – Ox executable for SGI (Irix)
```

As well as the files necessary to relink Ox:

    `ox/dev/linux`   – source, header and makefiles for Linux
    `ox/dev/sun`   – source, header and makefiles for Sun
    `ox/dev/hp`   – source, header and makefiles for Hewlett Packard
    `ox/dev/sgi`   – source, header and makefiles for SGI

Note that the time functions does not work properly on the Sun.

Part I

Introduction to Ox

Chapter 3

Getting started

3.1 A first Ox program

Ox is an object-oriented matrix language with a syntax similar to the C and C++ languages. This similarity is most clear in syntax items such as loops, functions, arrays and classes. A major difference is that Ox variables have no explicit type, and that special support for matrices is available. A comprehensive matrix function library is provided with Ox.

The advantages of object-oriented programming are that it potentially improves the clarity and maintainability of the code, as well as reducing coding effort through inheritance. Several useful classes are provided with Ox.

An Ox program consists of one or more source code files. As a first example consider the following small program:

```
#include <oxstd.h> // include the Ox standard library header

main()                  // function main is the starting point
{
    decl m1, m2;        // declare two variables, m1 and m2

    m1 = unit(3);       // assign to m1 a 3 x 3 identity matrix
    m2 = <0,0,0;1,1,1>;//m2 is a 2 x 3 matrix, the first row
                        // consists of zeros, the second of ones

    print("two matrices", m1, m2);      // print the matrices
}
```

Running this first program will produce the following result:

```
two matrices
        1.0000      0.00000      0.00000
        0.00000     1.0000       0.00000
        0.00000     0.00000      1.0000

        0.00000     0.00000      0.00000
        1.0000      1.0000       1.0000
```

The default extension of an Ox source code file is `.ox`, so the file name of this program could e.g. be `myfirst.ox`. The next section explains how to run the Ox program on your system. First we consider some aspects of the program.

- The first line includes the `oxstd.h` file into the source code (literally: the contents of the file are inserted at that point). This file contains the function declarations of the standard library, so that the function calls can be checked for number of arguments. The file name is between < >, indicating that the header file came with the Ox program.
- The function `main` is the starting point, and each program is only allowed one such function. Even though `main` has no arguments, it still requires `()`.
- Variables may be declared by using the `decl` statement, and have no type until the program is actually run.
- `unit` is a standard library function, which creates an identity matrix; here it is called with argument 3. The result is assigned to the variable `m1`. The type of `m1` has become *matrix*, and until a reassignment is made (or it goes out of scope), `m1` will keep its type and value.
- `<0,0,0;1,1,1>` is a *matrix constant*. Elements are listed by row, whereby rows are separated by a semicolon, and elements within a row by a colon. This value is stored in `m2`, which is now also of type matrix.
- `print` is a library function, which can print any type of variable or constant to the standard output screen. It can take any number of arguments. Here it has three: a *string constant* and two variables (which both happen to be matrices).

In ANSI C, the same program could be (assuming that the matrix and functions are all linked in, and PrintMat is supplied):

```
#include <stdio.h>      /* include the C standard io header */
#include "jdtypes.h"             /* include for type MATRIX */
#include "jdmath.h"          /* for MatAlloc, MatFree, MatI */

main()                 /* function main is the starting point */
{
    MATRIX m1, m2;     /* declare two variables, m1 and m2 */

    m1 = MatAlloc(3, 3);          /*   m1 is a 3 x 3 matrix */
    m2 = MatAlloc(2, 3);          /*   m2 is a 2 x 3 matrix */

    MatI(m1, 3);                  /* set m1 to identity matrix */
    m2[0][0] = m2[0][1] = m2[0][2] = 0;          /* setup m2 */
    m2[1][0] = m2[1][1] = m2[1][2] = 1;

    printf("two matrices");
    PrintMat(m1); PrintMat(m2);       /* print the matrices */

    MatFree(m1, 3, 3); MatFree(m2, 2, 3);
}
```

One important aspect of the C language emerges from the C program: array elements start at zero, so [0][0] is row 0, column 0, and [1][2] is row 1, column 2. This convention is also adopted the Ox language (but could be changed, see §12.8.3).

The advantage of Ox over C here is that we can directly work with matrices, and do not have to worry about memory allocation and deallocation. Native C is likely to be faster, although we have encountered several cases in which Ox performed better than a comparable C program.

3.2 Running the first Ox program

Although you might not run Ox under MS-DOS, please read the next section anyway, as much of the information in there is relevant for other Ox versions.

3.2.1 MS-DOS compiler

The Ox compiler under MS-DOS is called oxl; starting it without arguments produces:

```
Ox version 1.10 (MSDOS) (C) J.A. Doornik, 1994-96.
Ox Object-oriented matriX language
Usage:  Oxl filename[.ox] [switches]
Switches:
   -c          create object (.oxo) file
   -Dtoken     define tokens, e.g. -DOPTION1+OPTION2
   -lfilelist  link object file, e.g. -lfile1+file2+file3
   -ipath      add include/link path
   -x          clear include/link path
   -of         switch fast library function calling off
   -on         switch line numbering off
   -r-         do not run code
   -rc#,#      set matrix cache, default is
               -rc16,1000: 16 entries, max size 1000
   -rd         dump code (debug version only)
   -rf         switch FastMath off (saves memory)
   -rr         print cache report
   -rt         switch trace on (debug version only)
```

Provided Ox has been properly installed, you can type:

```
oxl myfirst
```

to run the myfirst.ox program (the .ox extension is automatically appended). The output appears on screen. It can be redirected to the file myfirst.out as follows:

```
oxl myfirst > myfirst.out
```

Dynamic link libraries (DLL) are *not* supported under MS-DOS.

The -c switch compiles the Ox source code into an object file (.oxo file). Such files are binary, and cross-platform compatible. This means that you can create an .oxo file under MS-DOS, then copy it to the Sun (using binary transfer), and use it directly. Thus it provides a way to distribute modules without the source code.

3.2.2 Linux, Sun, HP compilers

The Ox compiler under Linux is called `oxlinux`. The Ox compiler on the Sun (SunOS 4.1) is called `oxsun`, the version for the Hewlett-Packard workstation `oxhp`. Both have the same command line syntax as the MS-DOS compiler. Unlike the MS-DOS compiler, they cannot display graphs on screen (but graphs can be saved to a disk file and viewed with *GhostView*). Dynamic link libraries (DLL) are *not* supported on the Sun. It is possible to statically relink Ox with additional source code.

3.2.3 Windows command-line compiler

The Ox command-line compiler for Windows NT/Windows 95 is called `oxlw`. (The DEC-Alpha version is also called `oxlw`, but in the `ox/bina` directory, instead of `ox/bin`.) It has the same command line syntax as the MS-DOS and Linux compilers. Like the Linux compiler, it cannot display graphs on screen (but can save graphs to disk). Dynamic link libraries (DLL) are supported under Windows.

3.2.4 Windows compiler (OxRun)

OxRun is a small Windows front end to Ox. It offers the same services as the command-line compilers:

Filename:	the Ox program to compile
Link:	the object files to link in e.g.
	`file1+file2+file3`
Include/link path:	this field corresponds to the `-I` command line
	switch in `Oxl`, e.g.: `c:/ox/include`
Define:	arguments for the `-D` command line switch
Compile only:	corresponds to `-c`

    OxRun remembers previously run programs, and has a Browse button. Most importantly, it activates *GiveWin*, and text and graphics output from the Ox program will appear in *GiveWin*.

    OxRun and *GiveWin* are not part of the MS-DOS release of Ox.

3.3 Running programs with graphics

Several types of graphs are readily produced in Ox, such as graphs over time of several variables, cross-plots, histograms, correlograms, etc. Two simple examples are in Ch. 10.

    Although all graph saving will work on any system supported by Ox, the result on screen will not always be identical.

    A graph can be saved in various formats: encapsulated PostScript (`.eps`), PostScript (`.ps`), and GiveWin graphics file (`.gwg`). When using *GiveWin*, graphs can also be saved in Windows Metafile format (.wmf), and copied to the clipboard for pasting into wordprocessors.

3.3.1 MS-DOS graphics

ShowDrawWindow switches the system to graphics mode and shows the graph on screen. Use CloseDrawWindow to switch back to text mode. If you forget this, use the MS-DOS mode command to switch back, e.g.:

```
mode co80
```

3.3.2 Linux graphics

Oxlinux, oxhp, oxsun, and oxsgi cannot display graphics, but can save graphics.

3.3.3 Windows graphics from the command-line

Oxlw cannot display graphics, but can save graphics.

3.3.4 Windows graphics (*OxRun* and *GiveWin*)

Text and graphics output from the Ox program will appear in *GiveWin*. There, text and graphs can be edited further, or copied to the clipboard for pasting into other programs.

3.4 Multiple files

The source code of larger projects will often be spread over several source files. Usually the .ox file containing the main function is only a few tens of lines. We have already seen that information about other source files is passed on through included header files. However, to run the entire program, the code of those files needs to be linked together as well. Ox offers various ways of doing this. As an example, consider a mini-project consisting of two files: a source code file and a header file. The third file will contain the main function.

File 1: myfunc.ox

```
#include <oxstd.h>

static decl iCalls = 0;//calls counter, initialize to 0

MyFunction(const ma)
{
    ++iCalls;                       // increment calls counter
    print("MyFunction has been called ", iCalls,
          " times and prints:", ma);
}
```

File 2: myfunc.h

```
MyFunction(const ma);
```

The header file myfunc.h *declares* the MyFunction function, so that it can be used in other Ox files. Note that the declaration ends in a semicolon. The source code file contains the *definition* of the function, which is the actual code of the function. The header of the definition does not end in a semicolon, but is followed by the opening brace of the body of the function. The iCalls variable is declared outside any function, making it an *external* variable. Here we also use the static *type specifier*, which restricts the scope of the variable to the myfunc.ox file: iCalls is invisible anywhere else (and other files may contain their own iCalls variable). Without the static specifier, the iCalls variable can be seen from any other source file, provided it is declared in the header file. The m1 and m2 variables in the listing on page 11 are called *automatic*. Their life starts when they are declared, and finishes at the closing brace (matching the brace level of declaration).

3.4.1 Including the code into the main file

The first way of combining the mini project with the main function is to #include the actual code. In that case the myfunc.h header file is not needed:

File 3a: mymaina.ox

```
#include <oxstd.h>
#include "myfunc.ox"

main()
{
    MyFunction("one");
}
```

The result will be just one code file, and mymaina.ox can be run as explained in §3.2, e.g. as oxl mymaina.

3.4.2 Separate compilation and linkage

Ox source code files can be compiled into Ox object files. These files have the .oxo extension, and are binary. The format is identical across operating systems, but since they are binary, transfer from one platform to another has to be done in binary mode.

File 3b: mymainb.ox

```
#include <oxstd.h>
#include "myfunc.h"

main()
{
```

```
    MyFunction("one");
}
```

The second way of running the project is to first compile myfunc.ox into my-func.oxo. The next step is to compile mymainb.ox and *link* the two together. First compile myfunc.ox into an Ox object file using the -c switch:

```
oxl -c myfunc
```

This creates myfunc.oxo (the .oxo extension is automatically appended). Remember that a new myfunc.oxo needs to be created every time myfunc.ox changes. Next run mymainb.ox, linking in myfunc.oxo:

```
oxl mymainb -lmyfunc
```

The -l switch specifies the files to link in; with an additional myfunc2.oxo for example:

```
oxl mymainb -lmyfunc+lmyfunc2
```

3.4.3 Separate compilation, including link file

Finally, object files to be linked in can be included, comparable to including source code files. For this, the link pragma is used:

File 3c: mymainc.ox

```
#include <oxstd.h>
#include "myfunc.h"

#pragma link("myfunc.oxo")

main()
{
    MyFunction("one");
}
```

When mymainc.ox is run, the Ox object file myfunc.oxo is linked in at the specified place, and this file can be run as explained in §3.2.

3.5 Ox file extensions

Table 3.1 summarizes file types (by extension) used in Ox.

3.6 Command line arguments

3.6.1 General switches

-c Create an object (.oxo) file, there is no linking or running of the file. An .oxo file is a binary file which holds compiled Ox code. It can be linked in using the -l

Table 3.1   Ox extensions.

extension	description
.ox	Ox source code file
.h	Ox header file
.oxo	compiled Ox code (object file)
.eps	Encapsulated PostScript file
.ps	PostScript file
.gwg	*GiveWin* graphics file
.mat	ASCII matrix file
.dat	ASCII data file with load information,
.in7/.bn7	PcGive 7 data file (with corresponding .bn7 file)
.xls	Excel version 4 spread sheet file
.wks and .wk1	Lotus spread sheet file
.dht	Gauss data file (with corresponding .dat file)
.fmt	Gauss matrix file

switch, or using the link `pragma`.

-Dtoken Define tokens, e.g. -DOPTION1+OPTION2 corresponds to the preprocessor statements

```
#define OPTION1
#define OPTION2
```

-lfilelist Link object file, e.g. -lfile1+file2+file3, which links in the named files (the .oxo extension is assumed). If the file cannot be found as specified, the linker will search along the include path.

-ipath Appends path in front of the current include path. Initially, the include path is that specified in the INCLUDE environment variable; use this switch to prepend directories for searching. Use a semicolon to separate directories. The include path is used to search for files included in search code and link files.

-w0 Switches off parse warnings. Currently, the parser warns for

- `isolated ; is empty statement`
  This refers to expressions such as `if (i == 10);` where the semicolon terminates the expression. The warning is also issued for `;` after `for` and `while` statements.
- `assignment in test expression`
  This refers to expressions such as `if (i = 10)` where an assignment is made inside a test expression. The warning is also issued for assignments in `for`, `while`, and `do while` statements.

-x Clears the current include path. Use this prior to the `-i` switch if you do not wish to search in the directories specified by the INCLUDE environment variables.

3.6.2 Optimization switches

-of Switch fast library function calling off. By default this is on. There is no reason to switch it off, other than to to check for speed differences.

-on Switch line numbering off. Use this switch to prevent the emission of line numbers into the compiled code. This makes error messages less helpful; moreover, the speed improvement is virtually negligable.

3.6.3 Run-time switches

-r- Do not run code. The code will be compiled and linked. Could be useful to only do a syntax check.

-rc Sets the matrix cache. By default, the cache stores up to 16 matrices, but only matrices which have fewer than 1000 elements (which corresponds to 8 KBytes). The first number is the number of matrices, the second the size, separated by a colon (no spaces are allowed!), so the default corresponds to `-rc16,1000`. It seems that the marginal benefit of a larger cache, or caching larger matrices is small. (Note that the default cache consumes 128 Kbytes in a (highly unlikely) worse case.) The cache can be switched off with `-rc0,0`. Use `-rr` for a cache report when the program is done.

-rf Switch FastMath off (saves memory). FastMath significantly speeds up the following operations and functions: $X'X$, `correlation`, `determinant`, `invertsym`, `ols2c`, `variance`. In general, the overhead is a duplicate of the matrix.

-rr Prints a cache report, e.g. after running bench1.ox:
```
Cache status:  size 16 limit 1000
hits 189998 misses 6 flushes 0 skipped 0.
```

Chapter 4

Introduction to the Ox language

The previous chapter introduced the first Ox programs, showing the similarity between the syntax of Ox and that of the C language (the standard reference for C is Kernighan and Ritchie, 1988). We saw that a program always includes header files to define the standard library functions, and that it must have a `main` function, which is where program control starts. We also saw that the body of the function is enclosed in curly braces.

This chapter will give a brief overview of the important elements of the Ox language. Some discussion of object-oriented features is in the next chapter. A more formal description of the Ox syntax is in Ch. 12. That chapter also has many more examples.

4.1 Variables, types and scope

Variables are declared using the `decl` keyword. Unlike C, variables are *implicitly* typed. This means that variables do not have a type when they are declared, but get a type when values are assigned to them. So a variable can change type during its lifetime. The most important implicit types are *int* for an integer value, *double* for a real number, *string* for a text string and *matrix* for a matrix (two-dimensional array) of real numbers. The next Ox program illustrates implicit declaration and scope:

```
#include <oxstd.h>

main()
{
    decl i, d, m, s;

    i = 1;          // assign integer to i --> i is of type int
    d = 1.0;        // assign real number to d --> d is double
    s = "some text";   // assign string to s --> s is string
    m = zeros(3,3);    // assign to m a 3 x 3 matrix of zeros
                                // --> m is of type matrix
    print("i=", i, " d=", d, " s=", s, "\nm=", m);
}
```

20

This prints (\n is the newline character):

```
i=1 d=1 s=some text
m=
       0.00000        0.00000        0.00000
       0.00000        0.00000        0.00000
       0.00000        0.00000        0.00000
```

The *scope* of a variable refers to the parts of the program which can see the variable. This could be different from its lifetime: a variable can be 'alive' but not 'seen'. If a variable is declared outside any function, its scope is the remainder of the source file. It is possible to export such variables to other source files, as we shall see shortly.

Variables declared inside a function have scope until the closing brace of the level at which it is declared. The following example illustrates:

```
#include <oxstd.h>

decl mX;                                    // external variable
main()
{
    decl i = 0;                             // local variable

    {
        decl i = 1, j = 0;                         // new i
        mX = ones(3,3);
        print("i=", i, " j=", j);           // prints: i=1 j=0
    }                   // brace end: local i and j cease to exist
    print("\ni=", i);        // revert to old i, prints: i=0
}
```

The variable mX (here we use *Hungarian notation*, see §4.8), can be seen everywhere in the main function. To make sure that it can never be seen in other source files, prefix it with the word static. It is good programming practice to use static in such cases, because it is very useful to know that it is not used in any other files (we may than rename it, e.g., without any unexpected side effects). An example was given in myfunc.ox on page 15.

It is also possible to share variables between various source files, although there can be only one declaration (physical allocation) of the shared variable. The following modifications would do that for the myfunc.ox program: (1) delete the static keyword from the declaration, (2) add to myfunc.h the line:

```
extern decl iCalls;
```

Any code which includes myfunc.h can reference or change the iCalls variable.

4.2 Functions and function arguments

We have already used various functions from the standard library (such as print, ones and zeros), and written several new ones (MyFunction, various main functions).

Indeed, an Ox program is primarily a collection of functions. It is important to know that all function arguments are *passed by value*. This means that the function gets a copy which it can change without changing the original. For example:

```
#include <oxstd.h>

func(mA)
{
    mA = zeros(1,2);
    print("ma in func()", mA);
}
main()
{
    decl ma;

    ma = ones(1,2);
    print("ma before func()", ma);
    func(ma);
    print("ma after func()", ma);
}
```

which prints:

```
ma before func()
        1.0000          1.0000
ma in func()
        0.00000         0.00000
ma after func()
        1.0000          1.0000
```

If the function argument is not changed by the function, it is good programming style to prefix it with the `const` keyword, as in:

```
func(const mA)
{
    print("ma in func()", mA);
}
```

Then the compiler can generate much more efficient code, especially for matrices and strings.

Of course it is possible to return changed values from the function. If there is only one return value, this is most simply done by using the `return` statement:

```
#include <oxstd.h>

func(const r, const c)
{
    return rann(r, c);      // return r x c matrix of random
}                           // numbers from standard normal
main()
{
    print("return value from func():", func(1,2) );
}
```

Another way is to pass a *pointer* to the variable, rather than the variable itself, as for example in:

```
#include <oxstd.h>

func(const pmA)
{
    pmA[0] = zeros(1,2);
    print("ma in func()", pmA[0]);
}
main()
{
    decl ma;

    ma = ones(1,2);
    print("ma before func()", ma);
    func(&ma);
    print("ma after func()", ma);
}
```

which prints:

```
ma before func()
       1.0000          1.0000
ma in func()
       0.00000         0.00000
ma after func()
       0.00000         0.00000
```

Now the change to ma is permanent. The argument to the function was the address of ma, and func received that address as a pointer. In C one could reference what is pointed to as *pmA or pmA[0]. In Ox only the latter is possible; we modified what that pointer referred to by assigning a value to pmA[0]. When func has finished, ma has been changed permanently. Note that we gave the argument a const qualification. This was possible because we did not change pmA itself, but what pmA pointed to.

4.3 The for and while loops

Since Ox is a matrix language, there is much less need for loop statements than in C or C++. Indeed, because Ox is compiled and then interpreted, there is a speed penalty for using loop statements when they are not necessary.

The for, while and do while loops have the same syntax as in C. The for loop consists of three parts, an initialization part, a termination check, and an incrementation part. The while loops only have a termination check.

```
#include <oxstd.h>

main()
{
    decl i, d;
```

```
     for (i = 0; i < 5; ++i)
     {
         d = i * 0.01;
         print(d, "\n");
     }
}
```

which prints:

```
0
0.01
0.02
0.03
0.04
```

This could also be written, less elegantly, using `while` as follows:

```
#include <oxstd.h>

main()
{
    decl i, d;

    i = 0;
    while (i < 5)
    {
        d = i * 0.01;
        print(d, "\n");
        ++i;
    }
}
```

It is not uncommon to have more than one loop counter in the `for` statement, as the following code snippet illustrates:

```
decl i, j;

for (i = 0, j = 10; i < 5 && j > 0; ++i, --j)
    print(i * j, "\n");
```

The `&&` is *logical-and*, whereas `||` is *logical-or*. The `++i` statement is called (prefix) incrementation, and means 'add one to `i`'. Similarly, `--j` subtracts one from `j`. There is a difference between prefix and postfix incrementation (decrementation). For example, the second line in

```
i = 3;
j = ++i;
```

means: add one to `i`, and assign the result to `j`, which will get the value 4. But

```
i = 3;
j = i++;
```

means: leave the value of `i` on the stack for assignment, then afterwards increment `i`. So `j` will get the value 3. In the incrementation part of the `for` loop it does not matter whether you use the prefix or postfix form.

4.4 The `if` statement

The `if` statement allows for conditional program flow. In the following example we draw a uniform random number. Such a random number is always between zero and one. The `ranu` returns a matrix, unless we ask it to generate just one number. Then it returns a double, as is the case here.

```
decl d = ranu(1,1);

if (d < 0.5)
    print("less than 0.5\n");
else if (d < 0.75)
    print("less than 0.75\n");
else
    print("greater than 0.75\n");
```

Again, braces are used to group multiple statements together. They should also be used when nesting `if` statements, to avoid confusion about which `else` belongs to which `if`.

```
decl d1 = ranu(1,1), d2 = ranu(1,1);

if (d1 < 0.5)
{   print("d1 is less than 0.5\n");
}
else
{   if (d2 < 0.75)
        print("d1 >= 0.5 and d2 < 0.75\n");
    else
        print("d1 >= 0.5 and d2 <= 0.75\n");
}
```

The `if` part is executed if the expression evaluates to a non-zero value (*true*). The `else` part otherwise, i.e. when the expression evaluates to zero (*false*: either an integer 0, or a double 0.0). Some care is required when using matrices in `if` statements. A matrix expression is a true statement if all elements are true (non-zero). Even if only one element is zero, the matrix expression is false, so

```
#include <oxstd.h>

main()
{
    if (ones(2,2))  print("yes");
    else            print("no");
    if (unit(2))    print("yes");
    else            print("no");
    if (zeros(2,2)) print("yes");
    else            print("no");
}
```

prints: yesnono.

There are two forms of relational operators. There is < <= > >= == != meaning 'less', 'less than or equal', 'greater', 'greater than or equal', 'is equal' and 'is not equal'.

These always produce the integer value 1 (true) or 0 (false). If any of the arguments is a matrix, the result is only true if it is true for each element:

```
#include <oxstd.h>

main()
{
    if (ones(2,2) == 1)  print("yes");    // true for each
    else                 print("no");         // element
    if (unit(2) == 1)    print("yes");//not true for each
    else                 print("no");         // element
    if (zeros(2,2) == 1) print("yes");//not true for each
    else                 print("no");         // element
}
```

prints: yesnono.

The second form are the dot-relational operators .< .<= .> .>= .== . ! = meaning 'dot less', 'dot less than or equal', 'dot greater', 'dot greater than or equal', 'is dot equal' and 'is not dot equal'. If any of the arguments is a matrix, the result is a matrix of zeros and ones, with each element indicating the relevant result.

The any library function returns 1 (true) if *any* element of the matrix is non-zero, so that yesyesno will be printed by:

```
#include <oxstd.h>

main()
{
    if (any(ones(2,2)))  print("yes");
    else                 print("no");
    if (any(unit(2)))    print("yes");
    else                 print("no");
    if (any(zeros(2,2))) print("yes");
    else                 print("no");
}
```

To conclude: you can test whether all elements of a matrix m are equal to one (say) by writing: if (m == 1). To test whether any element is equal to one: if (any(m .== 1)). The expression if (m != 1), on the other hand, is only true if none of the elements is equal to one. So, use if (!(m == 1)) to test whether it is true that not all elements are equal to one.

4.5 Operations and matrix programming

To a large extent, the same operators are available in Ox as in C or C++. Some of the additional operators are power (^), horizontal concatenation (~), vertical concatenation (|) and the Kronecker product (**). One important distinction is that the operators are also available for matrices, so that, for example, two matrices can be added up directly.

For some operators, such as multiplication, there is a distinction between the dot operators (e.g. . * is element by element multiplication and * is matrix multiplication if both arguments are matrices). Not available in Ox are the bitwise operators, instead you need to use the library functions binand and binor.

Because Ox is implicitly typed, the result type of the expression will depend on the types of the variables in the expression. When a mixture of types is involved, the result is promoted upwards in the order integer, double, matrix. So in an expression consisting if an integer and a double, the integer will be promoted to a double. An expression of only integers yields an integer. However, there are two important exceptions to this rule:

(1) integer division is done in floating point and yields a double. *This is an important difference with C, where integer division is truncated to an integer.*
(2) power expressions involving integers which yield a result too large to be expressed as an integer give a double result.

To illustrate, we write the Fahrenheit to Celsius example of Kernighan and Ritchie (1988) in Ox:

```
#include <oxstd.h>

const decl LOWER = 0;
const decl UPPER = 100;
const decl STEP  = 20;
main()
{
    decl fahr;

    for (fahr = LOWER; fahr <= UPPER; fahr += STEP)
        print("%3d", fahr, " ",
                "%6.1f", (5.0/9.0) * (fahr-32), "\n");
}
```

which prints:

```
  0   -17.8
 20    -6.7
 40     4.4
 60    15.6
 80    26.7
100    37.8
```

In C we have to write 5.0/9.0, because 5/9 evaluates to zero. In Ox both expressions would be evaluated in floating point arithmetic.

In general we get more more efficient code by vectorizing each program as much as possible:

```
#include <oxstd.h>

const decl LOWER = 0;
const decl UPPER = 100;
```

```
const decl STEP   = 20;
main()
{
    decl fahr;

    fahr = range(LOWER, UPPER, STEP)';
    print("%6.1f",  fahr ~ (5.0/9.0) * (fahr-32) );
}
```

- As in the first version of the program, we declare three constants which define the Fahrenheit part of the table.
- The range() function creates a $1 \times n$ matrix with the values LOWER, LOWER+STEP, LOWER + 2STEP, ..., UPPER.
- The transpose operator ′ changes this into an $n \times 1$ matrix.
- The conversion to Celsius in the print statement works on the matrix as a whole: multiplication of a matrix by a scalar is equivalent to multiplication by the scalar of each element of the matrix.
- The ~ operator concatenates the two column vectors into an $n \times 2$ matrix.
- Finally, the print function is different from the printf in C. In Ox each variable to print is simply specified sequentially. It is possible, as done here with "%6.1f", to insert formatting strings for the next variable.

The program prints a table similar to the earlier output:

```
    0.0   -17.8
   20.0    -6.7
   40.0     4.4
   60.0    15.6
   80.0    26.7
  100.0    37.8
```

4.6 Arrays

The Ox syntax allows for arrays, so you may use, for example, an array of strings (often useful), an array of matrices, or even an array of an array of matrices (etc.). The following program gives an example.

```
#include <oxstd.h>

const decl MX_R = 2;
const decl MX_C = 2;
main()
{
    decl i, asc, asr, m;

    asr = new array[MX_R];
    asc = new array[MX_C];
```

```
    for (i = 0; i < MX_R; ++i)
        asr[i] = sprint("col ", i);
    for (i = 0; i < MX_R; ++i)
        asc[i] = sprint("row ", i);

    m = ranu(MX_R, MX_C);
    print("%r", asr, "%c", asc, m);
}
```
which prints

	row 0	row 1
col 0	0.020192	0.68617
col 1	0.15174	0.74598

- The new operator declares a new object. That could be a class object, as discussed in the next chapter, a matrix, a string, or, as used here, an array. The argument in square brackets is the size of the array. (When creating a matrix in this way, note that a matrix is always two-dimensional, and needs two arguments, as in: m = new matrix[2][2].)
- The sprint functions return a string, which is stored in the arrays.
- In print(), we use "%r" followed by an array of strings to specify row labels for the subsequent matrix. Columns labels use "%c".

4.7 Object-oriented programming

In some of the literature of recent years it has been claimed that object-oriented programming would solve all programming problems. My claims here are more modest. I see it as a useful addition, but believe thoughtless application could actually result in less readable programs. You may completely ignore the object-oriented features. However, you will then not be able to use the preprogrammed classes for data management and simulation. It is especially in the latter task that I found a considerable reduction in the required programming effort after writing the base class.

One of the drawbacks of C++, as compared with C, is that it is a much larger and considerably more complicated language, with all the extra overhead used for the object-oriented features. The standardization of C++ is also as yet an unfinished process. Ox only implements a subset of the C++ features. I tend to see that as a benefit rather than a drawback.

The *class* is the main vehicle for object-oriented programming. A class is nothing more than a group of variables (the data) and functions (the actions) packaged together. This makes it a supercharged struct (or record in Pascal terminology). Inheritance allows for a new class to add data and functions to the base class, or even redefine functionality of the base class.

In Ox, all data members of the class are private (only visible to class members), and all function members are public. Like C++, Ox has the virtual keyword to define functions which can be replaced by the derived class. Classes are used by dynamically creating objects of that class. No static objects exist in Ox. When an object is created, the *constructor* function is called, when the object is deleted, the *destructor* function is called.

More information on object-oriented programming is given in §12.5.6. Examples based on the preprogrammed classes are in Ch. 11.

4.8 Style and Hungarian notation

The readability and maintainability of a program is considerably enhanced when using a consistent style and notation, together with proper indentation and documentation. Style is a personal matter; this section describes the one I have adopted.

In my code, I always indent by four spaces at the next level of control (i.e. after each opening brace), jumping back on the closing brace.

Table 4.1　　Hungarian notation prefixes.

prefix	type	example
i	integer	iX
c	count of	cX
f	boolean (integer flag)	fX
	(b is also used)	
d	double	dX
m	matrix	mX
v	vector ($1 \times n$ matrix)	vX
s	string	sX
a	array	
as	array of strings	asX
am	array of matrix	amX
p	pointer (function argument)	pX
m_	class member variable	m_mX
g_	external variable with global scope	g_mX

I have found Hungarian notation especially useful (see e.g. Petzold, 1992, Ch. 1). Hungarian notation involves the decoration of variable names. There are two elements to Hungarian notation: prefixing of variable names to indicate type (Table 4.1), and using case to indicate scope (Table 4.2, remember that Ox is case sensitive).

As an example consider:

```
#include <oxstd.h>

const decl MX_R = 2;                              /* a constant */
```

Table 4.2 Hungarian notation, case sensitivity.

function	all lowercase
function (exported)	first letter uppercase
`static` external variable	type in lowercase, next letter uppercase
exported external variable	as above, but prefixed with `g_`
function argument	type in lowercase, next letter uppercase
local variables	all lowercase
constants	all uppercase

```
decl g_mX;                              /* exported matrix */
static decl iCount;             /* static external variable */

static func1(const pdX)   /* argument is pointer to double */
{
}
                                     /* exported function */
Func2(const mX, const asX, const cT, const cX)
{
    decl i, m;
}
```

`Func2` expects a `cT` × `cX` matrix, and corresponding array of `cX` variable names. The `c` prefix is used for the number of elements in a matrix or string. Note however, that it is not necessary in Ox to pass dimensions separately. You can ask `mX` and `asX` what dimensions they have:

```
Func2(const mX, const asX)
{
    decl i, m, ct, cx;
    cx = columns(mX);
    ct = rows(mX);
    if (cx != sizeof(asX))
        print("error: dimensions don't match");
}
```

4.9 Optimizing for speed

Ox is very fast: current benchmarks suggest that it is faster than several other commonly used matrix language interpreters. A program can never be fast enough though, and here are some tips to achieve higher speed:

- Use matrices as much as you can, avoiding loops and matrix indexing.
- Use the `const` argument qualifier when an argument is not changed in a function: this allows for more efficient function calling.
- Use built-in functions where possible.

- When optimizing a program with loops, it usually only pays to optimize the inner most loop. One option is to move loop invariants to a variable outside the loop.
- Avoid using 'hat' matrices, i.e. avoid using outer products over large dimensions when not necessary.
- If necessary, you can link in C or Fortran code, see Appendix A2.

Chapter 5

Numerical accuracy

Any computer program that performs numerical calculations is faced with the problem of (loss of) numerical accuracy. It seems a somewhat neglected area in econometric computations, which to some extent could be owing to a perception that the gradual and steady increase in computational power went hand in hand with improvements in accuracy. This, however, is not the case. At the level of software interaction with hardware, the major (and virtually the only) change has been the shift from single precision (4-byte) floating point computation to double precision (8-byte). Not many modern regression packages have problems with the Longley (1967) data set, which severely tests single precision implementations. Of course, there has been a gradual improvement in the understanding of numerical stability of various methods, but this must be offset against the increasing complexity of the calculations involved.

Loss of numerical accuracy is not a problem, provided we know when it occurs and to what extent. Computations are done with finite precision, so it will always be possible to design a problem with analytical solution which fails numerically. Unfortunately, most calculations are too complex to precisely understand to what extent accuracy is lost. So it is important to implement the most accurate methods, and increase understanding of the methods used. The nature of economic data will force us to throw away many correct digits, but only at the end of the computations.

Real numbers are represented as *floating point* numbers, consisting of a sign, a mantissa, and an exponent. A finite number of bytes is used to store a floating point number, so only a finite set can be represented on the computer. The main storage size in Ox is 8 bytes, which gives about 15 to 16 significant digits. Two sources of error result. The first is the *representation error*: most numbers can only be approximated on a computer. The second is *rounding error*. Consider the *machine precision* ϵ_m: this is the smallest number that can be added to one such that the result is different from one:

$$\epsilon_m = \operatorname*{argmin}_{\epsilon} \left(1 + \epsilon \neq 1\right).$$

So an extreme example of rounding error would be $(1 + \epsilon_m/10) - 1$, where the answer would be 0, rather than $\epsilon_m/10$. In Ox: $\epsilon_m \approx 2.2 \times 10^{-16}$.

Due to the accumulation of rounding errors, it is possible that mathematically equivalent formulae can have very different numerical behaviour. For example, computing $V[x]$ as $\frac{1}{T}\sum x_i^2 - \bar{x}^2$ is much less stable than $\frac{1}{T}\sum (x_i - \bar{x})^2$. In the first case, we potentially subtract two quite similar numbers, resulting in cancellation of significant digits (we could even get a negative number). A similar cancellation could occur in the computation of inner products (a very common operation, as it is part of matrix multiplication).

The Windows and MS-DOS versions of Ox accumulate inner products in extended 10-byte reals, leading to a higher accuracy. In general, one can expect small difference in the results from computations between versions of Ox. Often these are unnoticeable in the accuracy used for printing. The following code example can show the difference between 8 and 10-byte accumulation:

```
#include <oxstd.h>
#include <oxfloat.h>

main()
{
    decl x, y;

    x = <DBL_MAX; DBL_MAX; DBL_MAX-1;
        DBL_MAX; DBL_MAX>;
    y = <10; 10; 1; -10; -10>;

    print("%20.16g", x'y);
}
```

When using extended precision for inner products, it prints the value for DBL_MAX (see Ch. 9) else it prints infinity (the text of which is machine specific). When the computations work, it also shows that DBL_MAX - 1 equals DBL_MAX.

An interesting example of harmless numerical inaccuracies is in the case of a grid plot of an autoregressive parameter based on the concentrated likelihood function of an AR(k) model. Rounding errors make the likelihood function appear non-smooth (not differentiable). This tends to occur in models with many lags of the dependent variable and a high autoregressive order. It also occurs in an AR(1) model of the Longley data set, see Fig. 5.1, which is a grid of 2000 steps between -1 and 0, done in PcGive (ignoring the warning that numerical accuracy is endangered).

It is important to distinguish numerical accuracy from other problems that may occur. Multicollinearity, for example, is first and foremost a statistical problem. A certain parameterization of a model might make the estimates of one or more parameters statistically imprecise (cf. the concept of 'micronumerosity' playfully introduced by Goldberger in Kiefer, 1989). This imprecision could be changed (or moved) by altering the specification of the model. Multicollinearity could induce numerical instability, leading to loss of significant digits in some or all results.

Another example is the determination of the optimum of a non-linear function that is not concave. Here it is possible to end up in a local optimum. This is clearly not a problem of numerical stability, but inherent to non-linear optimization techniques. A good

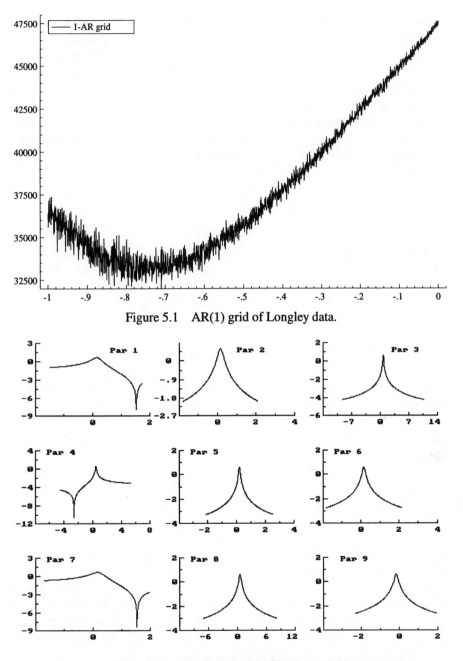

Figure 5.1   AR(1) grid of Longley data.

Figure 5.2   Likelihood grid of Klein model I.

example is provided by Klein model I. Figure 5.2 provides a grid plot of the FIML likelihood function for each parameter, centred around the maximum found with the 2SLS
estimates as a starting point. These grids are of a different type from the AR grid in
Fig. 5.1. In the former, all parameters but one are kept fixed, whereas the AR grid graphs
the concentrated likelihood. In the case of one autoregressive parameter, the actual optimum may be read off the graph, as is the case in the AR grid plot above.

Problems of numerical accuracy could also manifest themselves when using very
large matrices. An example was encountered by Mike Pitt, when computing eigenvalues
of the following type of matrix $A = (a_{ij})$ (of dimension $n \times n$)):

$$a_{ij} = 1 \quad i \le j + 1,$$
$$a_{ij} = 0 \quad i > j + 1.$$

Such a matrix has ones on and below the diagonal, and just above the diagonal. Figure
5.3 graphs the eigenvalue as a function of the size of the matrix. The matrix is not symmetric, so we used the `eigen` function. The eigenvalues are real, but a small complex
part starts to arise for large n. The maximum eigenvalue starts to behave erratically when
the dimension gets above 86 (similar behaviour occurs with other computer programs).

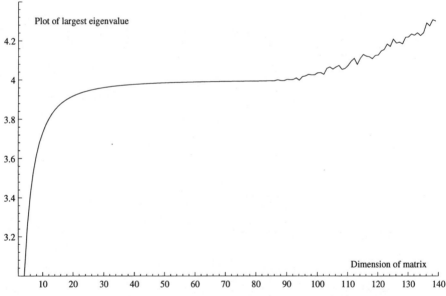

Figure 5.3   Maximum eigenvalue as a function of matrix dimension.

A matrix frequently used to show the limitations of numerical techniques is the Hilbert matrix. A Hilbert matrix of dimension n, H_n, has elements

$$h_{ij} = (i + j + 1)^{-1}, \quad i, j = 0, 1, \ldots, n - 1.$$

This matrix is very ill-conditioned, and many computations involving H_n break down even for n as small as 10. The inverse and determinant of H_n are known analytically, for example from Barnett (1990):

$$\det(H_n) = \prod_{k=0}^{n-1} \frac{(n-k-1)!(n-k-1)!k!}{(n+k)!}.$$

We could use the `loggamma` function to compute the (reciprocal of the) determinant: $\log \Gamma(z+1) = \log(z!)$. Then we give up some accuracy, the loggamma function has about 10 significant digits, but can make a stable computation up to $n = 23$. At $n = 24$ the `exp` function overflows. Restricting ourselves to the logarithm of the determinant, we can go quite a bit further. The `determinant` function breaks down much earlier: at $n = 4$ we have about 13 significant digits correct, at $n = 10$ just 5. At $n = 11$, the function reports that the matrix is singular. If we scale the matrix to keep the determinant under control, we get the message that the determinant is unreliable at $n = 11$, which is borne out by only two correct digits. Beyond that, there is no correct answer from the `determinant` function; using the `logdet` function does not help.

To conclude, we show that using floating point for computations which should result in integers could lead to unexpected results. Most of the time conversion to an integer works, but not always. The following code has been especially written to show that:

```
#include <oxstd.h>

intfuzzy(const d)
{
    return  d > 0 ? int(d * (1 + fuzziness(0)/2))
                  : int(d * (1 - fuzziness(0)/2));
}
main()
{
    decl i, j;

    for (i = 322, j = 122; i < 327; ++i, ++j)
        print("%20.16f", (i*0.1 - 20) * 10, " ",
            "%5d", int( ((i*0.1) - 20) * 10) - j,
            "%5d", int( ((i*0.1) - 20) * 10),
            "%5d", int(floor( ((i*0.1) - 20) * 10)),
            "%5d", int(ceil( ((i*0.1) - 20) * 10)), "\n");

    for (i = 322, j = 122; i < 327; ++i, ++j)
        print("%20.16f", (i*0.1 - 20) * 10, " ",
            "%20.16f", (i*0.1 - 20) * 10 * (1+fuzziness(0)/2),
            "%5d", intfuzzy( ((i*0.1) - 20) * 10) - j, "\n");
}
```

which has output on Windows (note that there could be minor differences on other platforms):

```
122.0000000000000300      0   122   122   123
123.0000000000000400      0   123   123   124
123.9999999999999900     -1   123   123   124
125.0000000000000000      0   125   125   125
126.0000000000000100      0   126   126   127

122.0000000000000300  122.0000000000000900      0
123.0000000000000400  123.0000000000001000      0
123.9999999999999900  124.0000000000000400      0
125.0000000000000000  125.0000000000000600      0
126.0000000000000100  126.0000000000000700      0
```

The last two zeros in the floating point print-out are beyond the precision, so can be ignored. We see however, that even then the results are not exact: in general most integers cannot be represented exactly in floating point notation (this is the representation error mentioned earlier). Once we start computing, these inexactitudes propagate. Conversion to an integer involves truncation, hence we find 123 for the third value, and not 124 as expected. This also affects the floor and ceil function. (Another example of this effect is given under the range library function.)

There is a potential solution, as shown in the code. Add a little bit to positive numbers (subtract for negative numbers), where the little bit is a fraction determined by the current fuzziness value. This is implemented in the truncf library function. Alternatively, one could round to the nearest integer, using the round function.

Note that, when indexing a matrix by another matrix, a problem like this could occur when the indices are the result from computation, rather than direct storage. Internally, the indices are converted to integers by truncation, so you could decide to round first. When using random indices (e.g. in bootstrapping), such rounding will produce indices out of range, and truncation is precisely what is required.

Chapter 6

How to ...

How to compute/get/achieve:

- bootstrap a data set, see under: 'take a random sample ...'.
- censored random variates, for example, a random normal censored at a and b (don't forget any dots):

```
x = rann(1000,1);
y = x .< a .? a .: x .> b .? b .: x;
```

- check if all elements in a matrix are equal to a value, 1 say:

```
if (x == 1)
```

- check if no element in a matrix is equal to a value, 1 say:

```
if (x != 1)
```

- check if any element in a matrix is not equal to a value, 0 say:

```
if ( !(x == 0) )
if ( max(x .== 0) )
```

- check if any element in a matrix is equal to a value, 1 say:

```
if ( any(x .== 1) )
```

- check if two matrices, x and y, are equal to each other:

```
if (x == y)
```

- check if two matrices, x and y, have any elements in common:

```
if ( any(x .== y) )
```

- concatenation of columns in a loop

```
m = new matrix[1][0];
for (i = 0; i < columns(mx); ++i)
    m ~= mx[][i];
```

- concatenation of rows in a loop

```
decl m = new matrix[0][1];
for (i = 0; i < rows(mx); ++i)
    m |= mx[i][];
```

- correlation matrix out of a variance matrix:

```
decl sdi = 1 ./ sqrt(diagonal(mvar));
corrm = sdi .* mvar .* sdi';
```

- create a tridiagonal matrix, symmetric, $n \times n$:

```
a * unit(n) + b * lag0(unit(n), 1) + b * lag0(unit(n), -1);
```

- delete rows with certain values:

```
mx[ vecindex( !sumr(x .== value) )][];
```

- element-by-element maximum (dot-maximum) (or minimum, etc.) of two matrices, or of a matrix and a number:

```
x = y .> 3 .? y .: 3;
x = y .> z .? y .: z;
```

- error function

```
erf = (2 * probn(x * sqrt(2)) - 1);
```

- factorial: see under the `loggamma()` library function, e.g. for $x!$:

```
fact = exp(loggamma(x + 1));
```

- gamma function: see under the `loggamma()` library function.
- index of the maximum value in each column

```
maxindc = limits(x)[2][]';
```

- maximum of each column:

```
maxc = limits(x)[0][];
```

- Numerical variance
  Following maximum likelihood estimation, compute the second derivative matrix Q using `Num2Derivative`. Then $-Q^{-1}$ is an estimate of the parameter variance matrix.
- π (this requires `#include <oxfloat.h>`):

```
pi = M_PI;
```

- select rows with certain values:

```
mx[ vecindex( sumr(x .== value) )][];
```

- second moments:

```
mom = x'x;
```

- sorted column index of a matrix x:

```
sortindex =
    sortc(x ~ range(0, rows(x)-1)')[][columns(x)-1];

// Now sortindex can be used to sort
// another matrix y conformably:
z = y[sortindex][];
```

- sequence from a to b of n equally spaced points. For example, how to generate a sequence of 20 equally spaced points from -1.1 to 1.1 (see under the range library function for more information):

```
seq = range(-110, 110, 11) / 100;
```

- substitute certain values only, say change all the 3's to 1 in a matrix x:

```
x = x .== 3 .? 1 .: x;
```

- take a random sample of size n with replacement from the rows of a matrix x:

```
y = x[ ranu(1,n) * n ][];
```

- trim the matrix x by deleting the first top and the last bot rows:

```
trim = x[top:rows(x)-bot-1][];
```

- truncated random variates (i.e. random numbers from truncated distributions, see Devroye, 1986, p.39), with the distribution F truncated on the left at a, and on the right at b:

$$F^{-1}\left\{F(a) + u \times [F(b) - F(a)]\right\},$$

where u is a uniform random number. In Ox code, for a random normal, truncated at a and b:

```
pa = probn(a);        // Pr{value <= a}
      // pa = 0 for no  left truncation
pb = probn(b);        // Pr{value <= b}
      // pb = 1 for no right truncation
y = quann( pa + ranu(1000,1) * (pb - pa) );
```

- two-sided critical values from a t(k) distribution:

```
pvalue = 2 * tailt(fabs(x), k);
```

- unsorting a matrix which is to be sorted by a column i.

```
sorted = sortbyc(x ~ range(0, rows(x)-1)', i)
unsorted = sortbyc(sorted, columns(sorted) - 1);
```

- $y \log y$:

```
y .* log(y .> 0 .? y .: 1);
```

Part II

Function and Language Reference

Chapter 7

Function summary

This chapter lists all library functions by category, and gives a brief description. More detailed descriptions with examples follow in Chapters 8–10.

general functions

any	returns TRUE if any element is TRUE
binand	binary *and* operation
binor	binary *or* operation
columns	get number of columns of argument
countc	count elements in columns in specified intervals
countr	count elements in rows in specified intervals
exit	exits Ox
fuzziness	set fuzziness parameter
isdotfeq	tests for dot fuzzy equality
isfeq	tests for fuzzy equality
limits	maximum/maximum values in matrix plus location
max	maximum value in arguments
min	minimum value in arguments
oxversion	returns the Ox version
prodc	compute column products
prodr	compute row products
rows	get number of rows of argument
sizeof	get size of element
spikes	spikes in matrix plus location
strlwr	convert a string to lower case
strupr	convert a string to upper case
strfind	finds a string in an array of strings
sumc	compute column sums
sumr	compute row sums
sumsqrc	compute column sum of squares
sumsqrr	compute row sum of squares
va_arglist	needed to access arguments in a variable argument list

type functions

isarray	tests if argument is an array
isclass	tests if argument is a class object
isdouble	tests if argument is a double
isfile	tests if argument is a file
isfunction	tests if argument is a function
isint	tests if argument is an integer
ismatrix	tests if argument is a matrix
isstring	tests if argument is a string

matrix functions

determinant	returns the determinant of a matrix
diagonalize	set off-diagonal elements to zero
invert	invert a matrix
inverteps	sets inversion/rank epsilon
invertsym	invert a symmetric matrix
logdet	returns the log and sign of the determinant
nullspace	returns the null space of a matrix
rank	returns the rank of a matrix
trace	returns the trace of a matrix

input/output

eprint	print to stderr
fclose	close a file
fopen	open a file
format	set default print format
fprint	print to a file
fread	read data in binary format from a file
fscan	read from a file
fseek	gets or repositions the file pointer
fwrite	write data in binary format from a file
loadmat	load a matrix
print	print to stdout
savemat	save a matrix
scan	read from the console
sprint	print to a string
sprintbuffer	resize the sprint buffer
sscan	read from a string

mathematical functions

`betafunc`	incomplete beta integral
`cabs`	complex absolute value
`cdiv`	complex division
`ceil`	ceiling
`cmul`	complex multiplication
`csqrt`	complex square root
`exp`	exponent
`fabs`	absolute value
`floor`	floor
`fmod`	floating point remainder
`gammafunc`	incomplete gamma function
`idiv`	integer division
`imod`	integer remainder
`log`	natural logarithm
`log10`	base-10 logarithm
`loggamma`	logarithm of gamma function
`polygamma`	derivatives of loggamma function
`round`	rounds to nearest integer
`sqr`	square
`sqrt`	square root
`trunc`	truncate towards zero
`truncf`	fuzzy truncation towards zero

matrix creation

`constant`	create a matrix and fill with a value
`diag`	create matrix with specified vector on diagonal
`ones`	create a matrix of ones
`range`	create a matrix consisting of a range of numbers (trend)
`toeplitz`	create a symmetric Toeplitz matrix
`unit`	create an identity matrix
`zeros`	create a matrix of zeros

matrix decomposition

`choleski`	Choleski decomposition of symmetric positive definite matrix
`decldl`	square root free Choleski decomposition of sym.pd. matrix
`decldlband`	Choleski decomposition of sym.pd. band matrix
`declu`	LU decomposition
`decsvd`	singular value decomposition
`eigen`	eigenvalues of matrix
`eigensym`	eigenvalues of symmetric matrix

`eigensymgen`	solves generalized symmetric eigen problem
`polydiv`	divides two polynomials
`polymul`	multiplies two polynomials
`polymake`	gets polynomial coefficients from the (inverse) roots
`polyroots`	computes the (inverse) roots of a polynomial
`solveldl`	solves AX=B when A is decomposed with `decldl`
`solveldlband`	solves AX=B when A is decomposed with `decldlband`
`solvelu`	solves AX=B when A is decomposed with `declu`
`solvetoeplitz`	solves AX=B when A is symmetric Toeplitz

matrix modification/reordering

`diagonal`	extract diagonal from a matrix
`lower`	return the lower diagonal of a matrix
`reflect`	reflect a matrix
`reshape`	reshape a matrix by row
`reversec`	reverse column elements
`reverser`	reverse row elements
`setdiagonal`	set the diagonal of a matrix
`setlower`	set the lower diagonal of a matrix
`setupper`	set the upper diagonal of a matrix
`shape`	reshape a matrix by column
`sortbyc`	sort one column, and remaining columns accordingly
`sortbyr`	sort one row, and remaining rows accordingly
`sortc`	sort columns of a matrix
`sortr`	sort rows of a matrix
`submat`	extract a submatrix
`thinc`	thin the columns of a matrix
`thinr`	thin the rows of a matrix
`upper`	return the upper diagonal of a matrix
`vec`	vectorize the columns of a matrix
`vech`	vectorize the lower diagonal only
`vecindex`	row indices of non-zero elements of the vec of a matrix
`vecr`	vectorize the rows of a matrix

probability

`densbeta`	$B(a, b)$ distribution density
`denschi`	χ^2 distribution density
`densf`	F-distribution density
`densn`	standard normal density
`denst`	Student t-distribution density

`quanchi`	χ^2 distribution quantiles
`quanf`	F-distribution quantiles
`quann`	standard normal quantiles
`quant`	Student t-distribution quantiles
`probbeta`	$B(a, b)$ distribution probabilities
`probchi`	χ^2 distribution probabilities
`probf`	F-distribution probabilities
`probgamma`	Γ-distribution probabilities
`probn`	standard normal probabilities
`probt`	Student t-distribution probabilities
`tailchi`	χ^2 distribution tail probabilities
`tailf`	F-distribution tail probabilities
`tailn`	standard normal tail probabilities
`tailt`	Student t-distribution tail probabilities

statistics

`correlation`	correlation matrix of matrix (data in columns)
`meanc`	compute column means
`meanr`	compute row means
`ols2c`	OLS based on normal equations (data in columns)
`ols2r`	OLS based on normal equations (data in rows)
`olsc`	OLS based on orthogonal decomposition (data in columns)
`olsr`	OLS based on orthogonal decomposition (data in rows)
`quantilec`	quantiles of a matrix (data in columns)
`quantiler`	quantiles of a matrix (data in rows)
`standardize`	standardize a matrix (data in columns)
`spline`	natural cubic spline smoother (data in columns)
`varc`	compute column variances
`variance`	variance matrix of matrix (data in columns)
`varr`	compute row variances

random numbers

`ranbeta`	$B(a, b)$ distributed random numbers
`ranbinomial`	binomially distributed random numbers
`ranchi`	χ^2 distributed random numbers
`ranexp`	$\exp(\lambda)$ distributed random numbers
`ranf`	F-distributed random numbers
`rangamma`	gamma-distributed random numbers
`rann`	standard normal distributed random numbers
`ranpoisson`	poisson distributed random numbers
`ranseed`	set and get seed of random number generator

`rant`	Student t-distributed random numbers
`ranu`	uniform $[0, 1]$ distributed random numbers

time series (data in columns)

`acf`	autocorrelation function of matrix
`arma0`	residuals of an ARMA(p, q) filter
`armaforc`	forecasts from an ARMA(p, q) process
`armagen`	fitted values of an ARMA(p, q) process
`armavar`	autocovariances of an ARMA(p, q) process
`cumsum`	cumulate autoregressive sum
`cumprod`	cumulate autoregressive product
`cumulate`	cumulate (vector) autoregressive process
`diff0`	ith difference, $(1 - L^i)y$
`diff0pow`	dth fractional difference, $(1 - L)^d y$
`fft`	fast fourier transform
`lag0`	ith lag
`pacf`	partial autocorrelation function of matrix
`periodogram`	periodogram, smoothed periodogram (spectral density)

trigonometric functions

`acos`	arccosine
`asin`	arcsine
`atan`	arctangent
`cos`	cosine
`cosh`	cosine hyperbolicus
`sin`	sine
`sinh`	sine hyperbolicus
`tan`	tangent
`tanh`	tangent hyperbolicus

time and date functions

`date`	returns a string with the current date
`time`	returns a string with the current time
`timer`	returns an integer representing the current time
`timespan`	returns the lapsed time

maximization and differentiation

`MaxBFGS`	maximize a function using BFGS
`MaxControl`	set maximum no of iterations and print control
`MaxControlEps`	set convergence tolerances
`MaxConvergenceMsg`	get convergence message

MaxSimplex	maximize a function using the simplex method
Num1Derivative	numerical computation of 1st derivative
Num2Derivative	numerical computation of 2nd derivative
NumJacobian	numerical computation of Jacobian matrix

graphics functions

CloseDrawWindow	Close the drawing window
SaveDrawWindow	Save the drawing to a file
SetDrawWindow	Set the name of the drawing window
SetTextWindow	Set the name of the text window
ShowDrawWindow	Show the drawing window

Draw	draw a matrix against an x-axis
DrawCorrelogram	draw a correlogram
DrawDensity	draw a histogram and/or density
DrawMatrix	draw a matrix against an x-axis
DrawQQ	draw a QQ plot
DrawSpectrum	draw a spectral density
DrawT	draw a matrix against time
DrawTMatrix	draw a matrix against time
DrawX	cross plot of a matrix against a vector
DrawXMatrix	cross plot of a matrix against a vector

Chapter 8

Function reference

Ox has implicit typing, so function declarations contain no type information. However, at run time, type information is known and checked for validity. The following argument types are distinguished in the function summary:

argument type	legal actual argument	conversion inside function
int	int, double	double $\rightarrow$ int
double	int, double	int $\rightarrow$ double
matrix	matrix	none
arithmetic type	int, double, matrix	int $\rightarrow$ double
any type	any type	none
string	string	none
array	array	none
address	address	none

Nearly all functions documented in this chapter require the `oxstd.h` header file, which must be included by writing

```
#include <oxstd.h>
```

at the top of your source code. A few functions need an additional header file, which is indicated explicitly.

acf

```
acf(const ma, const ilag);
```
   ma   in: arithmetic type, $T \times n$ matrix
   ilag   in: int, the highest lag, if $\geq T$ then $T - 1$ is used

Return value
   Returns a $(\text{ilag} + 1) \times n$ matrix with the autocorrelation function of the columns
   of ma up to lag ilag. Returns 0 if ilag ≤ 0. If any variance is $\leq 10^{-20}$, then
   the corresponding autocorrelations are set to 0.

Description
   Computes the autocorrelation functions of the columns of a $T \times n$ matrix
   $A = (a_0, a_1, \ldots, a_{n-1})$. The autocorrelation function of a T-vector $x = (x_0 \cdots x_{T-1})'$ up to lag k is defined as $r = (\hat{r}_0 \cdots \hat{r}_k)'$:

$$\hat{r}_j = \frac{\sum_{t=j}^{T-1}(x_t - \bar{x})(x_{t-j} - \bar{x})}{\sum_{t=0}^{T-1}(x_t - \bar{x})^2}, \tag{8.1}$$

   with the mean defined in the standard way as:

$$\bar{x} = \frac{1}{T}\sum_{t=0}^{T-1} x_t.$$

   Note that $\hat{r}_0 = 1$. The approximate standard error for r_j is $1/\sqrt{T}$.

See also
   DrawCorrelogram, pacf

Example

   The example computes a correlogram twice, once using the library function, and
   once 'manually' (in the matrix macf).

```
#include <oxstd.h>

main()
{
    decl i, m1 = rann(200,2), m1m, macf, ilag = 5;

    macf = new matrix[ilag + 1][2];
    m1m = m1 - meanc(m1);              // in deviation from mean

    for (i = 0; i <= ilag; ++i)
        macf[i][] = diagonal(m1m'lag0(m1m, i));
    macf = macf ./ macf[0][];          // scale by variance

    print( acf(m1, ilag) ~ macf);
}
```

produces

```
        1.0000          1.0000          1.0000          1.0000
      -0.028406       -0.027646       -0.028406       -0.027646
      -0.0010304       0.022494       -0.0010304       0.022494
       0.054407       -0.069012        0.054407       -0.069012
      -0.10231        -0.052104       -0.10231        -0.052104
      -0.016475        0.12511        -0.016475        0.12511
```

acos

```
acos(const ma);
```

    ma   in: arithmetic type

Return value

    Returns the arccosine of ma, of double or matrix type.

See also

    asin, atan, cos, cosh, sin, sinh, tan, tanh

Example

```
#include <oxstd.h>

main()
{
    print( acos(<0,1>) );
    print( asin(<0,1>) );
    print( atan(<0,1>) );
    print( cos(<0,1>) );
    print( cosh(<0,1>) );
    print( sin(<0,1>) );
    print( sinh(<0,1>) );
    print( tan(<0,1>) );
    print( tanh(<0,1>) );
}
```

produces

```
        1.5708          0.00000
        0.00000         1.5708
        0.00000         0.78540
        1.0000          0.54030
        1.0000          1.5431
        0.00000         0.84147
        0.00000         1.1752
        0.00000         1.5574
        0.00000         0.76159
```

any

```
any(const ma);
```
     ma   in: arithmetic type

Return value

    Returns TRUE if any element of ma is TRUE, of integer type.

Description

    If any element is non-zero, the return value is 1. This is in contrast with the `if` statement, which evaluates to TRUE if `all` elements are TRUE.

See also

    §12.7.9

Example

```
#include <oxstd.h>

main()
{
    decl m1 = unit(2), m2 = zeros(2,2);

    if (m1 == 0)        print ("TRUE ");
    else                print ("FALSE ");
    if (any(m1 .== 0))  print ("TRUE ");
    else                print ("FALSE ");
    if (!(m1 == 0))     print ("TRUE ");
    else                print ("FALSE ");
    if (any(m1 .!= 0))  print ("TRUE ");
    else                print ("FALSE ");

    if (m2 == 0)        print ("TRUE ");
    else                print ("FALSE ");
    if (any(m2 .== 0))  print ("TRUE ");
    else                print ("FALSE ");
    if (m2 != 0)        print ("TRUE ");
    else                print ("FALSE ");
    if (any(m2 .!= 0))  print ("TRUE ");
    else                print ("FALSE ");
}
```

    produces: FALSE TRUE TRUE TRUE TRUE TRUE FALSE FALSE

arma0

```
arma0(const ma, const vp, const cp, const cq);
```

ma	in:	$T \times n$ matrix A
vp	in:	$1 \times s$ matrix with autoregressive coefficients $\phi_1, \phi_2, \ldots, \phi_p$ followed by the moving average coefficients $\theta_1, \theta_2, \ldots, \theta_q$, $s \geq p + q$
cp	in:	int, no of autoregressive coefficients (could be 0)
cq	in:	int, no of moving average coefficients (could be 0)

Return value

Returns the residual from applying the ARMA(p, q) filter to each column of A. The result has the same dimensions as ma. The first p rows of the return value will be zero.

Description

For a column $a = (a_0, \ldots, a_{T-1})'$ of A, this function computes (see e.g. Harvey, 1993, §3.3):

$$\epsilon_t = 0 \qquad\qquad\qquad\qquad\qquad\qquad\qquad t = 0, \ldots, p - 1,$$
$$\epsilon_t = a_t - \phi_1 a_{t-1} \ldots - \phi_p a_{t-p} - \theta_1 \epsilon_{t-1} \ldots - \theta_q \epsilon_{t-q} \quad t = p, \ldots, T - 1,$$

using $\epsilon_t = 0$ for $t < 0$. For example when $p = 1$ and $q = 2$:

$$\epsilon_0 = 0$$
$$\epsilon_1 = a_1 - \phi_1 a_0 - \theta_1 \epsilon_0$$
$$\epsilon_2 = a_2 - \phi_1 a_1 - \theta_1 \epsilon_1 - \theta_2 \epsilon_0$$
$$\epsilon_t = a_t - \phi_1 a_{t-1} - \theta_1 \epsilon_{t-1} - \theta_2 \epsilon_{t-2} \quad t = p, \ldots, T - 1.$$

See also

armagen, armaforc, armavar, diff0, diff0pow, cumulate

Example

```
#include <oxstd.h>

main()
{
    decl mx = <1:5>';
    print( arma0(mx,<0.5, 0.5>, 1, 1)
         ~ arma0(mx,<0.5>, 0, 1) );
}
```

produces

```
0.00000        1.0000
1.5000         1.5000
1.2500         2.2500
1.8750         2.8750
2.0625         3.5625
```

armaforc

```
armaforc(const mx, const vp, const cp, const cq);
armaforc(const mx, const vp, const cp, const cq,
    const ma);
armaforc(const mx, const vp, const cp, const cq,
    const ma, const me);
```

mx	in:	$H \times n$ matrix X, fixed part of forecasts
vp	in:	$1 \times s$ matrix with autoregressive coefficients $\phi_1, \phi_2, \ldots, \phi_p$ followed by the moving average coefficients $\theta_1, \theta_2, \ldots, \theta_q$, $s \geq p + q$
cp	in:	int, no of autoregressive coefficients (could be 0)
cq	in:	int, no of moving average coefficients (could be 0)
ma	in:	(optional argument) $T \times n$ matrix A, pre-forecast data values (default is zero)
me	in:	(optional argument) $T \times n$ matrix E, pre-forecast residual values (default is zero)

Return value

Returns the forecasts from an ARMA(p, q) model, as an $H \times n$ matrix. The same model is applied to each column of mx.

Description

For a column $x = (x_0, \ldots, x_{H-1})'$ of X, as the first argument, and assuming the ma and me arguments are omitted, this function computes:

$$\hat{a}_0 = x_0$$
$$\hat{a}_1 = x_1 + \phi_1 \hat{a}_0$$
$$\hat{a}_2 = x_2 + \phi_1 \hat{a}_1 + \phi_2 \hat{a}_0$$
$$\ldots$$
$$\hat{a}_h = x_h + \phi_1 \hat{a}_{h-1} + \ldots + \phi_p \hat{a}_{h-p} \quad h = p, \ldots, H - 1,$$

The ma argument can be used to specify actual values $a = (a_0, \ldots, a_{T-1})'$, which are used in the beginning stages of the forecasting, e.g. when $p = 2$:

$$\hat{a}_0 = x_0 + \phi_1 a_{T-1} + \phi_2 a_{T-2}$$
$$\hat{a}_1 = x_1 + \phi_1 \hat{a}_0 + \phi_2 a_{T-1}$$
$$\hat{a}_2 = x_2 + \phi_1 \hat{a}_1 + \phi_2 \hat{a}_0$$
$$\hat{a}_h = x_h + \phi_1 \hat{a}_{h-1} + \phi_2 \hat{a}_{h-2} \quad h = 2, \ldots, H - 1,$$

Note that the actual values are taken from the end of ma: the first forecast will use the last two values, the second forecast the last value.

When a moving average component is present, it is necessary to specify the actual values for the error term. The me argument is used for this. As for the actual values, the errors are taken from the end of me, and are only used when lagged errors fall in the pre-forecast period. For an ARMA(2,2) model (see e.g. Harvey, 1993, §2.6):

$$\hat{a}_0 = x_0 + \phi_1 a_{T-1} + \phi_2 a_{T-2} + \theta_1 \epsilon_{T-1} + \theta_2 \epsilon_{T-2}$$
$$\hat{a}_1 = x_1 + \phi_1 \hat{a}_0 + \phi_2 a_{T-1} + \theta_2 \epsilon_{T-1}$$
$$\hat{a}_2 = x_1 + \phi_1 \hat{a}_1 + \phi_2 \hat{a}_0$$
$$\hat{a}_h = x_h + \phi_1 \hat{a}_{h-1} + \phi_2 \hat{a}_{h-2} \qquad\qquad h = 2, \ldots, H-1,$$

See also

arma0, armavar, cumulate

Example

We use an example from Harvey (1993, p.35):

$$y_t = 0.6y_{t-1} + 0.2y_{t-2} + \epsilon_t + 0.3\epsilon_{t-1} - 0.4\epsilon_{t-2}.$$

Using $y_T = 4$, $y_{T-1} = 5$, $\epsilon_T = 1$ and $\epsilon_{T-1} = 0.5$ four forecasts are computed. The two entries of 100 are ignored, because values are taken from the end:

```
#include <oxstd.h>

main()
{
    print( armaforc(zeros(4,1), <0.6,0.2,0.3,-0.4>, 2, 2,
        <100;100;5.0;4.0>, <0.5;1>) );
}
```

produces

```
        3.5000
        2.5000
        2.2000
        1.8200
```

armagen

```
armagen(const mx, const vp, const cp, const cq);
```

mx	in:	$T \times n$ matrix of known component X
me	in:	$T \times n$ matrix of errors E
vp	in:	$1 \times s$ matrix with autoregressive coefficients $\phi_1, \phi_2, \ldots, \phi_p$ followed by the moving average coefficients $\theta_1, \theta_2, \ldots, \theta_q$, $s \geq p + q$
cp	in:	int, no of autoregressive coefficients (could be 0)
cq	in:	int, no of moving average coefficients (could be 0)

Return value

Generates a an ARMA(p, q) series from an error term (me) and a mean term (mx). The result has the same dimensions as mx. The first p rows of the return value will be identical to those of mx; the recursion will be applied from the pth term onward (missing lagged errors are set to zero).

Description

For a column $(x_0, \ldots, x_{T-1})'$ of X, and a column $(\epsilon_0, \ldots, \epsilon_{T-1})'$ of E, this function computes:

$$a_t = x_t \qquad\qquad\qquad\qquad\qquad\qquad\qquad t = 0, \ldots, p - 1,$$
$$a_t = x_t + \phi_1 a_{t-1} \ldots \phi_p a_{t-p} + \epsilon_t + \theta_1 \epsilon_{t-1} \ldots \theta_q \epsilon_{t-q} \quad t = p, \ldots, T - 1,$$

using $\epsilon_t = 0$ for $t < 0$. For example when $p = 1$ and $q = 2$:

$$a_0 = x_0$$
$$a_1 = x_1 + \phi_1 a_0 + \epsilon_1 + \theta_1 \epsilon_0$$
$$a_2 = x_2 + \phi_1 a_1 + \epsilon_2 + \theta_1 \epsilon_1 + \theta_2 \epsilon_0$$
$$a_t = x_t + \phi_1 a_{t-1} + \epsilon_t + \theta_1 \epsilon_{t-1} + \theta_2 \epsilon_{t-2} \quad t = p, \ldots, T - 1.$$

This function could be used to generate an ARMA(p, q) series from random numbers. In that case it is common to discard intitial observations to remove the effect of starting up the recursion.

See also

arma0, armaforc, armavar, cumsum, cumulate

Example

```
#include <oxstd.h>

main()
{
    decl mx = ones(5,1), meps = rann(5,1) / 10;
    print( armagen(mx, meps, <0.5, 0.5>, 1, 1)
          ~ armagen(mx, meps, <0.5>, 0, 1) );
}
```

produces

```
      1.0000        0.93480
      0.97785       1.0503
      0.89928       0.95791
      0.87461       0.93760
      0.87471       0.93896
```

armavar

```
armavar(const vp, const cp, const cq, const dvar,
    const ct);
```
vp	in:	$1 \times s$ matrix with autoregressive coefficients $\phi_1, \phi_2, \ldots, \phi_p$ followed by the moving average coefficients $\theta_1, \theta_2, \ldots, \theta_q$, $s \geq p + q$
cp	in:	int, no of autoregressive coefficients (could be 0)
cq	in:	int, no of moving average coefficients (could be 0)
dvar	in:	double, variance of disturbance, σ_ϵ^2.
ct	in:	int, number of autocovariance terms required

Return value

Returns a $1 \times$ ct matrix with the autocovariances of the ARMA(p, q) process. Or 0 if the computations failed (e.g. when all autoregressive coefficients are zero).

Description

Computes the theoretical autocovariances c(i), $i = 0, \ldots, T - 1$ (see equation (8.4) on page 131 for a definition) of the ARMA(p, q) process specified as

$$a_t = \phi_1 a_{t-1} + \ldots + \phi_p a_{t-p} + \epsilon_t + \theta_1 \epsilon_{t-1} + \ldots + \theta_q \epsilon_{t-q}, \quad E\epsilon_t = 0, \ E\epsilon_t^2 = \sigma_\epsilon^2.$$

using $\epsilon_t = 0$ for $t < 0$. Stationary is assumed, but not verified. The computations are based on the algorithm given in McLeod (1975).

See also

arma0, pacf

Example

In the example below, we set σ_ϵ^2 such that we obtain the autocorrelation function:
```
#include <oxstd.h>

main()
{
    print( armavar(<0.5>, 1, 0, (1 - 0.5^2), 5)'
        ~ armavar(<-0.5>, 1, 0, (1 - (-0.5)^2), 5)'
        ~ armavar(<0.5>, 0, 1, 1 / (1 + 0.5^2), 5)' );
}
```

produces

```
     1.0000        1.0000        1.0000
     0.50000      -0.50000       0.40000
     0.25000       0.25000       0.00000
     0.12500      -0.12500       0.00000
     0.062500      0.062500      0.00000
```

asin

```
asin(const ma);
```
      ma   in: arithmetic type

Return value
    Returns the arcsine of ma, of double or matrix type. ·

See also
    acos (for examples), atan, cos, cosh, sin, sinh, tan, tanh

atan

```
atan(const ma);
```
      ma   in: arithmetic type

Return value
    Returns the arctangent of ma, of double or matrix type.

See also
    acos (for examples), asin, cos, cosh, sin, sinh, tan, tanh

betafunc

```
betafunc(const mx, const ma, const mb);
```
      mx   in: x, arithmetic type
      ma   in: a, arithmetic type
      mb   in: b, arithmetic type

Return value
    Returns the incomplete beta integral $B_x(a, b)$. Returns 0 if $a \leq 0, b \leq 0$ or $x \leq 0$.
    The accuracy is to about 10 digits.
    The return type is derived as follows:

returns	mx	ma,mb
$m \times n$ matrix	$m \times n$ matrix	scalar
$m \times n$ matrix	scalar	$m \times n$ matrix
$m \times n$ matrix	$m \times n$ matrix	$m \times n$ matrix
double	scalar	scalar

Description
    The incomplete beta integral is defined as:

$$B_x(a, b) = \int_0^x t^{a-1} (1 - t)^{b-1} \, dt, \quad a > 0, b > 0.$$

Note that the complete beta integral is:

$$B(a,b) = B_1(a,b) = \frac{\Gamma(a)\Gamma(b)}{\Gamma(a+b)}.$$

Using the loggamma function, $B(a,b)$ can be computed as:

```
exp(loggamma(a) + loggamma(b) - loggamma(a+b))
```

which avoids overflow in the gamma function.

Also note that betafunc computes the incomplete beta integral, and *not* $I_x(a,b) = B_x(a,b)/B(a,b)$. $I_x(a,b)$ corresponds to the beta distribution, and can be computed with probbeta.

The approximation is based on the continued fraction representation given in Press, Flannery, Teukolsky and Vetterling (1988, §6.3).

See also

gammafunc, probbeta, probf, tailf

binand, binor

```
binand(const ma, ...);
binor(const ma, ...);
      ma            in:   int
      ...           in:   additional integers
```

Return value

binand returns the result from *and*-ing all arguments (the & operator in C/C++).

binor returns the result from *or*-ing all arguments (the | operator in C/C++).

Example

```
#include <oxstd.h>

main()
{
    print( binand(1,2,4), " ", binor(1,2,4) );
}
```

produces

```
0 7
```


cabs, cdiv, cmul, csqrt

```
cabs(const ma);
cdiv(const ma, const mb);
cmul(const ma, const mb);
csqrt(const ma);
```

ma, mb   in: $2 \times n$ matrix (first row is real part, second row imaginary part), or $1 \times n$ matrix (real part only)

Return value

cabs returns a $1 \times n$ matrix with the absolute value of the vector of complex numbers.

cdiv returns a $2 \times n$ matrix with the result of the division of the two vectors of complex numbers. If both ma and mb have no imaginary part, the return value will be $1 \times n$.

cmul returns a $2 \times n$ matrix with the result of the multiplication of the two vectors of complex numbers. If both ma and mb have no imaginary part, the return value will be $1 \times n$.

csqrt returns a $2 \times n$ matrix with the square root of the vector of complex numbers.

Description

Using subscript r for the real part of a, b and subscript i for the imaginary part:

cabs: modulus of complex number: $(a_r^2 + a_i^2)^{1/2}$.

cmul: complex multiplication: $(a_r + ia_i)(b_r + ib_i)$.

cdiv: complex division: $(a_r + ia_i)/(b_r + ib_i)$.

csqrt: square root of complex number: $(a_r + ia_i)^{1/2}$.

Example

```
#include <oxstd.h>

main()
{
    decl v = <1, -1, -2>, rv = csqrt(v);
    rv[0][1] = 1;/* change to a more interesting value */

    print(v, rv, cabs(rv), cdiv(rv, rv), cmul(rv, rv),
        cmul(rv, cdiv(ones(1,3), rv)) );
}
```

produces

```
        1.0000        -1.0000        -2.0000

        1.0000         1.0000         0.00000
        0.00000        1.0000         1.4142

        1.0000         1.4142         1.4142

        1.0000         1.0000         1.0000
        0.00000        0.00000        0.00000

        1.0000         0.00000       -2.0000
        0.00000        2.0000         0.00000
```

```
             1.0000          1.0000          1.0000
             0.00000         0.00000         0.00000
```

In the second example the complex functions are used to check if the computed roots of a polynomial indeed correspond to zeros of the polynomial:

```
#include <oxstd.h>

main()
{
    decl v1, roots, cr;

    v1 = <-1, 1.2274, -0.017197, -0.28369, -0.01028>;

    polyroots(v1, &roots);

    cr = columns(roots);
    print("roots", roots,
            "inverse roots", cdiv(ones(1,cr), roots) );

    decl x1, x2, x3, x4, check;
    x1 = roots;
    x2 = cmul(x1, x1);                      /* roots ^ 2 */
    x3 = cmul(x2, x1);                      /* roots ^ 3 */
    x4 = cmul(x2, x2);                      /* roots ^ 4 */
    check = v1[0][4] * (ones(1,cr) | zeros(1,cr)) +
            v1[0][3] * x1 + v1[0][2] * x2 +
            v1[0][1] * x3 + v1[0][0] * x4;

    print("check (could be somewhat different "
            "with other Ox versions)", check);
}
```

which produces:

```
roots
        0.82865         0.82865        -0.39337        -0.036535
        0.16923        -0.16923         0.00000         0.00000
inverse roots
        1.1585          1.1585         -2.5422         -27.371
       -0.23659         0.23659         0.00000         0.00000
check (could be somewhat different with other Ox versions)
   1.6653e-016   1.6653e-016  -2.7756e-016  -1.3515e-017
  -2.2204e-016   2.2204e-016   0.00000       0.00000
```

ceil

```
ceil(const ma);
```
      ma   in: arithmetic type

Return value

Returns the ceiling of each element of ma, of double or matrix type. The ceiling is the smallest integer larger than or equal to the argument

See also

floor, round, trunc

Example

```
#include <oxstd.h>

main()
{
    print( ceil(<-1.8, -1.2, 1.2, 1.8>) );
    print( floor(<-1.8, -1.2, 1.2, 1.8>) );
    print( round(<-1.8, -1.2, 1.2, 1.8>) );
    print( trunc(<-1.8, -1.2, 1.2, 1.8>) );

    print( int(-1.8), " ", int(-1.2), " ",
           int(1.2), " ", int(1.8) );
}
```

produces

```
     -1.0000       -1.0000        2.0000        2.0000
     -2.0000       -2.0000        1.0000        1.0000
     -2.0000       -1.0000        1.0000        2.0000
     -1.0000       -1.0000        1.0000        2.0000
 -1 -1 1 1
```

choleski

```
choleski(const ma);
```
    ma   in: symmetric, positive definite $m \times m$ matrix A

Return value

Returns the Choleski decomposition of a symmetric positive definite matrix A: $A = PP'$; P is lower triangular (has zeros above the diagonal).
Returns 0 if the decomposition failed.

Error messages

choleski(): decomposition failed (this implies a negative definite or numerically singular matrix A).

See also

decldl, invertsym

Example

```
#include <oxstd.h>

main()
{
    decl mp;

    mp = choleski(<4,1;1,3>);
    print(mp, mp*mp');
}
```

produces

```
    2.0000        0.00000
 0.500000          1.6583

    4.0000         1.0000
    1.0000         3.0000
```

columns

```
columns(const ma);
```

    ma   in: any type

Return value

Returns an integer value with the number of columns in the argument ma:

type	returns
$m \times n$ matrix	n
string	number of characters in the string
array	number of elements in the array
file	number of columns in the file
	(only if opened with f format, see fopen)
other	0

See also

    rows

Example

```
#include <oxstd.h>

main()
{
    print( columns(<0,1;1,2;3,4>), " ",
        columns("taylor"), "\n" );
    print( rows(<0,1;1,2;3,4>), " ",
        rows("taylor"), "\n" );
    print( sizeof(<0,1;1,2;3,4>), " ",
        sizeof("taylor"));
}
```

produces

```
2 6
3 6
3 6
```

constant

```
constant(const dval, const r, const c);
    dval        in:  double
    r           in:  int
    c           in:  int
```

Return value
  Returns an r by c matrix filled with dval.

See also
  ones, unit, zeros

Example

```
#include <oxstd.h>

main()
{
    print( constant(1.5, 2, 2) );
}
```

produces

```
    1.5000      1.5000
    1.5000      1.5000
```

correlation

```
correlation(const ma);
    ma          in:  T × n matrix A
```

Return value
  Returns a $n \times n$ matrix holding the correlation matrix of ma. If any variance is $\leq 10^{-20}$, then the corresponding row and column of the correlation matrix are set to 0.

Description

Computes the correlation matrix $R = (r_{ij})$ of a $T \times n$ matrix $A = (a_{tj})$:

$$\bar{a}_j = \frac{1}{T} \sum_{t=0}^{T-1} a_{tj}$$

$$\hat{\sigma}_j^2 = \frac{1}{T} \sum_{t=0}^{T-1} (a_{tj} - \bar{a}_j)^2$$

$$r_{ij} = \frac{1}{T\hat{\sigma}_i\hat{\sigma}_j} \sum_{t=0}^{T-1} (a_{ti} - \bar{a}_i)(a_{tj} - \bar{a}_j)$$

Note that $r_{ii} = 1$.

See also

acf, meanc, meanr, standardize, varc, varr, variance

Example

```
#include <oxstd.h>

main()
{
    decl m1 = rann(100,2), m2;

    m2 = standardize(m1);
    print( correlation(m1), m2'm2/rows(m2) );
}
```

produces

```
     1.0000         0.10707
     0.10707        1.0000

     1.0000         0.10707
     0.10707        1.0000
```

cos, cosh

```
cos(const ma);
cosh(const ma);
```
      ma   in: arithmetic type

Return value

cos returns the cosine of ma, of double or matrix type.

cosh returns the cosine hyperbolicus of ma, of double or matrix type.

See also

acos (for examples), asin, atan, cosh, sin, sinh, tan, tanh

countc

```
countc(const ma, const va);
    ma            in:  m × n matrix
    va            in:  1 × q matrix
```

Return value

Returns a matrix r which counts of the number of elements in each column of ma which is between the corresponding values in va:

r[0][0] = # elements in column 0 of ma $\leq$ va[0][0]
r[1][0] = # elements in column 0 of ma $>$ va[0][0] and $\leq$ va[0][1]
r[2][0] = # elements in column 0 of ma $>$ va[0][1] and $\leq$ va[0][2]
r[q][0] = # elements in column 0 of ma $>$ va[0][q-1]

...

r[0][1] = # elements in column 1 of ma $\leq$ va[0][0]
r[1][1] = # elements in column 1 of ma $>$ va[0][0] and $\leq$ va[0][1]
r[2][1] = # elements in column 1 of ma $>$ va[0][1] and $\leq$ va[0][2]
r[q][1] = # elements in column 1 of ma $>$ va[0][q-1]

...

If ma is $m \times n$, and va is $1 \times q$ the returned matrix is $(q+1) \times n$ (any remaining columns of va are ignored).

Description

Counts the number of elements in each column which is in a supplied interval.

See also

countr

Example

```
#include <oxstd.h>

main()
{
    print( countc(<0:3;1:4;2:5>, <2,4>) );
    print( countr(<0:3;1:4;2:5>, <2>) );
}
```

produces

```
  3.0000        2.0000       1.0000       0.00000
  0.00000       1.0000       2.0000       2.0000
  0.00000       0.00000      0.00000      1.0000

  3.0000        1.0000
  2.0000        2.0000
  1.0000        3.0000
```

countr

```
countr(const ma, const va);
    ma          in:  m × n matrix
    va          in:  1 × q matrix
```

Return value

Returns a matrix `r` which counts of the number of elements in each row of `ma` which is between the corresponding values in `va`:

r[0][0] = # elements in row 0 of ma $\leq$ va[0][0]
r[0][1] = # elements in row 0 of ma $>$ va[0][0] and $\leq$ va[0][1]
r[0][2] = # elements in row 0 of ma $>$ va[0][1] and $\leq$ va[0][2]
r[0][q] = # elements in row 0 of ma $>$ va[0][q-1]
...

r[1][0] = # elements in row 1 of ma $\leq$ va[0][0]
r[1][1] = # elements in row 1 of ma $>$ va[0][0] and $\leq$ va[0][1]
r[1][2] = # elements in row 1 of ma $>$ va[0][1] and $\leq$ va[0][2]
r[1][q] = # elements in row 1 of ma $>$ va[0][q-1]
...

If ma is $m \times n$, and va is $1 \times q$ the returned matrix is $m \times (q+1)$ (any remaining columns of va are ignored).

Description

Counts the number of elements in each row which is in a supplied interval.

See also

`countc` (for an example)

cumprod

```
cumprod(const mfac);
cumprod(const mfac, const cp);
cumprod(const mfac, const cp, const mz);
    mfac        in:  T × n or 1 × n matrix of multiplication factors S
    cp          in:  int: autoregressive order p (optional argument; default is 1)
    mz          in:  (optional argument) T × n or 1 × n matrix of known com-
                     ponents Z (optional argument; default is 0)
```

Return value

Returns a $T \times n$ matrix with the cumulated autoregressive product. The first p rows of the return value will be identical to the sum of those in `mz` and `mfac`; the recursion will be applied from the pth term onward. If either `mz` or `mfac` is $1 \times n$, the same values are used for every t.

Description

For a column $(z_0, \ldots, z_{T-1})'$ of known values X, and multiplication factors $(s_0, \ldots s_{T-1})'$ the cumprod function computes:

$$
\begin{aligned}
a_t &= z_t + s_t, & t &= 0, \ldots, p-1, \\
a_t &= z_t + s_t(\phi_1 a_{t-1} \times \ldots \times \phi_p a_{t-p}) & t &= p, \ldots, T-1.
\end{aligned}
$$

See also

armagen, cumsum (for an example), cumulate

cumsum

```
cumsum(const mx, const vp);
cumsum(const mx, const vp, const mstart);
```
mx   in: $T \times n$ matrix of known component X

vp   in: $1 \times p$ or $n \times p$ matrix with autoregressive coefficients $\phi_1, \phi_2, \ldots, \phi_p$

mstart   in: (optional argument) $T \times s$ matrix of starting values S, $s \geq p$; default is mx

Return value

Returns a $T \times n$ matrix with the cumulated autoregressive sum. The first p rows of the return value will be identical to those of mstart; the recursion will be applied from the pth term onward.

If vp is $1 \times p$, the same coefficients are applied to each column; if vp is $n \times p$, each row will have coefficients specific to each column of the recursive series.

Description

For a column $(x_0, \ldots, x_{T-1})'$ of known values X, and starting values $(s_0, \ldots s_{p-1})'$ the cumsum function computes:

$$
\begin{aligned}
a_t &= s_t, & t &= 0, \ldots, p-1, \\
a_t &= x_t + \phi_1 a_{t-1} + \ldots + \phi_p a_{t-p}, & t &= p, \ldots, T-1.
\end{aligned}
$$

See also

armagen, cumprod, cumulate

Example

```
#include <oxstd.h>

main()
{
    decl mx = ones(5,1);
    print( mx
```

```
~  cumsum(mx, <0.5>)
~  cumsum(mx, <1, 0.5>, <1;2>)
~  cumprod(mx*2)
~  cumprod(mx*2, 2) );
```
}

produces

1.0000	1.0000	1.0000	2.0000	2.0000
1.0000	1.5000	2.0000	4.0000	2.0000
1.0000	1.7500	3.5000	8.0000	8.0000
1.0000	1.8750	5.5000	16.000	32.000
1.0000	1.9375	8.2500	32.000	512.00

cumulate

```
cumulate(const ma);
cumulate(const ma, const m1, ...);
```
     ma   in: $T \times n$ matrix A
     m1   in: $n \times n$ matrix, coefficients of first lags (optional argument)
     ...   in: $n \times n$ matrix, coefficients of lags 2, ...

Return value

Returns a $T \times n$ matrix.

The simplest version returns a matrix which holds the cumulated (integrated) columns of ma.

The second form cumulates (integrates) the (vector) autoregressive process with current values ma using the specified coefficient matrices. The function has a variable number of arguments, and the number of arguments determines the autoregressive order (minimum 2 arguments, which is an AR(1) process). Note that cumulate(m) corresponds to cumulate(m, unit(columns(m))).

Description

The version with one arguments cumulates the columns of its argument.

For the form with additional arguments, assume that ma and k coefficient matrices have been supplied ($k \geq 1$: at least two arguments) and write $A_0^{T-1} = A = $ ma, $M_1 = $ m1, $...M_k$. Also define A_{-i}^{T-1-i} as the ith lag, whereby each column is lagged: each column of A is shifted down, and missing values are replaced by zeros, so that e.g. $A_{-1}^{T-2} = $ lag0(ma, 1).

The cumulate function returns:

$$A_0^{T-1} + A_{-1}^{T-2}M_1 + A_{-2}^{T-3}M_2 + \cdots A_{-k}^{T-1-k}M_k,$$

which has the same dimensions as ma.

Perhaps easier to understand is the univariate case. For example, with three arguments, $(a_0, \ldots, a_{T-1})'$, β_0 and β_1, this function computes y_t:

$$y_0 = a_0,$$
$$y_1 = a_1 + \beta_0 y_0,$$
$$y_t = a_t + \beta_0 y_{t-1} + \beta_1 y_{t-1}, \quad t = 2, \ldots, T-1.$$

Comparison with the `arma0` function shows that in the univariate case `cumu-
late(y,a0,a1)` corresponds to `arma0(y,-(a0~a1),0,2)`.

See also

arma0, cumsum, lag0

Example

```
#include <oxstd.h>

main()
{
    print( ones(5,1)
           ~ cumulate(ones(5,1))
           ~ cumulate(ones(5,1), <0.5>)
           ~ cumulate(ones(5,1), <1>, <0.5>) );
}
```

produces

```
1.0000        1.0000        1.0000        1.0000
1.0000        2.0000        1.5000        2.0000
1.0000        3.0000        1.7500        3.5000
1.0000        4.0000        1.8750        5.5000
1.0000        5.0000        1.9375        8.2500
```

date

date();

Return value

A string holding the current date.

See also

time

Example

```
#include <oxstd.h>

main()
{
    print("\ntime=", time(), " date=", date(), "\n");
}
```

prints the current time and date.

decldl

```
decldl(const ma, const aml, const amd);
    ma          in:  symmetric, positive definite m × m matrix A
    aml         in:  address of variable
                out: m × m lower diagonal matrix L, LDL' = A
    amd         in:  address of variable
                out: 1 × m matrix with reciprocals of D
```

Return value

Returns the result of the Choleski decomposition:

  1 no error;
  0 the Choleski decomposition failed: the matrix is negative definite or the matrix is (numerically) singular.

Description

Computes the square root free Choleski decomposition of a symmetric positive definite matrix A stored in argument ma: $A = LDL'$. L has zeros above the diagonal and ones on the diagonal.

Note that the *reciprocals* of D are stored in amd.

Error messages

decldl(): decomposition failed

See also

choleski, decldlband, solveldl

Example

```
#include <oxstd.h>

main()
{
    decl ma = <4,1;1,3>, md, ml, mi;

    print("result = ", decldl(ma, &ml, &md));
    print(" L =", ml, "D =", md);
    print(ml*diag(1 ./ md)*ml');

    mi = solveldl(ml, md, unit(2));
    print(mi*ma);
}
```

produces (the final matrix could have values of around 1e-16 instead of 0):

```
result = 1 L =
        1.0000       0.00000
        0.25000       1.0000
D =
```

0.25000	0.36364

| 4.0000 | 1.0000 |
| 1.0000 | 3.0000 |

| 1.0000 | 0.00000 |
| 0.00000 | 1.0000 |

decldlband

```
decldlband(const ma, const aml, const amd);
```
ma	in: $p \times m$ vector specifying the A^b matrix
aml	in: address of variable
	out: holds $p \times m$ lower diagonal matrix L
amd	in: address of variable
	out: $1 \times m$ matrix with reciprocals of D

Return value

Returns the result of the Choleski decomposition:

    1 no error;

    0 the Choleski decomposition failed: the matrix is negative definite or the matrix is (numerically) singular.

Description

Computes the square root free Choleski decomposition of a symmetric positive definite band matrix A stored in argument ma: $A = LDL'$. L has zeros above the diagonal and ones on the diagonal. Note that the reciprocals of D are stored. If $A = (a_{ij}), i, j = 0, \ldots m - 1$ is the underlying $m \times m$ symmetric positive definite band matrix, with bandwidth $p - 1$, so that $a_{ij} = 0$ for $|i - j| \geq p$, then the input matrix ma $= A^b$ is formed as:

$$
\begin{pmatrix}
0 & \cdots & \cdots & 0 & a_{0,p-1} & \cdots & a_{m-p,m-1} \\
\vdots & & & & & & \vdots \\
0 & a_{0,1} & a_{1,2} & \cdots & \cdots & \cdots & a_{m-2,m-1} \\
a_{0,0} & \cdots & \cdots & \cdots & \cdots & \cdots & a_{m-1,m-1}
\end{pmatrix}
$$

The example below also shows how to create A^b out of A and vice versa.

Error messages

decldlband(): decomposition failed

See also

solveldlband, solvetoeplitz

Example

```
#include <oxstd.h>

main()
{
    decl i, j, k, m, ma, m1, ml, md, ct = 5, cb = 3;

    m1 = toeplitz(<5,4,3>, ct);
    for (i = 0; i < ct; ++i)
        m1[i][i] += i;

    ma = new matrix[cb][ct];      // create band matrix from
    for (i = 0; i < cb; ++i)      //    upper diagonal of m1
        for (j = cb-1-i, k = 0; j < ct; ++j, ++k)
            ma[i][j] = m1[k][j];

    print(m1, ma);

    if (decldlband(ma, &ml, &md))
        print( solveldlband(ml, md, <1;2;3;4;5>)' );

                          // store L in lower diagonal of m1
    for (i = 0, m = 1-cb; i < ct; ++i, m++)
        for (j = max(0,m), k = j - m; j < i; ++j, ++k)
            m1[i][j] =  ml[k][i];

    print(m1, m1);
}
```

produces

```
    5.0000        4.0000        3.0000        0.00000       0.00000
    4.0000        6.0000        4.0000        3.0000        0.00000
    3.0000        4.0000        7.0000        4.0000        3.0000
    0.00000       3.0000        4.0000        8.0000        4.0000
    0.00000       0.00000       3.0000        4.0000        9.0000

    0.00000       0.00000       3.0000        3.0000        3.0000
    0.00000       4.0000        4.0000        4.0000        4.0000
    5.0000        6.0000        7.0000        8.0000        9.0000

    0.012378      0.26172      -0.036251      0.17507       0.48983

    0.00000       0.00000       0.60000       1.0714        0.70000
    0.00000       0.80000       0.57143       0.53333       0.67290
    5.0000        6.0000        7.0000        8.0000        9.0000

    5.0000        4.0000        3.0000        0.00000       0.00000
    0.80000       6.0000        4.0000        3.0000        0.00000
    0.60000       0.57143       7.0000        4.0000        3.0000
    0.00000       1.0714        0.53333       8.0000        4.0000
    0.00000       0.00000       0.70000       0.67290       9.0000
```

declu

```
declu(const ma, const aml, const amu, const amp);
```

ma	in:	square $m \times m$ matrix A
aml	in:	address of variable
	out:	$m \times m$ matrix lower diagonal matrix L, has ones on the diagonal
amu	in:	address of variable
	out:	$m \times m$ matrix upper diagonal matrix U, $LU = PA$
amp	in:	address of variable
	out:	$2 \times m$ matrix, the first row holds the permutation matrix P', $A = (LU)[P'][]$, the second row holds the interchange permutations

Return value

Returns the result of the LU decomposition:

1 no error;
2 the decomposition could be unreliable;
0 the LU decomposition failed: the matrix is (numerically) singular.

Description

Computes the LU decomposition of a matrix A as: $PA = LU$ by Gaussian elimination (using accumulation of inner-products) with partial pivoting, as described, e.g. in Wilkinson (1965, §4.39) (also see Golub and Van Loan, 1989 §3.4 for an analysis). *Note that L has ones on the diagonal.*
The permutation matrix P' is stored as row indices so that $A = (LU)[P'][]$ (see the example below). The actual permutation matrix $P' = P^{-1}$ can be created as pt = (unit(rows(ma)))[mp][] where ma is the original matrix, and mp holds the row indices as returned by declu. P can be computed as mp[][mp]. The second row of mp holds the interchange permutations p, such that rows $p[0][i]$ and i are swapped.

Error messages

declu(): decomposition failed

See also

determinant, invert, solvelu

Example

```
#include <oxstd.h>

main()
{
    decl ma, ml, mu, vp, mx;
```

```
    ma = <3,17,10;2,4,-2;6,18,-12>;
    declu(ma, &ml, &mu, &vp);
    print( (ml*mu)[ vp[0][] ][],
           (unit(rows(ma)))[ vp[0][] ][] );

    mx = solvelu(ml, mu, vp, ma);
    print(mx);
}
```

produces (note that the last matrix is the identity matrix: whether it has zeros, or nearly zeros, could dependent on which Ox version was used):

```
        3.0000              17.000              10.000
        2.0000              4.0000             -2.0000
        6.0000              18.000             -12.000

        0.00000             1.0000              0.00000
        0.00000             0.00000             1.0000
        1.0000              0.00000             0.00000

        1.0000     4.4409e-016                 0.00000
   -3.7007e-017         1.0000                 0.00000
    1.8504e-017     5.5511e-017                 1.0000
```

decsvd

```
decsvd(const ma, const amu, const amw);
decsvd(const ma, const amu, const amw, const amv);
```

ma	in:	$m \times n$ matrix $A, m \geq n$
amu	in:	address of variable
	out:	$m \times n$ matrix $U, U'U = I_n$
amw	in:	address of variable
	out:	$1 \times n$ matrix with diagonal of W
amv	in:	(optional argument) address of variable
	out:	if not 0 on input: $n \times n$ matrix $V, UWV' = A, V'V = I_n$

Return value

Returns the result of the singular value decomposition:

0 no error;

k if the k-th singular value (with index $k - 1$) has not been determined after 50 iterations.

Note that the singular values are in *decreasing order*, with the columns of U, V sorted accordingly.

Description

Decomposes a $m \times n$ matrix A, $m \geq n$, $\mathrm{rank}(A) = r > 0$, into $A = UWV'$:

U is $m \times n$ and $U'U = I_n$,

W is $n \times n$ and diagonal, with positive diagonal elements,

V is $n \times n$ and $V'V = I_n$.

The rank of A is the number of non-zero diagonal elements of W.

Error messages

decsvd(): needs m >= n

decsvd(): svd failed

See also

§12.7.5.1, §12.7.5

Example

```
#include <oxstd.h>

main()
{
    decl mu, mv, mw;

    print("result = ", decsvd(<2,1;3,1>, &mu, &mw, &mv));
    print(" W =", mw, "A =", mu * diag(mw) * mv');
}
```

produces

```
result = 0 W =
    3.8643        0.25878
A =
    2.0000        1.00000
    3.0000        1.00000
```

densbeta, denschi, densf, densn, denst

```
densbeta(const ma, const a, const b);
denschi(const ma, const df);
densf(const ma, const df1, const df2);
densn(const ma);
denst(const ma, const idf);
```

ma	in:	arithmetic type
a,b	in:	arithmetic type, arguments for Beta distribution
df	in:	arithmetic type, degrees of freedom
df1	in:	arithmetic type, degrees of freedom in the numerator
df2	in:	arithmetic type, degrees of freedom in the denominator
idf	in:	int, degrees of freedom

Return value

Returns the requested density at ma (the returned densities are positive):

densbeta   Beta (a, b) density

denschi $\chi^2(df)$ density

densf $F(df1, df2)$ density

densn   standard normal density

denst   student-t(df) density

The return type is derived as follows:

returns	ma	degrees of freedom arguments
$m \times n$ matrix	$m \times n$ matrix	scalar (int for denst)
$m \times n$ matrix	scalar	$m \times n$ matrix
$m \times n$ matrix	$m \times n$ matrix	$m \times n$ matrix
double	scalar	scalar (int for denst)

See also

prob..., quan..., tail...

determinant

```
determinant(const ma);
```
    ma   in: $m \times m$ matrix

Return value

Returns the determinant of ma. Return type is double.

Description

Computes the determinant of a matrix. The determinant is obtained from the LU decomposition of the matrix (see declu). Use invert if both the inverse and determinant are required. Note that for ill-conditioned or large matrices, the determinant could be a very large or very small number.

Error messages

determinant(): overflow (determinant set to DBL_MAX_E_EXP)

determinant(): underflow (determinant set to 0)

determinant(): matrix is singular (determinant set to 0)

determinant(): unreliable (this is a warning)

See also

declu, invert, logdet

Example

```
#include <oxstd.h>

main()
{
    print( determinant(<2,1;1,4>) );
}
```

produces: 7

diag

```
diag(const ma);
```
  ma   in: double, or $m \times 1$ or $1 \times m$ matrix

Return value
  Returns a $m \times m$ matrix with ma on the diagonal.

See also
  diagonal, diagonalize, toeplitz

Example

```
#include <oxstd.h>

main()
{
    print( diag(<1,1>), diag(<1;1>) );
}
```

produces

```
    1.0000      0.00000
    0.00000     1.0000

    1.0000      0.00000
    0.00000     1.0000
```

diagonal

```
diagonal(const ma);
```
  ma   in: arithmetic type

Return value
  A matrix with the diagonal from the specified matrix in the first row. *Note that the diagonal is returned as a row vector, not a column.* If ma is $m \times n$, the returned matrix is $\min(m, n) \times \min(m, n)$; if ma is scalar, the returned matrix is 1×1.

See also
  diag, diagonalize, setdiagonal

Example

```
#include <oxstd.h>

main()
{
    print( diagonal(<2,1;1,4>) );
}
```

produces

```
    2.0000        4.0000
```

diagonalize

```
diagonalize(const ma);
    ma              in:   arithmetic type
```

Return value

Returns a matrix with the diagonal of ma on its diagonal, and zeros in off-diagonal elements. If ma is $m \times n$, the returned matrix is $m \times n$; if ma is scalar, the returned matrix is 1×1.

See also

diag, diagonal, setdiagonal

Example

```
#include <oxstd.h>

main()
{
    print( diagonalize( constant(2, 3, 4) ) );
}
```

produces

```
        2.0000        0.00000        0.00000        0.00000
        0.00000        2.0000        0.00000        0.00000
        0.00000        0.00000        2.0000        0.00000
```

diff0

```
diff0(const ma, const ia);
diff0(const ma, const ia, const dmisval);
    ma          in:   $T \times n$ matrix $A$
    ilag        in:   int, lag length of difference
    dmisval     in:   (optional argument) double, value to set missing observations
                      to (default is 0)
```

Return value

Returns a $T \times n$ matrix with the ilagth difference of the specified matrix, whereby missing values are replaced by zero. E.g. the result matrix r using second differences (ilag = 2) is:

```
r[0][0] = 0                    r[0][1] = 0                    ...
r[1][0] = 0                    r[1][1] = 0                    ...
r[2][0] = ma[2][0]-ma[0][0]    r[2][1] = ma[2][1]-ma[0][1]   ...
r[3][0] = ma[3][0]-ma[1][0]    r[3][1] = ma[3][1]-ma[1][1]   ...
r[4][0] = ma[4][0]-ma[2][0]    r[4][1] = ma[4][1]-ma[2][1]   ...
...
```

The result has the same dimensions as ma.

Description

Differences the specified matrix, missing values are replaced by zero (unless a missing value is specified as the third argument). Using the lag operator L, for a column $a = (a_0, \ldots, a_{T-1})'$ of A, this function computes $(1 - L^d)a$. For $d = 1$, this is: $(0, a_1 - a_0, \ldots, a_{T-1} - a_{T-2})'$. The value of d must be integer, but may be negative (a forward difference). Note that $(1 - L^0)a = 0$.

See also

lag0, diff0pow

Example

```
#include <oxstd.h>

main()
{
    print( diff0(<1:5>',2) );
}
```

produces

```
      0.00000
      0.00000
      2.0000
      2.0000
      2.0000
```

diff0pow

```
diff0pow(const ma, const d);
diff0pow(const ma, const d, const dmisval);
```

ma	in:	$T \times n$ matrix A
d	in:	double, length of difference d, $|d| \leq 10000$
dmisval	in:	(optional argument) double, value to set missing observations to (default is 0)

Return value

Returns a $T \times n$ matrix with $(1 - L)^d A$. The result has the same dimensions as ma.

Description

Differences the specified matrix, missing values are replaced by zero (unless a missing value is specified as the third argument). For a column $a = (a_0, \ldots, a_{T-1})'$ of A, this function computes $(1 - L)^d a$.

For integer d, this is a repeated application of $(1 - L)^{sign(d)}$, so that the first observation of the return value will be 0 if d is a non-zero integer.

For real d, write $d = d^* + k$, with $-0.5 < d^* < 0.5$. Then first $a^* = (1 - L)^{d^*} a$ is computed:

$$a_t^* = (1 - L)^{d^*} a_t = \sum_{j=0}^{t} \frac{(-d^*)_j}{j!} a_{t-j}, \quad t = 0, \ldots, T - 1,$$

where the $(\cdot)_j$ symbol is defined as:

$$
\begin{aligned}
(z)_0 &= 1, \\
(z)_j &= z(z + 1) \ldots (z + j - 1) && \text{for } j > 0 \\
(z)_j &= 1/\left((z - 1)(z - 2) \ldots (z - j)\right) && \text{for } j < 0
\end{aligned}
$$

and using $a_k = 0$ for $k < 0$. This is followed by a repeated application of $(1 - L)^{sign(k)}$ on a^*.

See also

arma0, diff0

Example

In this example, fracdiff replicates part of the functionality of the library function diff0pow.

```
#include <oxstd.h>

fracdiff(const mY, const d)
{
    decl i, mu = mY, fac = -d;

    for (i = 1; i < rows(mY); ++i, fac *= (-d+i-1)/i)
        mu += fac * lag0(mY,i);

    return mu;
}
main()
{
    decl mx = <1:5>';
    print( diff0pow(mx,2) ~ diff0(diff0(mx,1),1) ~
```

```
            diff0pow(mx,-2) ~ diff0(diff0(mx,-1),-1) );
      print( diff0pow(mx,0.2) ~ fracdiff(mx,0.2) ~
         diff0pow(mx,-0.2) ~ fracdiff(mx,-0.2) );
   }
```

produces

```
         0.00000      0.00000      0.00000      0.00000
         1.0000       1.0000       0.00000      0.00000
         0.00000      0.00000      0.00000      0.00000
         0.00000      0.00000     -1.0000      -1.0000
         0.00000      0.00000      0.00000      0.00000

         1.0000       1.0000       1.0000       1.0000
         1.8000       1.8000       2.2000       2.2000
         2.5200       2.5200       3.5200       3.5200
         3.1920       3.1920       4.9280       4.9280
         3.8304       3.8304       6.4064       6.4064
```

double

```
double(const ma);
```
    ma   in: arithmetic type

Return value

Casts the argument to a double:

input	returns
integer	converted to a double
double	unchanged
matrix	element 0,0
string	element 0 as a double
other types	error

See also

    int, matrix, string §12.7.2.3

eigen, eigensym

```
eigen(const ma, const amval);
eigen(const ma, const amval, const amvec);
eigensym(const ms, const amsval);
eigensym(const ms, const amsval, const amsvec);
```

ma	in:	$m \times m$ matrix A
amval	in:	address of variable
	out:	$2 \times m$ matrix with eigenvalues of A first row is real part, second row imaginary part *The eigenvalues are not sorted.*
amvec	in:	address of variable
	out:	$n \times m$ matrix with eigenvectors of A in columns
ms	in:	symmetric $m \times m$ matrix A^s
amsval	in:	address of variable
	out:	$1 \times m$ matrix with eigenvalues of A^s, sorted in decreasing order
amsvec	in:	address of variable
	out:	$n \times m$ matrix with eigenvectors of A^s in columns

Return value

Returns the result of the eigenvalue decomposition:

0 no error;

1 maximum no of iterations (50) reached.

Description

Computes the eigenvalues of a real matrix and a symmetric real matrix. The ei-gensym function delivers the eigenvalues sorted, with the *largest first*. If eigenvectors are requested, these are in corresponding order.

The eigen function uses the balanced form of the matrix. (eigensym: if the matrix has elements of widely varying order of magnitude, the smaller elements should be in the bottom right hand corner.)

Sources: these routines are based on algorithms by J.H. Wilkinson and colleagues in Numerische Mathematik (Martin, Reinsch and Wilkinson, 1968, Martin and Wilkinson, 1968b, Martin and Wilkinson, 1968a, Parlett and Reinsch, 1969, Peters and Wilkinson, 1970, Dubrulle, 1970)

Error messages

eigen(): maximum no. of iterations reached

eigensym(): maximum no. of iterations reached

Example

```
#include <oxstd.h>

main()
{
    decl meval, mevec;

    print("result=", eigensym(<2,1;1,3>, &meval, &mevec));
    print(" eigenvalues:", meval, "eigenvectors:", mevec);
```

```
    print("result=", eigen(<2,1;-3,1>, &meval));
    print(" eigenvalues:", "%r",
        {"real", "imaginary"}, meval);
}
```

produces

```
result=0 eigenvalues:
    3.6180        1.3820
eigenvectors:
  -0.52573       0.85065
  -0.85065      -0.52573
result=0 eigenvalues:
real             1.5000        1.5000
imaginary        1.6583       -1.6583
```

eigensymgen

eigensymgen(const ma, const mb, const amval,const amvec);

ma	in:	symmetric $m \times m$ matrix A
mb	in:	symmetric positive definite $m \times m$ matrix B
amval	in:	address of variable
	out:	$1 \times m$ matrix with sorted eigenvalues of A
amvec	in:	address of variable
	out:	$n \times m$ matrix eigenvectors of A in columns

Return value

Solves the general eigenproblem $Ax = \lambda Bx$. returning the result of the eigen-value decomposition:

  0 no error;
  1 maximum no of iterations (50) reached.
 −1 Choleski decomposition failed.

Description

Solves the general eigenproblem $Ax = \lambda Bx$, where A and B are symmetric, B is also positive definite. The problem is transformed in standard eigenproblem by decomposing $B = CC' = LDL'$ and solving $Py = \lambda y$, where $y = C'x$, $P = C^{-1}AC'^{-1}$

Error messages

eigensymgen(): matrices not conformant
eigensymgen(): maximum no. of iterations reached
eigensymgen(): decomposition failed (Choleski decomposition)

See also

decldl, eigensym

Example

```
#include <oxstd.h>

main()
{
    decl meval, mevec;

    print("result = ",
        eigensymgen(<2,1;1,3>,<1,0;0,1>, &meval, &mevec));
    print(" generalized eigenvectors:", mevec);
}
```

produces

```
result = 0 generalized eigenvectors:
    -0.52573        0.85065
    -0.85065       -0.52573
```

eprint

```
eprint(const a, ...);
```

a	in:	any type
...	in:	any type

Return value

Returns the number of arguments supplied to the function.

Description

Prints to stderr. See print for a further description.

See also

fprint, print, sprint

Example

```
#include <oxstd.h>

main()
{
    eprint( "\nerror message\n" );
}
```

produces

```
error message
```

exit

```
exit(const iexit);
     ma              in:   integer, exit code
```
Description

    Exits Ox, with the specified exit code.

No return value.

exp

```
exp(const ma);
     ma              in:   arithmetic type
```
Return value

    Returns the exponent of each element of ma, of double or matrix type.

See also

    `log`

Example

```
#include <oxstd.h>

main()
{
    print( exp(<0,1>) );
}
```
produces

```
    1.0000          2.7183
```

fabs

```
fabs(const ma);
     ma              in:   int, double, matrix
```
Return value

    Returns the absolute value of each element of ma, of the same type as ma.

Example

```
#include <oxstd.h>

main()
{
    print( fabs(<-1.1,1.1>) );
}
```
produces

```
    1.1000          1.1000
```

fclose

```
fclose(const file);
    file        in:  an open file which is to be closed
```

Return value

Returns 0.

Description

Closes the specified file, which was previously opened by a call to `fopen`. All open files are automatically closed when the program exits. On some operating systems, there is a limit on the number of open files.

See also

`fopen`, `fprint` (for an example)

fft

```
fft(const ma);
fft(const ma, const inverse);
    ma          in:  2×n matrix (first row is real part, second row imaginary part),
                     or 1 × n matrix (real part only, imaginary part is zero)
    inverse     in   (optional argument), int: if equal to 1 an inverse FFT is done
```

Return value

If only one argument is used, the return value is a $2 \times s$ matrix which holds the Fourier transform; s is the smallest power of 2 which is $\geq n$.

If `inverse` equals 1, the return value is a $2 \times s$ matrix which holds the inverse Fourier transform; s is the smallest power of 2 which is $\geq n$.

Description

Performs an (inverse) fast Fourier transform. The code is derived from Dobbe (1995).

Example

```
#include <oxstd.h>

main()
{
    print( fft(<1,0,1>), fft(fft(<1,0,1>), 1) );
}
```

produces

```
        2.0000        0.00000        2.0000        0.00000
        0.00000       0.00000        0.00000       0.00000

        1.0000        0.00000        1.0000        0.00000
        0.00000       0.00000        0.00000       0.00000
```

floor

```
floor(const ma);
```
     ma   in: arithmetic type

Return value

    Returns the floor of each element of ma, of double or matrix type. The floor is the largest integer less than or equal to the argument.

See also

    ceil (for an example), round, trunc

fmod

```
fmod(const da, const db);
```
     ma   in: arithmetic type
     mb   in: arithmetic type

Return value

    Returns the floating point remainder of ma / mb. The sign of the result is that of ma. The return type is double if both ma and mb are int or double. If ma is a matrix, the return type is a matrix of the same size, holding the floating point remainders $ma[i][j]/db$, etc. The return type is derived as follows:

returns	ma	mb
$m \times n$ matrix	$m \times n$ matrix	scalar
$m \times n$ matrix	scalar	$m \times n$ matrix
$m \times n$ matrix	$m \times n$ matrix	$m \times n$ matrix
double:	scalar	scalar

See also

    imod

Example

```
#include <oxstd.h>

main()
{
    print( fmod(3,2), " ", fmod(-3,2), " ",
           fmod(3,-2), " ", fmod(-3,-2) );
}
```

produces: 1 -1 1 -1

fopen

```
fopen(const filename);
fopen(const filename, const smode);
```
     `filename`   in: name of file to open
     `smode`   in: text with open mode

Return value

    Returns the opened file if successful, otherwise the value 0.

Description

    Opens a file. The first form, without the `smode` argument opens a file for *reading* (equivalent to using `"r"`). The `smode` argument can be:

    `"w"` .   open for writing
    `"wb"`   open for writing (binary)
    `"a"`   open for appending
    `"ab"`   open for appending (binary)
    `"r"`   open for reading
    `"rb"`   open for reading (binary)

    The binary mode makes a difference under MS-DOS and Windows, but only for the treatment of end-of-line characters. Binary leaves a \n as \n, whereas non-binary translates \n to \r\n on output (and vice versa on input).

    In addition, when the file has a `.fmt` extension, and the letter f is appended to the format (as e.g. `"rbf"`), the matrix file is opened in formatted mode. In that case, reading and writing can occur by blocks of rows. When writing, the file must be explicitly closed through a call to `fclose`. Note that `.fmt` files written by Gauss on Unix platforms cannot be opened this way.

See also

    `fclose`, `fprint` (for an example), `fread`, `fscan`, `fseek`, `fwrite`

format

```
format(const sfmt);
```
     `sfmt`   in: string: new default format for double or int
                    int: new line length for matrix printing

No return value.

Description

    Use this function to specify the default format for double and int types. The function automatically recognizes whether the format string is for int or double (otherwise it is ignored). The specified double format will also be used for printing

matrices. See under the `print` function for a complete description of the formatting strings.

Use an integer argument to set the line length for matrix printing (default is 80,
the maximum is 1024).

The default format strings are:

int	`"%d"`
double	`"%g"`
matrix	each element `"%#12.5g"`, 6 elements on a line (depending on the line length).

Notes:

- The `print` function allows setting of format for the next argument only.
- Be careful with the `%f` format. For example, when printing 1e-300, the out-
  put field will need 302 characters.
- By default, integers are printed without leading spaces, to use a space
  as separator: `format(" %d");` alternatively specify a wider field:
  `format("%6d");`.
- Matrices always use one space between elements.

See also

    `fprint, print, sprint`

fprint

`fprint(const file, const a, ...);`

file	in:	file which is open for writing
a	in:	any type
...	in:	any type

Return value

    Returns the number of arguments supplied to the function.

Description

    Prints to the specified file. See `print` for a further description.

See also

    `fclose, fopen, print`

Example

```
#include <oxstd.h>

main()
{
    decl file = fopen("test.tmp", "w");
```

```
        fprint(file, "some text\n" );

        fclose(file);
}
```

produces a file test.tmp with the specified text.

fread

```
fread(const file, const am);
fread(const file, const am, const type);
fread(const file, const am, const type, const r);
fread(const file, const am, const type, const r,const c);
```

file	in:	file which is open for writing
am	in:	address, address for storing read item
type	in:	(optional argument), type of object to read, see below
r	in:	(optional argument), number of rows to read; default is 1 if argument is omitted
c	in:	(optional argument), number of columns to read; default is 1 if argument is omitted, unless file is opened with f, in which case the number of columns is read from the file

Return value

Returns an integer:

  −1 nothing read, because end-of-file was reached;
   0 nothing read, unknown error;
 > 0 object read, return value is size which was actually read:

type	data type read	return value
'i', 'd'	integer	1
'e', 'f'	double	1 (r and c omitted, or both equal to 1)
'e', 'f'	matrix	$r \times c$
'e', 'f'	matrix	r (number of complete columns read; file opened with f in format)
'c'	integer	1 (if $r = 1$: just one byte read)
'c'	string	r (if $r > 1$: r bytes read)

When reading a matrix, for example as fread(file,&x,'f',r,c), the size of x will always be r by c. If less than rc elements could be read, the matrix is padded with zeros. If no elements could be read at all, because the end of the file was reached, the return value is −1.

Description

Reads binary data from the specified file. The byte ordering is the platform specific ordering, unless the f format was used (also see fopen and fwrite).

See also

fclose, fopen, fscan, fseek, fwrite (for example using f format)

Example

A number of input/output examples is in the samples/inout directory. Below is inout7.ox. The programs inout10 and inout11 show how data can be read and written in blocks when the file is not a .fmt file.

This example writes a matrix as a .fmt file using savemat. Then the matrix is written using fread, in such a way that the same format is used.

Note that under Windows and MS-DOS these files are identical, but that on some platforms (such as the Sun) the files differ: iotest7.ox is little endian, but reading here assumes the platform ordering (which is big endian on a Sun).

```
#include <oxstd.h>

main()
{
    decl file, x = rann(2,3);

    x[0][] = double("tinker");

    savemat("iotest7.fmt", x);

    decl s, r, c, rc8;

    file = fopen("iotest7.fmt");
    fread(file, &s, 'c', 4);

    if (s == "\xDD\xEE\x86")
        print("signature OK\n");
    else
    {   print("signature NOT OK!\n");
        exit(1);
    }

    fread(file, &r, 'i');
    fread(file, &c, 'i');
    fread(file, &rc8, 'i');
    fread(file, &x, 'f', r, c);

    print("-1 indicates eof: ", fread(file, &s, 'c', 1),
        "\n");
    fclose(file);

    print("rows=", r, " columns=", c, string(x[0][0]),
        x[1:][]);
}
```

produces:

```
signature OK
-1 indicates eof: -1
rows=2 columns=3tinker
      -0.64953      -0.65276        0.75399
```

fscan

```
fscan(const file, const a, ...);
    file      in:  file which is open for writing
    a         in:  any type
    ...       in:  any type
```

Return value

Returns the number of arguments successfully scanned and assigned, or -1 when the end of the file was encountered and nothing was read.

Description

Reads text from a file. The arguments are a list of scanning strings and the addresses of variables.

A scanning string consists of text, optionally with a format specifier which starts with a % symbol. The string is truncated after the format. Any text which preceeds the format, is skipped in the file. A space character will skip any white space in the file.

If the scanning string holds a format (and assignment is not suppressed in the format), the string must be followed by the address of a variable.

The format specification is similar to that for the scanf function of the C language:

$$\%[\text{* or \#}][width]type$$

The *width* argument specifies the width of the input field. A * suppresses assignment. A # can only be used with m and M.

Notes:

- The " %m " and " %M " formats can be used to read a matrix from a file. They first read the number of rows and columns, and then the matrix row by row; this corresponds to the format used by loadmat.
  No dimensions are read by " %#m " and " %#M ", in that case the scanning string has to be followed by two integers indicating the number of rows and columns to be read.
- The " %z " format reads a whole line up to \n, the \n (and \r) are removed from the return value. The line can be up to 2048 characters long (or whatever buffer size is set with sprintbuffer). If the line in the file is too long, the remainder is skipped.

Table 8.1   Formatting types for scanning.

double *type*:	
e,f,g	field is scanned as a double value
le,lf,lg	field is scanned as a double value
integer *type*:	
d	signed decimal notation,
i	signed decimal notation,
o	unsigned octal notation,
x	unsigned hexadecimal notation,
u	unsigned decimal notation,
c	(no width) scan a single character (i.e. one byte),
string *type*:	
s	scan a string up to the next white space,
z	scan a whole line,
c	(width > 1) scan a number of characters,
matrix *type*:	
m,M	scan a matrix row by row.

- When scanning a string, the maximum string length which can be read is 2048. The sprintbuffer function can be used to enlarge the buffer size.

See also
> fprint, fread, scan, sscan (for another example)

Example
> The example writes a file, and reads it twice. The first time, the string read is tinker123, but then reading gets stuck, because the word tailor can not be read is an integer, double or matrix. Failure to read the matrix dimension generates an error message.
> The second time, the file is read properly.

```
#include <oxstd.h>

main()
{

    decl file;

    file = fopen("iotest2.txt", "w");
    fprint(file,
```

```
            "tinker123\ntailor456.78\n 2 2 1 0 0 1\n");
        fclose(file);

        decl c = -2, s, i = 0, d = 0, m = 0;

        file = fopen("iotest2.txt");
        c = fscan(file, "%s", &s, "%d", &i, "%f", &d,
            "%m", &m);                     // stops after &s
        fclose(file);

        print("\nitems read=", c, " s=", s, " int=", i,
            " dbl=", d, " mat=", m);

        file = fopen("iotest2.txt");
        c = fscan(file, "tinker%d", &i, " tailor%f", &d,
            "%m", &m);
        fclose(file);

        print("\nitems read=", c, " int=", i, " dbl=", d,
            " mat=", m);
    }
```

produces

```
load matrix: no matrix elements

items read=1 s=tinker123 int=0 dbl=0 mat=0
items read=3 int=123 dbl=456.78 mat=
        1.0000          0.00000
        0.00000         1.0000
```

fseek

```
fseek(const file);
fseek(const file, const type);
fseek(const file, const type, const r);
```

file	in:	file which is open for writing
type	in:	(optional argument), type of object use in seeking, see below
r	in:	(optional argument), number of rows to read; default is 1 if argument is omitted

Return value

The first form, with only the `file` argument, tells the current position in the file as an offset from that start of the file (as the standard C function `ftell`.

The second and third form return 0 if the seek was successful, else a non-zero number,

Description

Repositions the file pointer. The `type` argument is interpreted as follows:

type	seek data type	byte equivalent
'i', 'd'	integer	$4r$
'e', 'f'	double	$8r$
'e', 'f'	matrix rows	$16 + 8rc$ (file opened with f in format)
'c'	character	r

So when a file is opened as "rbf", fseek(file,'f',r) moves the file pointer to row r in the .fmt file.

See also
      fclose, fopen

Example
      This example reads and writes to a matrix opened with the f format. In that case, the number of columns applies to the whole file, and seeking is by row. Once the file file holds data, each subsequent write must match the number of columns already in the file.

```
#include <oxstd.h>

main()
{
    decl file, x, i;

    file = fopen("iotest9.fmt", "wbf");   // write

    fwrite(file, ones(1, 4));
    fwrite(file, 1 + ones(1, 4));
    fwrite(file, zeros(27, 4));

    fclose(file);

    file = fopen("iotest9.fmt", "abf");   // append
    print("file is ", rows(file), " by ",
        columns(file), "\n");

    fwrite(file, 2 + ones(1, 4));
    fclose(file);

    file = fopen("iotest9.fmt", "rbf");    // read
    print("file is ", rows(file), " by ",
        columns(file), "\n");

    fseek(file, 'f', 1);                    // second row
    fread(file, &x, 'f', 1);                // read it
    print("row of twos:", x);

    fseek(file, 'f', rows(file)-1);  // second row
    fread(file, &x, 'f', 1);    // read it
    print("row of threes:", x);
}
```

produces:

```
file is 29 by 4
file is 30 by 4
row of twos:
        2.0000        2.0000        2.0000        2.0000
row of threes:
        3.0000        3.0000        3.0000        3.0000
```

fwrite

```
fwrite(const file, const a);
    file      in:  file which is open for writing
    a         in:  int, double, matrix or string
```

Return value

Returns 0 if failed to write, or the number of items written to the file:

input	return value (integer)
integer	1,
double	1,
$m \times n$ matrix	number of elements written (normally $m \times n$),
$m \times n$ matrix	opened with f format: no of rows written (normally m),
string	number of characters written.

Description

Writes binary data to the specified file. The byte ordering is the platform specific ordering, unless the f format was used (also see fopen), in which case writing is to a .fmt file in little-endian mode (also see savemat). When data is written to a .fmt file, the number of columns must match that already in the file (use columns(file) to ask for the number of columns in the file).

See also

fclose, fopen, fread, fseek (for example using f format)

Example

A number of input/output examples is in the samples/inout directory. Below is inout6.ox, which saves a matrix as a .ftm file using savemat. Then the matrix is written using fwrite, in such a way that the same format is used. See under fread for a read example.

Note that under Windows and MS-DOS these files are identical, but that on some platforms (such as the Sun) the files differ: iotest6a.fmt is little endian, but iotest6b.fmt big endian. So on a Sun, using loadmat on iotest6b.fmt fails to read the matrix correctly.

The example also shows how a short string can be stores in matrix, and retrieved
from it.

```
#include <oxstd.h>

main()
{
    decl file, x = rann(2,3);

    x[0][] = double("tinker");

    savemat("iotest6a.fmt", x);

    file = fopen("iotest6b.fmt", "wb");

//  two ways if writing signature, first:
//  decl s = new string[4];        // need four bytes
//  s[0:2] = "\xDD\xEE\x86";       // signature is DDEE8600
//  fwrite(file, s);
//
//  and second way:
    fprint(file, "%c", 0xdd, "%c", 0xee,
        "%c", 0x86, "%c", 0x00);

    fwrite(file, rows(x));
    fwrite(file, columns(x));
    fwrite(file, rows(x) * columns(x) * 8);
    fwrite(file, x);
    fclose(file);

    decl y = loadmat("iotest6b.fmt");

    print(string(x[0][0]), string(y[0][0]),
        x[1][1] - y[1][1]);
}
```

produces: `tinkertinker0`

fuzziness

```
fuzziness(const deps);
    deps       in:   double, 0 or new fuzziness value
```

Return value

Sets and returns the new fuzziness parameter if deps > 0. If deps ≤ 0, no
new fuzziness value is set, but the current one is returned. The default fuzziness
is 10^{-15}.

See also

isfeq

gammafunc

```
gammafunc(const dx, const dr);
```
mx	in:	x, arithmetic type
mr	in:	r, arithmetic type

Return value

Returns the incomplete gamma function $G_x(r)$. Returns 0 if $r \leq 0$ or $x \leq 0$. The accuracy is to about 10 digits.

The return type is derived as follows:

returns	mx	mr
$m \times n$ matrix	$m \times n$ matrix	scalar
$m \times n$ matrix	scalar	$m \times n$ matrix
$m \times n$ matrix	$m \times n$ matrix	$m \times n$ matrix
double	scalar	scalar

Description

The incomplete gamma function is defined as:

$$G_x(r) = \int_0^t \frac{1}{\Gamma(r)} x^{r-1} e^{-t} dt, \quad t > 0, r > 0.$$

Source: gammafunc uses Applied Statistics algorithm AS 239 (Shea, 1988).

See also

betafunc, loggamma, probgamma

Example

```
#include <oxstd.h>

main()
{
    print(probgamma(5.99, 1, 0.5), " ",
        gammafunc(5.99 * 0.5, 1) );
}
```

produces

```
0.949963 0.949963
```

idiv, imod

```
idiv(const ia, const ib);
imod(const ia, const ib);
```
ia	in:	int
ib	in:	int

Return value

The imod function returns the integer remainder of int(ia) / int(ib). The sign of the result is that of ia. The return type is int.

The idiv function returns the result of the integer division int(ia) / int(ib). The return type is int.

See also

fmod

Example

```
#include <oxstd.h>

main()
{
    print( idiv(3,2), " ", idiv(-4,2), " ",
            idiv(3,-2), " ", idiv(-4,-2), " ");
    print( imod(3,2), " ", imod(-3,2), " ",
            imod(3,-2), " ", imod(-3,-2) );
}
```

produces: 1 -2 -1 2 1 -1 1 -1

int

```
int(const ma);
```
        ma   in: arithmetic type

Return value

Casts the argument to an integer:

input	returns
integer	unchanged
double	rounded towards zero
matrix	element 0,0 rounded towards zero
string	element 0
other types	error

See also

ceil (for an example), double, matrix, trunc, §12.7.2.3

invert, invertsym

```
invert(const ma);
invert(const ma, const alogdet, const asign);
invertsym(const mas);
```

ma	in:	$m \times m$ real matrix A
alogdet	in:	(optional argument) address of variable
	out:	double, the *logarithm* of the absolute value of the determinant of A
asign	in:	(optional argument) address of variable
	out:	int , the sign of the determinant of A; 0: singular; $-1, -2$: negative determinant; $+1, +2$: positive determinant; $-2, +2$: result is unreliable
mas	in:	symmetric, positive definite $m \times m$ matrix A^s

Return value

Returns the inverse of A, or the value 0 if the decomposition failed.

Description

Inverts the matrix A. The `invert` function uses the LU decomposition (see under `declu`), `invertsym` function uses the Choleski decomposition (see under `decldl`). The exponent of the log-absolute-determinant can only be computed for values $\leq$ DBL_MAX_E_EXP and $\geq$ DBL_MIN_E_EXP (see Ch. 9).

Note that 1 / ma also returns the inverse (more precisely: if ma is square, `invert` is tried, if that fails, or the matrix is not square, the generalized inverse is used), see §12.7.5.

Error messages

invertsym(): inversion failed
invert(): inversion failed

See also

`decldl`, `declu`, `logdet`

Example

```
#include <oxstd.h>

main()
{
    decl mp;

    mp = <4,1;1,3>;
    print(invert(mp)*mp, invertsym(mp)*mp);
}
```

produces (note that the both matrices are the identity matrix: whether it has zeros, or nearly zeros, could dependent on which Ox version was used):

```
     1.0000 -2.7756e-017
     0.00000      1.0000

     1.0000 -2.7756e-017
     0.00000      1.0000
```

inverteps

```
inverteps(const dEps);
```
    dEps   in: sets the inversion epsilon ϵ_{inv} to dEps if dEps > 0, to the default if dEps < 0; leaves the value unchanged if dEps $==$ 0

Return value

    Returns the inversion epsilon (the new value if dEps != 0).

Description

    The following functions return singular status if the pivoting element is less than or equal to ϵ_{inv}: decldl, declu, decldlband, invert, invertsym, orthmgs. Less than $10\epsilon_{inv}$ is used by olsc and olsr.

    A singular value is considered zero when less than $\|A\|_\infty 10\epsilon_{inv}$ in rank, null-space, and when using the generalized inverse.

    The default value for ϵ_{inv} is $1000 \times$ DBL_EPSILON.

isarray, isclass, isdouble, isfile, isfunction, isint, ismatrix

```
isarray(const a);
isclass(const a);
isdouble(const a);
isfile(const a);
isfunction(const a);
isint(const a);
ismatrix(const a);
isstring(const a);
```
    a   in: any type

Return value

    Returns TRUE (i.e. the value 1) if the argument is of the correct type, FALSE (0) otherwise.

isdotfeq, isfeq

```
isdotfeq(const ma, const mb);
isfeq(const ma, const mb);
```
    ma   in: arithmetic type
    mb   in: arithmetic type

Return value

    isfeq always returns an integer: it returns 1 if the argument ma is fuzzy equal to mb, 0 otherwise.

isdotfeq returns a matrix if either argument is a matrix; the matrix consists of 0's and 1's: 1 if the comparison holds, 0 otherwise. If both arguments are scalar, isdotfeq is equal to isfeq.

In both cases the current fuzziness value is used.

See also

    fuzziness

Example

```
#include <oxstd.h>

main()
{
    decl m1 = <1+1e-17,1-1e-17;1+1e-17,1-1e-17 >;
    decl m2 = <1+1e-17,1-1e-10;1+1e-17,1-1e-17 >;

    print( "m1 is ", isfeq(m1,1) ? "" : "*** not *** ",
        "fuzzy equal to 1\n");
    print( "m2 is ", isfeq(m2,1) ? "" : "*** not *** ",
        "fuzzy equal to 1\n");

    print(isdotfeq(m1,1));
}
```

produces

```
m1 is fuzzy equal to 1
m2 is *** not *** fuzzy equal to 1

        1.0000          1.0000
        1.0000          1.0000
```

lag0

```
lag0(const ma, const ia);
lag0(const ma, const ia, double dmisval);
```

ma	in:	$T \times n$ matrix
ia	in:	int
dmisval	in:	(optional argument) double, value to set missing observations to (default is 0)

Return value

Returns a $T \times n$ matrix with the lags of the specified matrix, whereby missing values are replaced by zero. E.g. the result matrix r using two lags is:

```
r[0][0] = 0         r[0][1] = 0          ...
r[1][0] = 0         r[1][1] = 0          ...
r[2][0] = m[0][0]   r[2][1] = m[0][1]    ...
r[3][0] = m[1][0]   r[3][1] = m[1][1]    ...
...
```

The result has the same dimensions as ma.

Description

Lags the specified matrix, missing values are replaced by zero (unless a missing value is specified as the third argument). Using the lag operator (also called back-shift operator) L: this computes:

$$L^k a_t = a_{t-k} \quad \text{for} \quad t - k \geq 0,$$

and 0 for $t - k < 0$.

See also

diff0

Example

```
#include <oxstd.h>

main()
{
    print( lag0(<1:5>',2) );
}
```

produces

```
     0.00000
     0.00000
     1.0000
     2.0000
     3.0000
```

limits

```
limits(const ma);
```
      ma   in: $m \times n$ matrix

Return value

Returns a $4 \times n$ matrix:

    1st row: minimum of each column of ma

    2nd row: maximum of each column of ma

    3rd row: row index of minimum (lowest index if more than one exists)

    4th row: row index of maximum (lowest index if more than one exists)

See also

min, max, spikes

Example

```
#include <oxstd.h>

main()
{
    decl m = rann(7,2);
    print( m, limits(m) );
}
```

produces

```
    -0.65201        0.46053
    -0.39088       -0.64953
    -0.65276        0.75399
     1.0880         0.99745
     0.57228       -0.20805
    -0.59315        0.36607
     1.0833         1.5079

    -0.65276       -0.64953
     1.0880         1.5079
     2.0000         1.0000
     3.0000         6.0000
```

loadmat

```
loadmat(const sname);
loadmat(const sname, const iFormat);
```

sname	in:	string containing an existing file name
iFormat	in:	(optional argument, .mat matrix file only)

1: file has no matrix dimensions; then the matrix is returned as a column vector, and shape could be used to create a differently shaped matrix.

Return value

Returns the matrix which was read, or 0 if the operation failed.

Description

The type of file read depends on the extension of the file name:

.mat	matrix file (ASCII), described below,
.dat	ASCII data file with load information,
.in7	PcGive 7 data file (with corresponding .bn7 file),
.xls	Excel version 4 spread sheet file,
.wks and .wk1	Lotus spread sheet file,
.dht	Gauss data file (with corresponding .dat file),
.fmt	Gauss matrix file,
any other	as .mat file.

This function does not retrieve information on data frequency, sample periods and variable names. To retrieve such information, use the `Database` class.

A matrix file holds a matrix, preceded by two integers which specify the number of rows and columns of the matrix. It will normally have the `.mat` extension. If a symbol is found which is not a number, then the rest of the line will be skipped (so, e.g. everything following ; or // is treated as comments). An example of a matrix file is:

```
2 3            //<-- dimensions, a 2 by 3 matrix
//comment      //<-- a line of comment
1 0 0          //<-- first row of the matrix
0 1 .5         //<-- second row of the matrix
```

If the `iFormat` argument equals 1, the file is assumed not to contain matrix dimension (if it does, they will be the first two elements in the matrix).

The other file formats are described in more detail in the the `Database` class, under the Load functions, and in the *GiveWin* book. Note that all file formats work identically on whatever platform Ox runs on. So an `.xls` file could be written with Ox on a Sun, then transferred (in binary mode) to a Windows machine, and read into Ox for Windows. Ox takes care of differences in byte ordering when writing and reading binary files (always using little-endian format). This also means that a `.fmt` written by Ox on the Sun can be read by Ox under Windows. Gauss under Unix writes `.fmt` files in a different format.

Error messages

loadmat(): file not found
loadmat(): no matrix elements
loadmat(): not enough matrix elements

See also

Database class, savemat, shape

Example

```
#include <oxstd.h>

main()
{
    decl m = unit(2);

    savemat("t.mat", m);
    print(m, loadmat("t.mat"));
}
```

produces

```
    1.0000        0.00000
    0.00000       1.0000

    1.0000        0.00000
    0.00000       1.0000
```

and a file called t.mat:

```
2  2
   1.000000000000000e+000
   0.000000000000000e+000

   0.000000000000000e+000
   1.000000000000000e+000
```

log, log10

```
log(const ma);
log10(const ma);
```
      ma   in: arithmetic type

Return value

The log function returns the natural logarithm of each element of ma, of double or matrix type.

The log10 function returns the logarithm (base 10) of each element of ma, of double or matrix type.

See also

    exp

Example

```
#include <oxstd.h>

main()
{
    print( log(<1,10>) );
    print( log10(<1,10>) );

    // the following shows how to prevent log(0)
    // in the computation of y*log(y) using the
    // dot-conditional operator:
    decl y = range(0,4);
    print(y .* log(y .> 0 .? y .: 1));
}
```

produces

```
    0.00000    2.3026
    0.00000    1.0000
    0.00000    0.00000    1.3863    3.2958    5.5452
```

logdet

```
logdet(const ma, const asign);
```
     ma   in: $m \times m$ real matrix A

     asign   in: address of variable

                out: int, the sign of the determinant of A; 0: singular; $-1, -2$: negative determinant; $+1, +2$: positive determinant; $-2, +2$: result is unreliable

Return value

    Returns a double: the *logarithm* of the absolute value of the determinant of A (1.0 if the matrix is singular).

Description

    Computes the determinant (the log of the absolute value and the sign) of a matrix using the LU decomposition of the matrix (see declu). The exponent of log-absolute-determinant can only be computed for values $\leq$ DBL_MAX_E_EXP and $\geq$ DBL_MIN_E_EXP (see Ch. 9).

See also

    determinant, invert

loggamma

```
loggamma(const ma);
```
     ma   in: arithmetic type

Return value

    Returns the logarithm of the complete gamma function at the value of each element of ma, of double or matrix type.

    Returns zero for any argument less than or equal to zero.

Description

    Computes the logarithm of the gamma function at the argument:

$$\log \Gamma(a) = \log \int_0^\infty x^{a-1} e^{-x} dx \quad \text{for } a > 0.$$

If $a = i$ is integer then $\Gamma(i + 1) = i!$.

Often the ratio of two gamma functions needs te be computed. This can be done as $\Gamma(a)/\Gamma(b) = \exp(\log \Gamma(a) - \log \Gamma(b))$, thus reducing the risk of overflow for large arguments. The gamma function is also defined for negative (non-integer) arguments. For negative arguments one could use the relation

$$\Gamma(a) = -\frac{\pi}{sin(\pi a) a \Gamma(-a)}$$

or use

$$a\Gamma(a) = \Gamma(a+1).$$

The function is accurate to about 14 to 15 significant digits (a table is used to look up integer values up to 50). The approximation uses the recurrence relation to obtain an argument greater than 8.5; then an asymptotic formula with eight terms is applied (see Abramowitz and Stegun, 1984, §6.1.40).

See also

gammafunc, polygamma

Example

```
#include <oxstd.h>

main()
{
    print( loggamma(<0.5,1,10>) );
}
```

produces

```
       0.57236        0.00000        12.802
```

lower

```
lower(const ma);
```
    ma   in: $m \times n$ matrix

Return value

Returns the lower diagonal (including the diagonal) of a matrix, the strict upper diagonal elements are set to zero.

See also

setdiagonal, setupper, setlower, upper

Example

```
#include <oxstd.h>

main()
{
    print( lower(ones(3,3)) );
    print( upper(ones(3,3)) );
}
```

produces

```
        1.0000        0.00000        0.00000
        1.0000        1.0000        0.00000
        1.0000        1.0000        1.0000

        1.0000        1.0000        1.0000
        0.00000        1.0000        1.0000
        0.00000        0.00000        1.0000
```

matrix

```
matrix(const ma);
      ma            in:   arithmetic type
```

Return value

Casts the argument to a matrix:

input	returns
integer	a 1 × 1 matrix
double	a 1 × 1 matrix
matrix	unchanged
string	a 1 × 1 matrix
other types	error

See also

int, double, §12.7.2.3

max

```
max(const a,  ...);
      a             in:   arithmetic type
      ...           in:   arithmetic type
```

Return value

Returns the maximum value in all the arguments. The return type is int if all arguments are of type int; otherwise the return type is double.

Description

Finds the maximum value in the arguments.

Use the dot-relational operator to find the element-by-element maximum, see Ch. 6.

See also

limits, min

Example

```
#include <oxstd.h>

main()
{
    print( max(<1.5,12.5>, 1, 6) );
}
```

produces: 12.5

MaxBFGS

```
#include <maximize.h>
MaxBFGS(const func, const avP, const adFunc,
    const amHessian, const fNumDer);
```

func	in:	a function computing the function value, optionally with derivatives
avP	in:	address of $p \times 1$ matrix with starting values
	out:	$p \times 1$ matrix with final coefficients
adFunc	in:	address
	out:	double, final function value
amHessian	in:	address of $p \times p$ matrix, initial quasi-Hessian; a possible starting value is the identity matrix
	out:	final quasi-Hessian (not reliable as estimate of actual Hessian)
fNumDer	in:	0: func provides analytical first derivatives
		1: use numerical first derivatives

The supplied func argument should have the following format:

```
func(const vP, const adFunc, const avScore, const amHessian);
```

vP	in:	$p \times 1$ matrix with coefficients
adFunc	in:	address
	out:	double, function value at vP
avScore	in:	0, or an address
	out:	if !0 on input: $p \times 1$ matrix with first derivatives at vP
amHessian	in:	always 0 for MaxBFGS, as it does not need the Hessian
returns		1: successful, 0: function evaluation failed

Return value

Returns the status of the iterative process:

MAX_CONV *Strong convergence*
   Both convergence tests (8.2) and (8.3) were passed, using tolerance $\epsilon = \epsilon_1$.

MAX_WEAK_CONV *Failed to improve in line search: weak convergence*
   The step length s_i has become too small. The convergence test (8.2) was passed, using tolerance $\epsilon = \epsilon_2$.

MAX_MAXIT *Maximum number of iterations reached: no convergence!*

MAX_LINE_FAIL *Failed to improve in line search: no convergence!*
   The step length s_i has become too small. The convergence test (8.2) was not passed, using tolerance $\epsilon = \epsilon_2$.

MAX_FUNC_FAIL *Function evaluation failed: no convergence!*

The chosen default values for the tolerances are:

$$\epsilon_1 = 10^{-4}, \ \epsilon_2 = 5 \times 10^{-3}.$$

Description

MaxBFGS maximizes a function, using the quasi-Newton method developed by Broyden, Fletcher, Goldfarb, Shanno (BFGS). The function either uses supplied analytical first derivatives, or numerical first derivatives (in which case only the function values need to be available: this uses the function Num1Derivative). Using numerical derivatives saves programming (and thinking) time, but analytical dervatives tend to be computable with higher accuracy and over a wider parameter range. The iteration process is unaffected by this choice, other than caused by the slight numerical differences between the two methods (and the lower robustness of numerical derivatives).

A Newton scheme is used to maximize the unconstrained function $f(\theta)$:

$$\theta(k+1) = \theta(k) + s(k)\mathbf{Q}(k)^{-1}\mathbf{q}(k),$$

with

$\theta(k)$ parameter values at iteration k;
$s(k)$ steplength, normally 1;
$\mathbf{Q}(k)$ symmetric positive definite matrix (at iteration k);
$\mathbf{q}(k)$ first derivative of the function (the score vector);
$\delta(k)$ $= \theta(k) - \theta(k-1)$, the change in the parameters;
$\gamma(k)$ $= \mathbf{q}(k) - \mathbf{q}(k-1)$, the change in the score.

The BFGS method updates $\mathbf{H} = \mathbf{Q}^{-1}$ directly, avoiding the need for second derivatives. A linear line search is used if necessary.

Owing to numerical problems it is possible (especially close to the maximum) that the calculated δ_i does not yield a higher likelihood. Then an $s_i \in [0,1]$ yielding a higher function value is determined by a line search. Theoretically, since the direction is upward, such an s_i should exist; however, numerically it might be impossible to find one. When using BFGS with numerical derivatives, it often pays to scale the data so that the initial gradients are of the same order of magnitude.

The *convergence* decision is based on two tests. The first uses likelihood elasticities ($\partial \ell / \partial \log \theta$, switching notation from $f(\theta)$ to $\ell(\theta)$):

$$\begin{aligned} |q_{i,j}\theta_{i,j}| \le \epsilon \quad &\text{for all } j \text{ when } \theta_{i,j} \ne 0, \\ |q_{i,j}| \le \epsilon \quad &\text{for all } j \text{ with } \theta_{i,j} = 0. \end{aligned} \quad (8.2)$$

The second is based on the one-step-ahead relative change in the parameter values:

$$|\delta_{i+1,j}| \leq 10\epsilon |\theta_{i,j}| \quad \text{for all } j \text{ with } \theta_{i,j} \neq 0,$$
$$|\delta_{i+1,j}| \leq 10\epsilon \quad \text{for all } j \text{ when } \theta_{i,j} = 0. \tag{8.3}$$

The final quasi-Hessian can not reliably used to estimate standard errors. When, for example, iteration starts in the maximum with an identity matrix as initial quasi-Hessian, the final-Hessian will also be the identity matrix. Instead, it is possible to take the inverse of minus the numerical second derivatives.

See also

`MaxControl`, `MaxConvergenceMsg`, `Num1Derivative`,
`Num2Derivative`

Example

The following example minimizes the so-called Rosenbrock function (see Fletcher, 1987):

$$f(\alpha, \beta) = 100 * \left(\beta - \alpha^2\right)^2 + (1 - \alpha)^2.$$

No data are involved. It is easily seen that the minimum is at $(1, 1)$ with function value 0. The contours are rather banana-shaped. The program maximizes the function twice, starting from (0,0), once with analytical derivatives, once without:

```
#include <oxstd.h>
#include <maximize.h>

#pragma link("maximize.oxo")

fRosenbrock(const vP, const adFunc, const avScore,
    const amHessian)
{
    adFunc[0] = -100 * (vP[1][0] - vP[0][0] ^ 2) ^ 2
        - (1 - vP[0][0]) ^ 2;                // function value

    if (avScore)                        // if !0: compute score
    {   // this bit is not needed for numerical derivatives
        (avScore[0])[0][0] = 400 * (vP[1][0] - vP[0][0]^2)
            * vP[0][0] + 2 * (1 - vP[0][0]);
        (avScore[0])[1][0]=-200 * (vP[1][0] - vP[0][0]^2);
    }
    return 1;                           // 1 indicates success
}

main()
{
    decl vp, dfunc, ir, mhess;

    vp = zeros(2, 1);                   // starting values
```

```
        fRosenbrock(vp, &dfunc, 0, 0); // start function value

        MaxControl(1000, 50);
        mhess = unit(2);                                    // maximize
        ir = MaxBFGS(fRosenbrock, &vp, &dfunc, &mhess, FALSE);

        print("\n", MaxConvergenceMsg(ir),
            " using analytical derivatives",
            "\nFunction value = ", dfunc, "; parameters:", vp);

        vp = zeros(2, 1);                              // starting values
        fRosenbrock(vp, &dfunc, 0,0);//starting function value

        mhess = unit(2);                                    // maximize
        ir = MaxBFGS(fRosenbrock, &vp, &dfunc, &mhess, TRUE);

        print("\n", MaxConvergenceMsg(ir),
            " using numerical derivatives",
            "\nFunction value = ", dfunc, "; parameters:", vp);
}
```

produces

```
 Starting values
 parameters
       0.00000      0.00000
 gradients
       2.0000       0.00000
 Initial function = -1

 Position after 25 BFGS iterations
 Status: Strong convergence
 parameters
       1.0000       1.0000
 gradients
 -6.1526e-006  3.0477e-006
 Initial function= -1 function value= -2.4039328142e-014


Strong convergence using analytical derivatives
Function value = -2.40393e-014; parameters:
       1.0000
       1.0000

 Starting values
 parameters
       0.00000      0.00000
 gradients
       2.0000       0.00000
 Initial function = -1

 Position after 25 BFGS iterations
 Status: Strong convergence
```

```
parameters
        1.0000            1.0000
gradients
-6.1526e-006   3.0477e-006
Initial function= -1 function value= -2.37783658052e-014


Strong convergence using numerical derivatives
Function value = -2.37784e-014; parameters:
        1.0000
        1.0000
```

MaxControl, MaxControlEps

```
#include <maximize.h>
MaxControl(const mxIter, const iPrint);
MaxControlEps(const dEps1, const dEps2);
```
    mxIter   in: int, maximum number of iterations; default is 1000, use -1 to leave the current value unchanged

    dEps1   in: double, ϵ_1, default is 10^{-4}

    dEps2   in: double, ϵ_2, default is 5×10^{-3}

    iPrint   in: int, print results every iPrint'th iteration; default is 0, use -1 to leave the current value unchanged

Return value

    No return value.

Description

    The MaxControl and MaxControlEps functions provide control over some iteration parameters. Use a value of -1 for mxIter, iPrint, dEps1 or dEps2 to leave the current value unchanged.

See also

    MaxBFGS (for an example), MaxSimplex

MaxConvergenceMsg

```
#include <maximize.h>
MaxConvergenceMsg(const iCode);
```
    iCode   in: int, code returned by MaxBFGS or MaxSimplex

Return value

    Returns the text corresponding to the convergence code listed under the return values of MaxBFGS.

See also

MaxBFGS (for an example), MaxSimplex

MaxSimplex

```
#include <maximize.h>
MaxSimplex(const func, const avP, const adFunc, vDelta);
```
func	in:	a function computing the function value
avP	in:	address of $p \times 1$ matrix with starting values
	out:	$p \times 1$ matrix with coefficients at convergence
adFunc	in:	address
	out:	double, function value at convergence
vDelta	in:	0, or the initial simplex

The supplied func argument should have the same format as in **MaxBFGS**.

Return value

Returns the status of the iterative process, as documented under MaxBFGS.

Description

Maximizes a function using the simplex method, see for example Applied Statistics algorithm AS 47 (O'Neil, 1970). The simplex method can be rather slow. For reasonably well behaved functions, a preferred derivative free method is MaxBFGS using numerical derivatives.

See also

MaxBFGS

Example

```
#include <oxstd.h>
#include <oxfloat.h>
#include <maximize.h>

#pragma link("maximize.oxo")


fRosenbrock(const vP, const adFunc, const avScore,
    const amHess)
{
    adFunc[0] = -100 * (vP[1][0] - vP[0][0] ^ 2) ^ 2
        - (1 - vP[0][0]) ^ 2;

return 1;
}
fPowell(const vP,const adFunc,const avScore,const amHess)
{
```

```
    adFunc[0] = - (
          (vP[0][0] + 10*vP[1][0]) ^ 2
          + 5 * (vP[2][0] - vP[3][0]) ^ 2
       + (vP[1][0] - 2*vP[2][0]) ^ 4
          + 10 * (vP[0][0] + vP[3][0]) ^ 4);
return 1;
}
fQuad(const vP, const adFunc, const avScore, const amHess)
{
    adFunc[0] = -double(sumc(vP .^ 4));

return 1;
}

main()
{
    decl vp, vf, mh;

    MaxControl(-1,1000);

    vp = <-1.2;1>;   mh = unit(2);
    MaxBFGS(fRosenbrock, &vp, &vf, &mh, TRUE);
    vp = <-1.2;1>;   mh = unit(2);
    MaxSimplex(fRosenbrock, &vp, &vf, 0 /*<1;1>*/);

    vp = <3;-1;0;1>;   mh = unit(4);
    MaxBFGS(fPowell, &vp, &vf, &mh, TRUE);
    vp = <3;-1;0;1>;   mh = unit(4);
    MaxSimplex(fPowell, &vp, &vf, 0 /*<1;1;1;1>*/);

    vp = ones(10,1); mh = unit(10);
    MaxBFGS(fQuad, &vp, &vf, &mh, TRUE);
    vp = ones(10,1); mh = unit(10);
    MaxSimplex(fQuad, &vp, &vf, 0 /*vp*/);
}
```

produces after some editing of the output:

```
Position after 33 BFGS iterations
Status: Strong convergence
parameters    1.0000         1.0000
gradients    -9.7639e-006  5.2062e-006
Initial function= -24.2 function value= -1.76138959216e-013

Position after 132 Simplex iterations
Status: Strong convergence
parameters    1.0000         1.0000
gradients     3.1016e-005 -1.5515e-005
Initial function= -24.2 function value= -6.01783258199e-013

Position after 52 BFGS iterations
Status: Strong convergence
parameters
```

```
      0.00026873 -2.6873e-005   -0.00011152   -0.00011152
 gradients
 -1.5527e-010 -2.7204e-011  5.4559e-011 -1.4957e-010
 Initial function= -2615 function value= -7.58890166505e-015

 Position after 239 Simplex iterations
 Status: Strong convergence
 parameters
  -0.00081637  8.1527e-005   0.00029861    0.00029848
 gradients
  2.2133e-006  2.2078e-005 -1.3407e-006  1.3452e-006
 Initial function= -2615 function value= -2.09841509889e-012

 Position after 1 BFGS iterations
 Status: Strong convergence
 parameters
 -6.5512e-012 -6.5512e-012 -6.5512e-012 -6.5512e-012
 -6.5512e-012 -6.5512e-012 -6.5512e-012 -6.5512e-012
 -6.5512e-012 -6.5512e-012
 gradients
  6.5512e-022  6.5512e-022  6.5512e-022  6.5512e-022
  6.5512e-022  6.5512e-022  6.5512e-022  6.5512e-022
  6.5512e-022  6.5512e-022
 Initial function= -10 function value= -1.84197825689e-044
 steplen = 0.25

 Position after 454 Simplex iterations
 Status: Strong convergence
 parameters
  0.00012390  -0.00040964   0.00099913  7.2798e-005
 -0.00027496   0.00085512  -0.00076729  -0.00081975
  0.00052821  -0.00060839
 gradients
 -7.6214e-012  2.7501e-010 -3.9896e-009 -1.5505e-012
  8.3175e-011 -2.5012e-009  1.8070e-009  2.2036e-009
 -5.8956e-010  9.0080e-010
 Initial function= -10 function value= -2.57837611055e-012
```

meanc, meanr

```
meanc(const ma);
meanr(const ma);
```
      ma   in: $T \times n$ matrix A

Return value

    The meanc function returns a $1 \times n$ matrix holding the means of the columns of ma.

    The meanr function returns a $T \times 1$ matrix holding the means of the rows of ma.

See also

sumc, sumr, varc, variance (for an example), varr

min

```
min(const a, ...);
```
      a   in: arithmetic type
      ...   in: arithmetic type

Return value

Returns the minimum value in all the arguments. The return type is int if all arguments are of type int; otherwise the return type is double.

Description

Finds the minimum value in the arguments.

Use the dot-relational operator to find the element-by-element maximum, see Ch. 6.

See also

limits, max

Example

```
#include <oxstd.h>

main()
{
    print( min(<1.5,12.5>, 1, 6) );
}
```

produces: 1

nullspace

```
nullspace(const ma);
```
      ma   in: $m \times n$ matrix A, $m \geq n$

Return value

Returns the null space of ma, or 0 (ma is square and full rank), -1 (SVD failed).

Description

Uses the SVD to compute the null space $A_\perp$ of an $m \times n$ matrix A, with $m \geq n$, as explained in Appendix A4. If $\text{rank}(A) = r$, the rank of the null space is $p = m - r$, and $A_\perp$ is an $m \times p$ matrix such that $A'_\perp A_\perp = I$ and $A' A_\perp = 0$. The rank of A is the number of non-zero singular values, which is determined as explained under inverteps.

Error messages
    nullspace(): needs m $>=$ n
    nullspace(): svd failed

See also
    decsvd, inverteps

Example

```
#include <oxstd.h>

main()
{
    decl ma;

    ma = zeros(4,2);
    ma[0][0] = ma[0][1] = 1;

    print(ma, nullspace(ma));
}
```

produces

```
        1.0000          1.0000
        0.00000         0.00000
        0.00000         0.00000
        0.00000         0.00000

        0.00000         0.00000         0.00000
        1.0000          0.00000         0.00000
        0.00000         0.00000         1.0000
        0.00000         1.0000          0.00000
```

Num1Derivative, Num2Derivative

```
#include <maximize.h>
Num1Derivative(const func, vP, const avScore);
Num2Derivative(const func, vP, const amHessian);
```
func	in:	a function computing the function value, optionally with derivatives
vP	in:	$p \times 1$ matrix with parameter values
mHessian	in:	$p \times p$ matrix, initial Hessian
avScore	in:	an address
	out:	$p \times 1$ matrix with 1st derivatives at vP
amHessian	in:	an address
	out:	$p \times p$ matrix with 2nd derivatives at vP

The supplied `func` argument should have the format as documented under `MaxB-FGS`.

Return value

Returns 1 if successful, 0 otherwise.

Description

These functions take numerical first and second differences of a function based on a central finite difference approximation. The numerical derivatives are calculated using:

$$\frac{f(\theta + \epsilon\imath) - f(\theta - \epsilon\imath)}{\mu} \simeq \frac{\partial f(\theta)}{\partial(\imath'\theta)}$$

where $\imath$ is a unit vector (for example, $(1\ 0\ldots 0)'$ for the first element of θ), ϵ is a suitably chosen step length. Thus, ϵ represents a compromise between round-off error (cancellation of leading digits when subtracting nearly equal numbers) and truncation error (ignoring terms of higher order than ϵ in the approximation). Although the Ox code chooses ϵ carefully, there may be situations where the numerical derivative performs poorly.

If in `Num1Derivative` one-side fails, the procedure will use a one-sided difference.

The numerical values of second derivatives can be computed in a corresponding way using:

$$\frac{f(\theta + \epsilon_1\imath + \epsilon_2\jmath) + f(\theta - \epsilon_1\imath - \epsilon_2\jmath) - f(\theta - \epsilon_1\imath + \epsilon_2\jmath) - f(\theta + \epsilon_1\imath - \epsilon_2\jmath)}{4\epsilon_1\epsilon_2}$$

where $\imath$ or $\jmath$ is zero except for unity in the ith or j^{th} position.

See also

`MaxBFGS`

Example

The following example is based on the Rosenbrock function (see `MaxBFGS`):

```
#include <oxstd.h>
#include <maximize.h>

#pragma link("maximize.oxo")

fRosenbrock(const vP, const adFunc, const avScore,
    const amHessian)
{
    adFunc[0] = -100 * (vP[1][0] - vP[0][0] ^ 2) ^ 2
        - (1 - vP[0][0]) ^ 2;                // function value

    if (avScore)                    // if !0: compute score
    {   // this bit is not needed for numerical derivatives
        (avScore[0])[0][0]= 400 * (vP[1][0] - vP[0][0]^2)
```

```
                    * vP[0][0] + 2 * (1 - vP[0][0]);
            (avScore[0])[1][0]=-200 * (vP[1][0] - vP[0][0]^2);
        }
    return 1;
    }

    main()
    {
        decl vp, dfunc, vscore, mhess;

        vscore = vp = zeros(2, 1);                    // starting values

        fRosenbrock(vp, &dfunc, &vscore, 0);
        print("analytical first derivative at <0;0>", vscore);

        if (Num1Derivative(fRosenbrock, vp, &vscore))
            print("numerical 1st derivative at <0;0>", vscore);

        if (Num2Derivative(fRosenbrock, vp, &mhess))
            print("numerical 2nd derivative at <0;0>", mhess);
    }
```

produces

```
analytical first derivative at <0;0>
        2.0000
        0.00000
numerical 1st derivative at <0;0>
        2.0000
        0.00000
numerical 2nd derivative at <0;0>
        -2.0000        0.00000
        0.00000        -200.00
```

NumJacobian

```
#include <maximize.h>
NumJacobian(const func, vU, const amJacobian);
```

func	in:	function mapping from restricted to unrestricted parameters
vU	in:	of $u \times 1$ matrix with parameters
amJacobian	in:	address
	out:	$r \times u$ Jacobian matrix corresponding to mapping

The supplied func argument should have the following format:

```
func(const avR, const vU);
```

avR	in:	address
	out:	$r \times 1$ matrix with restricted coefficients
vU	in:	$u \times 1$ matrix with unrestricted coefficients
returns		1: successful, 0: function evaluation failed

Return value

Returns 1 if successful, 0 otherwise.

Description

Computes the Jacobian matrix of the restrictions imposed of the form $\theta = f(\phi)$: $J = \partial f(\phi)/\partial \theta'$; $f(\cdot)$ is an r-vector, ϕ is an u-vector.

See also

Num1Derivative

Example

```
#include <oxstd.h>
#include <maximize.h>

#pragma link("maximize.oxo")

fMap(const avR, const vU)
{
    decl cu = rows(vU);

    avR[0] = vU[0 : cu-2][] .^ 2;// drop last row, square

return 1;
}

main()
{
    decl vp, mjacob;

    if (NumJacobian(fMap, ones(4, 1), &mjacob))
        print("numerical Jacobian at <1;1;1;1>", mjacob);

    if (NumJacobian(fMap, zeros(4, 1), &mjacob))
        print("numerical Jacobian at <0;0;0;0>", mjacob);
}
```

produces

```
numerical Jacobian at <1;1;1;1>
        2.0000      0.00000      0.00000      0.00000
       0.00000       2.0000      0.00000      0.00000
       0.00000      0.00000       2.0000      0.00000
numerical Jacobian at <0;0;0;0>
       0.00000      0.00000      0.00000      0.00000
       0.00000      0.00000      0.00000      0.00000
       0.00000      0.00000      0.00000      0.00000
```

ols2c, ols2r, olsc, olsr

```
ols2c(const my, const mx, const amb);
ols2c(const my, const mx, const amb, const amxtxinv);
ols2c(const my, const mx, const amb, const amxtxinv,
    const amxtx);

olsc(const my, const mx, const amb);
olsc(const my, const mx, const amb, const amxtxinv);
olsc(const my, const mx, const amb, const amxtxinv,
    const amxtx);
```

my	in:	$T \times n$ matrix Y
mx	in:	$T \times k$ matrix X
amb	in:	address of variable
	out:	$k \times n$ matrix of OLS coefficients, B
amxtxinv	in:	(optional argument) address of variable
	out:	$k \times k$ matrix $(X'X)^{-1}$,
amxtx	in:	(optional argument) address of variable
	out:	$k \times k$ matrix $(X'X)$,

```
ols2r(const my, const mx, const amb);
ols2r(const my, const mx, const amb, const amxtxinv);
ols2r(const my, const mx, const amb, const amxtxinv,
    const amxtx);

olsr(const my, const mx, const amb);
olsr(const my, const mx, const amb, const amxtxinv);
olsr(const my, const mx, const amb, const amxtxinv,
    const amxtx);
```

my	in:	$n \times T$ matrix Y'
mx	in:	$k \times T$ matrix $X', T \geq k$
amb	in:	address of variable
	out:	$n \times k$ OLS coefficient matrix, B'
amxtxinv	in:	(optional argument) address of variable
	out:	$k \times k$ matrix $(X'X)^{-1}$,
amxtx	in:	(optional argument) address of variable
	out:	$k \times k$ matrix $(X'X)$,

Return value

0:	out of memory,
1:	success,
2:	ratio of diagonal elements of $X'X$ is large, rescaling is advised,
-1:	$(X'X)$ is (numerically) singular,
-2:	combines 2 and -1.

Description

olsc and olsr do ordinary least squares using the Householder QR decomposition with pivoting (see, e.g., Golub and Van Loan, 1989, Ch. 5).

ols2c and ols2r form $(X'X)$ and solve the normal equations using the Choleski decomposition (see decldl).

The QR based method for computing OLS is more accurate, but about half as fast (unless $T \approx k$), and more memory intensive (it needs to make a copy of the data to work on) than the normal equations approach.

If $(X'X)$ is singular, the QR based method computes B and $(X'X)^{-1}$ with zeros at the positions corresponding to the singular variables; $X'X$ remains based on the full X. The normal equation approach does not produce a meaningful result in case of singularity.

Example

```
#include <oxstd.h>

main()
{
    decl mx, my, cy = 2, ct = 50, ck = 3, mb, mxtx, mxtxi;
    mx = ranu(ct,ck);
    my = rann(ct,cy) / 10 + mx * ones(ck,1);

    olsc(my, mx, &mb);
    print(mb);
    olsr(my', mx', &mb, &mxtxi, &mxtx);
    print(mb, mxtx ~ mxtxi);

    print((1/mx)*my, mx'mx ~ invert(mx'mx));
}
```

produces:

```
0.97854    1.0523
1.0839    0.98610
0.93317    0.96965

0.97854    1.0839    0.93317
1.0523    0.98610    0.96965

16.388    11.428    12.531    0.17007    -0.063128    -0.085047
11.428    15.468    11.372    -0.063128    0.15353    -0.057459
12.531    11.372    16.618    -0.085047    -0.057459    0.16363
```

```
    0.97854    1.0523
    1.0839   0.98610
    0.93317   0.96965

   16.388    11.428    12.531     0.17007   -0.063128   -0.085047
   11.428    15.468    11.372    -0.063128   0.15353    -0.057459
   12.531    11.372    16.618    -0,085047  -0.057459    0.16363
```

ones

```
ones(const r, const c);
    r           in:  int
    c           in:  int
```

Return value

    Returns an r by c matrix filled with ones.

See also

    constant, unit, zeros

Example

```
#include <oxstd.h>

main()
{
    print( ones(2, 2) );
}
```

produces

```
    1.0000         1.0000
    1.0000         1.0000
```

oxversion

```
oxversion();
```

Return value

    Returns an integer with the version of Ox multiplied by 100. So for version 1.10 the return value is 110.

pacf

```
pacf(const macf);
```

```
macf        in:  arithmetic type, (m + 1) × n matrix of autocovariances or
                 autocorrelations
```

Return value

Returns a $m \times n$ matrix with the partial autocorrelation function of the columns of `macf`. Returns 0 if the computations fail (the stochastic process has a root on the unit circle).

Description

Given autocovariance (or autocorrelation) functions in the columns of `macf`, this function solves the Yule-Walker equations using Durbin's method as described in Golub and Van Loan (1989, §4.7.2).

For the theoretical PACF of an ARMA(p, q) process, use the results from `armavar` as input. For the sample PACF, use the results from `acf`.

See also

`acf, armavar`

Example

```
#include <oxstd.h>

main()
{
    print( pacf(
          armavar(<0.5>,  1,  0,  (1 - 0.5^2),   10)'
        ~ armavar(<-0.5>, 1,  0,  (1 - (-0.5)^2), 10)'
        ~ armavar(<0.5>,  0,  1,  1 / (1 + 0.5^2), 10)'
              )[:4][]  );
}
```

produces

```
    0.50000      -0.50000       0.50000
    0.00000       0.00000      -0.25000
    0.00000       0.00000       0.12499
    0.00000       0.00000      -0.062485
    0.00000       0.00000       0.031220
```

periodogram

```
periodogram(const ma, const itrunc, const cpoints,
    const imode);
```

ma	in:	arithmetic type, $T \times n$ matrix
itrunc	in:	int, truncation parameter m, if $\geq T$ then $T - 1$ is used
cpoints	in:	int, no of points N at which to evaluate periodogram, resulting in evaluation at frequencies: $0, \pi/(N-1), \ldots, \pi$.
imode	in:	0: (truncated) periodogram,
		1: smoothed periodogram using Parzen window,
		2: estimated spectral density using Parzen window (as option 1, but divided by c_0).

Return value

Returns a (cpoints) $\times n$ matrix with the periodogram of the columns of ma using autocovariances up to lag itrunc. Returns 0 if ilag ≤ 0.

Description

Computes the periodogram of the columns of a $T \times n$ matrix $A = (a_0, a_1, \ldots, a_{n-1})$.

Define the autocovariance function of a T-vector $x = (x_0 \cdots x_{T-1})'$ up to lag k as $c = (\hat{c}_0 \cdots \hat{c}_k)'$:

$$\hat{c}_j = \frac{1}{T-j} \sum_{t=j}^{T-1} (x_t - \bar{x})(x_{t-j} - \bar{x}), \tag{8.4}$$

with the mean defined in the standard way as:

$$\bar{x} = \frac{1}{T} \sum_{t=0}^{T-1} x_t$$

Note that $\hat{r}_j = \hat{c}_j/\hat{c}_0$, see equation (8.1) on page 53.

The periodogram is then defined as:

$$p(\omega) = \frac{1}{2\pi} \sum_{j=-m}^{m} K(j)\hat{c}_{|j|} \cos(j\omega), \quad 0 \leq \omega \leq \pi, \tag{8.5}$$

where $|\cdot|$ takes the absolute value, so that, for example, $c_{|-1|} = c_1$. The $K(\cdot)$ function is called the *lag window*, m is called the *lag truncation parameter*.

The value of the imode parameter affects the computations as follows:

0: uses $K(j) = 1$ for all j.

1: computes the smoothed periodogram. The smoothing is achieved using the Parzen window:

$$K(j) = 1 - 6\left(\frac{j}{m}\right)^2 + 6\left|\frac{j}{m}\right|^3, \qquad \left|\frac{j}{m}\right| \leq 0.5,$$

$$= 2\left(1 - \left|\frac{j}{m}\right|\right)^3, \qquad 0.5 \leq \left|\frac{j}{m}\right| \leq 1.0,$$

$$= 0, \qquad \left|\frac{j}{m}\right| > 1.$$

2: As 1, but using the autocorrelations $\hat{r}$ instead of the autocovariances $\hat{c}$.

We have that $K(-j) = K(j)$, so that the sign of j does not matter. The c_js are based on fewer observations as j increases. The window function attaches decreasing weights to the autococorrelations, with zero weight for $j > m$. The larger m, the less smooth the spectrum becomes, but the lower the bias. For more information see Priestley (1981, Ch.6) and Granger and Newbold (1986, §2.6). In each case, the periodogram is evaluated at N frequencies between 0 and π:

$$0, \frac{\pi}{N-1}, \frac{2\pi}{N-1}, \ldots, \frac{(N-1)\pi}{N-1} = \pi,$$

so that the horizontal axis could be computed as:

`M_PI * range(0, cpoints-1) / (cpoints-1).`

See also
> `DrawSpectrum` (for an example).

polydiv

`polydiv(const ma, const mb, const cp);`

ma	in:	$1 \times m$ matrix $A = (a_0 \ldots a_{m-1})$ specifying the A polynomial (see below)	
mb	in:	$1 \times n$ matrix $B = (b_0 \ldots b_{n-1})$ specifying the B polynomial (see below)	
cp	in:	int, required length, p, of polynomial resulting from division	

Return value
> Returns a $1 \times p$ matrix with the coefficients of polynomial resulting from dividing the A polynomial by the B polynomial. The integer 0 is returned when b_0 is 0, or $p = 0$.

Description
> Defining the two polynomials

$$A(x) = a_0 + a_1 x + a_2 x^2 + \ldots a_{m-1} x^{m-1},$$
$$B(x) = a_0 + b_1 x + b_2 x^2 + \ldots b_{n-1} x^{n-1},$$

> `polydiv` returns (p is specified in the function call):

$$D(x) = A(x)/B(x) = d_0 + d_1 x + d_2 x^2 + \ldots d_{p-1} x^{p-1}.$$

See also
> `polymake`, `polymul` (for an example), `polyroots`

polygamma

```
polygamma(const ma, const mn);
```
    ma   in: arithmetic type
    mn   in: arithmetic type, order of derivative: 0 = first derivative, 1 =
                          second derivative, etc.

Return value

Returns the derivative of the logarithm of the complete gamma function at the value of each element of ma, of double or matrix type. The second argument specifies the order of the derivative.

Returns zero for any argument less than or equal to zero, or derivative order less than 0.

The return type is derived as follows:

returns	ma	order arguments
$m \times n$ matrix	$m \times n$ matrix	scalar (int)
$m \times n$ matrix	scalar	$m \times n$ matrix
$m \times n$ matrix	$m \times n$ matrix	$m \times n$ matrix
double	scalar	scalar (int)

Description

Computes the derivatives of the loggamma function at the argument a:

$$\psi^{(n)}(a) = \frac{d^{n+1}}{da^{n+1}} \log \Gamma(a) \quad \text{for } a > 0.$$

Most commonly used are:

    $n = 0$ digamma (psi) function
    $n = 1$ trigamma function
    $n = 2$ tetragamma function
    $n = \ldots$ etc.

The function is accurate to about 15 significant digits. The approximation uses the recurrence relation

$$\psi^{(n)}(a + 1) = \psi^{(n)}(a) + (-1)^n n! z^{-n-1}.$$

to obtain an argument greater than 8.5; then an asymptotic formula with eight terms is applied (see Abramowitz and Stegun, 1984, §6.4.11).

See also

    loggamma

Example

```
#include <oxstd.h>
#include <oxfloat.h>

main()
{
    print(polygamma(<0.5,1>, 0),
          -M_EULER-2*log(2) ~ -M_EULER);
    print("%12.7g", polygamma(0.5, <0,1,2,3>));
}
```

produces

```
-1.9635      -0.57722
-1.9635      -0.57722
-1.96351     4.934802     -16.8288     97.40909
```

polymake

`polymake(const roots);`

roots   in: $2 \times m$ matrix with (inverse) roots of the polynomial, first row is real part, second row imaginary part (or $1 \times m$ matrix if all roots are real).

Return value

Returns the coefficients of the polynomial ($a_0 = 1$) as a $2 \times (m+1)$ matrix if the roots had a complex part, else $1 \times (m+1)$.

Description

Computes the polynomial coefficients from the inverse roots. The constant term (a_0) is set to one, so returned is the a_i from:

$$1 + a_1 x + a_2 x^2 + \dots a_m x^m.$$

See also

    `polyroots` (for an example)

polymul

`polymul(const ma, const mb);`

ma   in: $1 \times m$ matrix $A = (a_0 \dots a_{m-1})$ specifying the A polynomial (see below)

mb   in: $1 \times n$ matrix $B = (b_0 \dots b_{n-1})$ specifying the B polynomial (see below)

Return value

Returns a $1 \times m + n - 1$ matrix with the coefficients of the product of the polynomials.

Description

Defining the two polynomials

$$A(x) = a_0 + a_1 x + a_2 x^2 + \ldots a_{m-1} x^{m-1},$$
$$B(x) = a_0 + b_1 x + b_2 x^2 + \ldots b_{n-1} x^{n-1},$$

the `polymul` function returns:

$$C(x) = A(x)B(x) = c_0 + c_1 x + c_2 x^2 + \ldots c_{p-1} x^{p-1}, \quad p = m + n - 1.$$

See also

polydiv, polymake, polyroots

Example

```
#include <oxstd.h>

main()
{
    decl a, b;

    a = <1,-0.9>;   b = <1,-0.8,-0.1>;

    print(polymul(a, b));
    print(polydiv(polymul(b, a), a, 6));
}
```

produces

```
     1.0000          -1.7000        0.62000       0.090000

     1.0000          -0.80000      -0.10000 -3.4139e-017
-3.0725e-017 -2.7652e-017
```

polyroots

polyroots(const ma, const amroots);

ma	in:	$1 \times (m+1)$ matrix $A = (a_0 \ldots a_m)$ specifying the polynomial of order m (see below)
amroots	in:	address of variable
	out:	$2 \times m$ matrix with roots of the polynomial, first row is real part, second row imaginary part (all zeros if the roots are real). The roots are *not* sorted.

Return value

Returns the result of the eigenvalue decomposition:

0 no error;

1 maximum no of iterations (50) reached.

Description

Computes the inverse roots of a polynomial

$$a_0 + a_1x + a_2x^2 + \ldots a_mx^m.$$

The inverse roots are found as the eigenvalues of the companion matrix (which is already in upper Hessenberg form), e.g. when $m = 4$ and $a_0 = 1$:

$-a_1$	$-a_2$	$-a_3$	$-a_4$
1	0	0	0
0	1	0	0
0	0	1	0

Note that the implementation assumes that $a_0 \neq 0$. Also note that the inverse roots of

$$1 + a_1x + a_2x^2 + \ldots a_mx^m.$$

correspond to the roots of

$$x^m + a_1x^{m-1} + a_2x^{m-2} + \ldots a_1.$$

Error messages

polyroots(): maximum no. of iterations reached

See also

cabs (for another example), eigen, polydiv, polymake, polymul

Example

```
#include <oxstd.h>

main()
{
    decl v1, roots, cr;

    v1 = <-1, 1.2274, -0.017197, -0.28369, -0.01028>;

    polyroots(v1, &roots);

    cr = columns(roots);
    print(v1, "roots", roots,
        "inverse roots", cdiv(ones(1,cr), roots),
        "polynomial", polymake(roots) );
}
```

produces

```
        -1.0000        1.2274     -0.017197      -0.28369     -0.010280
roots
        0.82865        0.82865    -0.39337      -0.036535
        0.16923       -0.16923     0.00000        0.00000
inverse roots
         1.1585         1.1585    -2.5422        -27.371
        -0.23659        0.23659    0.00000         0.00000
polynomial
         1.0000        -1.2274     0.017197       0.28369       0.010280
         0.00000        0.00000    0.00000        0.00000       0.00000
```

print

```
print(const a, ...);
    a           in:   any type
    ...         in:   any type
```

Return value

Returns the number of arguments supplied to the function.

Description

Each argument is printed to stdout using default formatting. A formatting string can be input in the input stream: a formatting string starts with a % symbol, and is followed by one or more characters. If a formatting string is encountered, it is not printed, but applied to the next argument.

There is an additional option to add column and row labels for a matrix:

%r   the next argument contains row labels (array of strings)

%c   the next argument contains column labels (array of strings)

The default format strings are:

no value	`"null"`
int	`"%d"`
double	`"%g"`
matrix	`"\n"`, then each element `"%#12.5g"`, 6 elements on a line (5 if row is labelled), no labels.
string	`"%s"`
array	`"&0x%p"`
function	`"&%d"`
class	`"&0x%p"`
library function	`"&0x%p"`

The format function may be used to set a different default format; it also lists the format options.

The format specification is similar to that for the printf function of the C language:

$$\%[flag][width][.precision]type$$

Table 8.2   Formatting flags for doubles and integers.

flag	
–	left adjust in output field,
+	always print a sign,
space	prefix space if first character is not a sign
0	pad with leading zeros,
#	alternate output form:
	type is o: first digit will be 0,
	type is xX: prefix with 0x or 0X (unless value is 0),
	type is eEfgG: always print decimal point,
	type is gG: keep trailing zeros.
	type is mM: omit dimensions.

The *width* argument specifies the width of the output field. The *precision* argument specifies the number of significant digits (type is gG) number of digits after the decimal point (type is eEf); the default is 6 if *precision* is absent.

Table 8.3 explains the format strings; some notes:

- The `format` function allows setting a default format.
- Be careful with the `%f` format, for example, when printing 1e-300, the output field will need 302 characters.
- By default, integers are printed without leading spaces, to use a space as separator: `" %d"` alternatively specify a wider field: `"%6d"`.
- Matrices always use one space between elements.
- The `"%m"` and `"%M"` formats must be followed by a matrix. First the number of rows and columns is written, which is followed by the matrix, row by row; this corresponds to the format used by `savemat`. The dimensions are omitted by `"%#m"` and `"%#M"`.

  This format is most useful when the matrix has to be read from a file at a later stage.

See also

    `eprint, format, fprint, fscan, fwrite, sprint`

Example

```
#include <oxstd.h>

main()
{
    print( "%r", {"row 1", "row 2"},
```

Table 8.3   Formatting types for printing.

double *type*:	(also used for matrices)
g,G	%e or %E if the exponent is < -4 or $>=$ *precision*; else use %f,
e,e	scientific notation: with exponent,
f	print without exponent,
integer *type*:	
d,i	signed decimal notation,
o	unsigned octal notation,
x,X	unsigned hexadecimal notation,
u	unsigned decimal notation,
c	print as a single character (i.e. one byte),
string *type*:	
s	string format.
matrix *type*:	
m	print matrix row by row using %25.26e.
M	print matrix row by row using default format.

```
            "%c", {"col 1", "col 2"}, "%5.1g", unit(2) );
}
```

produces

```
          col 1 col 2
row 1         1     0
row 2         0     1
```

probbeta, probchi, probf, probgamma, probn, probt

```
probbeta(const ma, const a, const b);
probchi(const ma, const df);
probf(const ma, const df1, const df2);
probgamma(const ma, const dr, const da);
probn(const ma);
probt(const ma, const idf);
```

ma	in:	arithmetic type
a,b	in:	arithmetic type, arguments for Beta distribution
df	in:	arithmetic type, degrees of freedom
df1	in:	arithmetic type, degrees of freedom in the numerator
df2	in:	arithmetic type, degrees of freedom in the denominator
dr	in:	arithmetic type
da	in:	arithmetic type
idf	in:	int, degrees of freedom

Return value

Returns the requested probabilities at ma (the returned probabilities are between zero and one):

probbeta	probabilities from Beta(a, b) distribution,
probchi	probabilities from $\chi^2(df)$ distribution,
probf	probabilities from F$(df1, df2)$ distribution,
probgamma	probabilities from the Γ distribution,
probn	one-sided probabilities from the standard normal N$(0, 1)$,
probt	one-sided probabilities from student-t(df) distribution.

The probabilities are accurate to about 10 digits.

The return type is derived as follows:

returns	ma	degrees of freedom arguments
$m \times n$ matrix	$m \times n$ matrix	scalar (int for probt)
$m \times n$ matrix	scalar	$m \times n$ matrix
$m \times n$ matrix	$m \times n$ matrix	$m \times n$ matrix
double	scalar	scalar (int for probt)

Description

The Beta distribution is defined as $I_x(a, b)$ under betafunc.

The Gamma distribution, $\Gamma(z; r, a)$, is defined as:

$$\Gamma(z; r, a) = \int_0^z \frac{a^r}{\Gamma(r)} x^{r-1} e^{-ax} dx, \quad z > 0, r > 0, a > 0. \tag{8.6}$$

so that $\Gamma(z; r, 1)$ corresponds to the incomplete gamma function. Note that $\chi(df)$ can be computed as $\Gamma(\cdot; 0.5df, 0.5)$.

Sources: probchi uses gammafunc, probf uses betafunc, probn and tailn use Applied Statistics algorithm AS 66 (Hill, 1973), probt uses AS 3 (Cooper, 1968).

See also

betafunc, gammafunc, dens..., quan..., tail...

Example

```
#include <oxstd.h>

main()
{
    decl m = <0,4.61,5.99>;

    print("%r", {"chi:"},      probchi(m, 2));
    print("%r", {"gamma:"},    probgamma(m, 1, 0.5));
    print("%r", {"normal:"},   probn(<-1.96, 0, 1.96>) );
    print("%r", {"t:"},        probt(<-1.96, 0, 1.96>, 4) );

                        /* additional argument types: */
    print("%r", {"chi:"},      probchi(5.99, <2,3,4>),
          "%r", {"chi:"},      probchi(<6,7,8>, <2,3,4>) );
}
```

produces

```
chi:               0.00000       0.90024       0.94996
gamma:             0.00000       0.90024       0.94996
normal:            0.024998      0.50000       0.97500
t:                 0.060777      0.50000       0.93922
chi:               0.94996       0.88790       0.80010
chi:               0.95021       0.92810       0.90842
```

prodc, prodr

```
prodc(const ma);
prodr(const ma);
```
    ma   in: $T \times n$ matrix A

Return value

The prodc function returns a $1 \times n$ matrix r which holds the product of all column elements of ma.

The prodr function returns a $T \times 1$ matrix which holds the product of all row elements of ma.

See also

    sumc, sumr

Example

```
#include <oxstd.h>

main()
{
    print( prodc(<0:3;1:4;2:5>) );
    print( prodr(<0:3;1:4;2:5>) );
}
```

produces

```
0.00000          6.0000          24.000          60.000

0.00000
24.000
120.00
```

quanchi, quanf, quann, quant

```
quanchi(const ma, const df);
quanf(const ma, const df1, const df2);
quann(const ma);
quant(const ma, const idf);
```

ma	in:	arithmetic type, probabilities: all values must be between 0 and 1
df	in:	arithmetic type, degrees of freedom
df1	in:	arithmetic type, degrees of freedom in the numerator
df2	in:	arithmetic type, degrees of freedom in the denominator
idf	in:	int, degrees of freedom

Return value

Returns the requested quantiles (inverse probability function; percentage points) at ma:

quanchi	quantiles from $\chi^2(df)$ distribution
quanf	quantiles from $F(df1, df2)$ distribution
quann	standard normal quantiles
quant	quantiles from student-t(df) distribution

The quantiles are accurate to about 10 digits.

The return type is derived as follows:

returns	ma	degrees of freedom arguments
$m \times n$ matrix	$m \times n$ matrix	scalar (int for quant)
$m \times n$ matrix	scalar	$m \times n$ matrix
$m \times n$ matrix	$m \times n$ matrix	$m \times n$ matrix
double	scalar	scalar (int for quant)

Description

Sources: quanchi uses a modified version of Applied Statistics algorithm AS 91 (Best and Roberts, 1975) and AS R85 (Shea, 1991), quanf uses AS 109 (Cran, Martin and Thomas, 1977) and AS 64 (Majunder and Bhattacharjee, 1973) to obtain starting values for a Newton Raphson refinement (it does not use the iterative procedure from AS 109 because this was found to be not accurate enough; AS R83 (Berry, Mielke Jr and Cran, 1977) does not seem to solve this), quann uses

AS 241 (Wichura, 1988), quant uses an approximation from Abramowitz and Stegun (1984), and Newton Raphson to refine this.

See also

    dens..., prob..., tail...

Example

```
#include <oxstd.h>

main()
{
    decl t = range(1,10), tt = (t - 5) / 5;

    print("%20.10g",
        probf(t,10,10)' ~ quanf(probf(t,10,10),10,10)' );
    print("%20.10g",
        probt(tt,2)' ~ quant(probt(tt,2),2)' );
}
```

produces

```
        0.5000000001               1
        0.855154194                2
        0.9510726929               3
         0.98041856                4
        0.9910499384               5
        0.9954702686               6
        0.9975177199               7
        0.9985507194               8
         0.99910908                9
        0.9994284475              10

        0.253817018             -0.8
        0.3047166335            -0.6
        0.3639172365            -0.4
        0.4299859958            -0.2
             0.5                  0
        0.5700140042             0.2
        0.6360827635             0.4
        0.6952833665             0.6
         0.746182982             0.8
        0.7886751346               1
```

quantilec, quantiler

```
quantilec(const ma);
quantiler(const ma);
quantilec(const ma, const mq);
quantiler(const ma, const mq);
```

ma   in: $T \times n$ matrix A

mq   in: (optional argument) $1 \times q$ matrix of quantiles

Return value

The quantilec function returns a $q \times n$ matrix holding the requested quantiles of the columns of ma. If no second argument is used the return value is a $1 \times n$ matrix holding the medians.

The quantiler function returns a $T \times q$ matrix holding the requested quantiles of the rows of ma. If no second argument is used the return value is a $T \times 1$ matrix holding the medians.

Description

The q-th quantile ξ_q, $0 \le q \le 1$, of a random variable X is defined as the smallest ξ which satisfies $P(X \le \xi) = q$. So $\xi_{0.5}$, the median, divides the distribution in half.

For a sample of size T, $x = (x_0 \cdots x_{T-1})'$, the q-th quantile is found by interpolating the nearest two values. Write $(y_0 \cdots y_{T-1})$ for the ordered x-values, $y_0 \le y_1 \le \cdots \le y_{T-1}$, the quantiles are computed as:

$$\xi_q = [k + 1 - q\,(T-1)]\,y_k + [q\,(T-1) - k]\,y_{k+1}, \qquad (8.7)$$

where

$$k = \text{int}[q\,(T-1)].$$

when $q(T-1)$ is integer, the expression simplifies to $\xi_q = y_k$.

For example, for the quartiles ($\xi_{0.25}$, $\xi_{0.5}$ and $\xi_{0.75}$) when $T = 4$: $q(T-1) = 0.75, 1.5, 2.25$ and $k = 0, 1, 2$ respectively. In this case, the median is the average of the middle two observations: $\xi_{.5} = 0.5 y_1 + 0.5 y_2$, and the lower quartile: $\xi_{.25} = 0.25 y_0 + 0.75 y_1$.

The example below shows how to obtain quantiles without using interpolation.

See also

meanc, meanr, varc, varr

Example

```
#include <oxstd.h>

main()
{
    print( quantilec(<3;2;1;4>, <1/4,2/4,3/4>) );
    print( quantilec(<3;2;1;4>) );

    decl m = rann(2,10000);          /* generate m */

    print( quantiler(m, <0.8,0.9,0.95,0.975>) );
    print( quantilec(m', <0.8,0.9,0.95,0.975>) );
```

```
      m = sortr(m);                          /* sort m */
      print( m[][columns(m) * <0.8,0.9,0.95,0.975> ] );
}
```

produces:

```
      1.7500
      2.5000
      3.2500

      2.5000

      0.84237        1.2728        1.6360        1.9725
      0.82746        1.2619        1.6338        1.9409

      0.84237        0.82746
      1.2728         1.2619
      1.6360         1.6338
      1.9725         1.9409

      0.84267        1.2741        1.6388        1.9734
      0.82828        1.2626        1.6343        1.9414
```

ranbeta, ranbinomial, ranchi, ranexp, ranf, rangamma, rann, ranno, ranpoisson, rant

```
ranbeta(const r, const c, const a, const b);
ranbinomial(const r, const c, const n, const p);
ranchi(const r, const c, const df);
ranexp(const r, const c, const lambda);
ranf(const r, const c, const df1, const df2);
rangamma(const r, const c, const dr, const da);
rann(const r, const c);
ranno(const r, const c);
ranpoisson(const r, const c, const mu);
rant(const r, const c, const idf);
```

r	in:	int, number of rows
c	in:	int, number of columns
a,b	in:	arithmetic type, arguments for Beta distribution
n	in:	int, number of trials
p	in:	double, probability of success
lambda	in:	double
df	in:	double, degrees of freedom
df1	in:	double, degrees of freedom in the numerator
df2	in:	double, degrees of freedom in the denominator
dr	in:	double
da	in:	double
mu	in:	double, mean of poisson
idf	in:	int, degrees of freedom

Return value

Returns a r × c matrix of random numbers from the selected distribution:

function	Generates random numbers from
ranbeta	Beta(a, b) distribution,
ranbinomial	Binomial(n, p) distribution,
ranchi	$\chi^2(df)$ distribution,
ranexp	$\exp(\lambda)$ distribution with mean $1/\lambda$,
ranf	$F(df1, df2)$ distribution,
rangamma	Gamma(r, a) distribution, see (8.6) on p. 140,
rann	standard normal distribution,
ranpoisson	Poisson(μ) distribution,
rant	Student $t(df)$ distribution.

The matrix is filled by row. Note that, if both r and c are 1, the return value is a scalar of type double!

Description

All these functions use uniform random numbers generated as described under ranu.

The rangamma function uses algorithms 3.19 and 3.20 from Ripley (1987), rann uses the Polar-Marsaglia method, ranbinomial is based on a simple execution of the Bernoulli trials, ranpoisson uses algorithms 3.3 and 3.15 from Ripley (1987). Drawings from the Beta distribution are generated as a ratio of Gamma's.

For ranno *the matrix is not filled by row*; instead, each row is split in two, and each half filled simultaneously. ranno was called rann in Ox version 1.08 and before, and is supplied only for backward compatibility.

See also

ranseed, ranu

Example

```
#include <oxstd.h>

main()
{
    print( sumc( ranchi(1000,1,5) ) / 1000 );
    print( sumc( ranexp(1000,1,5) ) / 1000 );
    print( sumc( rann(1000,1) ) / 1000 );

    ranseed(-1);
    print(rann(1,5));
    ranseed(-1);
    print(rann(1,3) ~ rann(1,2));
}
```

produces

```
      5.0298
      0.20113
     -0.0054037

     -0.65201      0.46053     -0.39088     -0.64953     -0.65276
     -0.65201      0.46053     -0.39088     -0.64953     -0.65276
```

range

```
range(const min, const max);
range(const min, const max, const step);
```

min	in:	int or double, first value m
max	in:	int or double, last value n
step	in:	int or double, (optional argument) increment

Return value

Returns a $1 \times (n - m + 1)$ matrix with the values with values $m, m + 1, ..., n$. If $n < m$, range returns a $1 \times (m - n + 1)$ matrix with the values with values $m, m - 1, ..., n$.

The version which uses the step argument uses that as the incrementor (rather than the default $+1$ or -1), the returned matrix is a row vector of the required length.

Description

When all arguments are integers, the incrementation arithmetic is done using integers, else using doubles. Integer arithmetic could be a bit more precise when using longer ranges. The following example illustrates the difference:

```
range(-1.1, 1.1, 0.11);
range(-110, 110, 11) / 100;
```

The first line has the loop using floating point arithmetic, and will not have exactly zero, but something like -1.9e-16 as its 11th element. In the second line, the loop is incremented in integer arithmetic before conversion to floating point numbers. Here the 11th number will be exactly zero.

See also

> constant

Example

```
#include <oxstd.h>

main()
{
    print( range(1,4), range(4,1), range(1,6,2));
    print( range(1.2,4), range(1,6,2.1));
}
```

produces

1.0000	2.0000	3.0000	4.0000
4.0000	3.0000	2.0000	1.0000
1.0000	3.0000	5.0000	
1.2000	2.2000	3.2000	
1.0000	3.1000	5.2000	

rank

```
rank(const ma);
```
> ma　　　　　　in:　arithmetic type

Return value

> Returns the rank of a matrix, of type int. The rank of a scalar is 1.

Description

> Computes the rank of a matrix A. The rank is the number of singular values $> 10\epsilon_{inv}||A||_\infty$, with ϵ_{inv} is set by the inverteps function (the default is the machine precision for doubles ($\approx 2 \times 10^{-16}$ times 1000) and

$$||A||_\infty = \max_{0\leq i<m} \sum_{j=0}^{n-1} |a_{ij}|.$$

See also

> decsvd, inverteps

Example

```
#include <oxstd.h>

main()
{
    print( rank(<1,0;1,0>) );
}
```

produces: 1

ranseed

```
ranseed(const iseed);
    iseed        in:   int
```

Return value

Returns the current seed of the random number generator, of type int, after setting the seed to iseed. A call to ranseed(0) only returns the current seed, without changing it; ranseed(-1) resets to the initial seed and returns the initial seed.

Description

Sets the seed of the random number generator to iseed, unless iseed is 0. The initial seed is 198195252.

See also

ran..., ranu

Example

```
#include <oxstd.h>

main()
{
    print( ranseed(0) );
    print( meanc( rann(1000,2) ) );
    print( meanc( rann(1000,2) ) );
    ranseed(-1);
    print( meanc( rann(1000,2) ) );
}
```

produces

```
198195252
  -0.00079415     -0.010349
   0.0016709      -0.0037005
  -0.00079415     -0.010349
```

ranu

```
ranu(const r, const c);
     r              in:   int
     c              in:   int
```

Return value

Returns a r × c matrix of uniform random numbers. The matrix is filled by row.

Description

Generates random numbers uniformly distributed in the range 0 to 1. Each call to ranu will produce a different set of numbers, unless the seed is reset (this is achieved through the ranseed function).

The random number generator is the modified Park and Miller generator (based on Park and Miller, 1988, with modifications due to Park). It is a linear congruential generator, which in C form can be written as (assuming an int is 32 bits):

```
#define PM_A   48271
#define PM_M   2147483647L
#define PM_Q   (PM_M / PM_A)
#define PM_R   (PM_M % PM_A)
#define PM_INIT 198195252
static double dMinv = 1.0 / (double)PM_M;
static int iOldran = PM_INIT;

double ran(void)
{
    int  lo, hi, test;

    lo = iOldran % PM_Q;  hi = iOldran / PM_Q;
    test = lo * PM_A - hi * PM_R;
    iOldran = (test > 0) ? test : test + PM_M;

    return iOldran * dMinv;
}
```

The period of the generator is $2^{31} - 1$.

See also

ran..., ranseed

Example

```
#include <oxstd.h>

main()
{
    print( ranu(2,3) );
}
```

produces

```
      0.020192      0.68617       0.15174
      0.74598       0.27669       0.12892
```

reflect

```
reflect(const ma);
     ma              in:   square m × m matrix
```

Return value
Returns the reflected version of ma.

Description
Reflects a matrix around its secondary diagonal (from element $m-1, 0$ to element $0, m-1$. A matrix which is unchanged under reflection is called *persymmetric*.

See also
transpose operator '

Example

```
#include <oxstd.h>

main()
{
    print( reflect(<2,1;1,4>) );
}
```

produces

```
4.0000          1.0000
1.0000          2.0000
```

reshape

```
reshape(const ma, const r, const c);
     ma              in:   arithmetic type
     r               in:   int
     c               in:   int
```

Return value
Returns an r × c matrix, filled by row from vec(ma). If there are less than rc elements in ma, the input matrix is repeated.

Description
Reshapes a matrix. It runs through the rows of ma from top to bottom. When all the elements of ma are used, the function starts again at the begining of ma.

See also
shape

Example

```
#include <oxstd.h>

main()
{
    print( reshape(<1:3>, 4, 3)' );
}
```
produces

1.0000	1.0000	1.0000	1.0000
2.0000	2.0000	2.0000	2.0000
3.0000	3.0000	3.0000	3.0000

reversec, reverser

```
reversec(const ma);
reverser(const ma);
```
    ma   in: $m \times n$ matrix A

Return value

The reversec function returns an $m \times n$ matrix which has the columns of ma in reverse order.

The reverser function returns an $m \times n$ matrix which has the rows of ma in reverse order.

See also

    sortc, sortr

Example

```
#include <oxstd.h>

main()
{
    decl m = <0:3;4:7;8:11;12:15>;
    print( m, reversec(m), reverser(m) );
}
```
produces:

0.00000	1.0000	2.0000	3.0000
4.0000	5.0000	6.0000	7.0000
8.0000	9.0000	10.000	11.000
12.000	13.000	14.000	15.000
12.000	13.000	14.000	15.000
8.0000	9.0000	10.000	11.000
4.0000	5.0000	6.0000	7.0000
0.00000	1.0000	2.0000	3.0000
3.0000	2.0000	1.0000	0.00000
7.0000	6.0000	5.0000	4.0000
11.000	10.000	9.0000	8.0000
15.000	14.000	13.000	12.000

round

```
round(const ma);
```
      ma   in: arithmetic type

Return value

Returns the rounded elements of ma, of double or matrix type. Rounds to the nearest integer.

See also

ceil (for an example), floor, trunc

rows

```
rows(const ma);
```
      ma   in: any type

Return value

Returns an integer value which is the number of rows in the argument:

type	returns
$m \times n$ matrix	m
string	number of characters in the string
array	number of elements in the array
file	number of rows in the file
	(only if opened with f format, see fopen)
other	0

Description

Computes the number of rows in the argument.

See also

columns (for an example)

savemat

```
savemat(const sname, const ma);
savemat(const sname, const ma, const iFormat);
```
   sname   in: string containing an existing file name
   ma   in: matrix
   iFormat in: (optional argument)
                       1: omit the matrix dimensions, for matrix file only.

Return value

Returns 0 if the operation failed, 1 otherwise.

Description

The type of file saved depends on the extension of the file name:

.mat	ASCII matrix file,
.dat	ASCII data file with load information,
.in7	PcGive 7 data file (with corresponding .bn7 file),
.xls	Excel version 4 spread sheet file,
.wks and .wk1	Lotus spread sheet file,
.fmt	Gauss matrix file (32 bit),
any other	as .mat file.

The `loadmat` function has a discussion of the formats. Where required, the sample start is set to 1 (1), the frequency to 1, and the variable names to `Var1`, `Var2`, ... The `Database` class allows proper treatment of sample periods and variable names.

When writing a matrix file (see `loadmat` for an example), the values are written to full precision (16 significant digits).

All written files (including .fmt) are identical on each platform, so that a file can be written under Windows, transferred to a Sun in binary mode, and then read again using `loadmat`. So, the files are written in Windows byte ordering (little endian; also see `fwrite`). Gauss under Unix writes .fmt files in a different format.

Error messages

savemat(): cannot open file

Can only save ... variables

See also

`Database` class, `loadmat` (for an example)

scan

```
scan(const a, ...);
```
a	in:	any type
...	in:	any type

Return value

Returns the number of arguments successfully scanned and assigned.

Description

This function works as f scan, but reading from the console, not a file. Any text in the scanning string which does not have an input format is *echoed to the console* (this is different from the standard C scanf function).

See also

fscan, fwrite, sscan

Example

The following example reads one input line at a time (leading spaces in each line are skipped, because of the starting space in " %z", and reads from that string using scan. The * in "%*d" suppresses assignment, so the integer is skipped in the file.

```
#include <oxstd.h>

main()
{
    decl c, i, d, m;

    c = scan("Enter an integer: %d", &i,
            "Enter a double:   %f", &d);
    print("items read=", c, " int=", i, " dbl=", d, "\n");

    c = scan("Enter a 2 x 2 matrix: %#m", 2, 2, &m);
    print("items read=", c, " mat=", m);

    c = scan("Enter a matrix with dimensions: %m", &m);
    print("items read=", c, " mat=", m);
}
```

This program produces (keyboard input is written in italics):

```
Enter an integer: 24
Enter a double:    25
items read=2 int=24 dbl=25
Enter a 2 x 2 matrix: 1
0
0
1

items read=1 mat=
       1.0000        0.00000
       0.00000       1.0000

Enter a matrix with dimensions: 2
2
1
```

> *0*
> *0*
> *1*

```
items read=1 mat=
        1.0000        0.00000
        0.00000        1.0000
```

setdiagonal, setlower, setupper

```
setdiagonal(const ma, const mdiag);
setlower(const ma, const ml);
setupper(const ma, const mu);
setlower(const ma, const ml, const mdiag);
setupper(const ma, const mu, const mdiag);
```

ma	in:	$m \times n$ matrix
mdiag	in:	$1 \times \min(m,n)$ or $\min(m,n) \times 1$ or matrix $m \times n$ matrix or scalar
ml	in:	scalar or $m \times n$ matrix with new strict lower diagonal
mu	in:	scalar $m \times n$ matrix with new strict upper diagonal

Return value

setdiagonal returns a matrix with the diagonal replaced by mdiag, which is either a vector with the new diagonal elements, or a matrix from which the diagonal is copied. If mdiag is scalar, all diagonal elements of the returned matrix have that value.

setlower returns ma with the strict lower diagonal replaced by that of ml.   setlower(ma, ml, mdiag) corresponds to setdiagonal(setlower(ma, ml), mdiag).

setupper returns ma with the strict upper diagonal replaced by that of ml. setupper(ma, ml, mdiag) corresponds to setdiagonal(setupper(ma, ml), mdiag).

See also

diag, diagonal, diagonalize, lower, upper

Example

```
#include <oxstd.h>

main()
{
    decl ma = ones(2,2);
    print(setdiagonal(ma, zeros(2,1)),
```

```
                setdiagonal(ma, 0),
                setdiagonal(ma, zeros(2,2)) );

        ma = ones(3,3);
        decl mb = rann(3,3);

        print(setlower(ma, mb, mb), setupper(ma, 0),
                setupper(ma, 0, 2) );
    }
```
produces

```
        0.00000         1.0000
        1.0000          0.00000

        0.00000         1.0000
        1.0000          0.00000

        0.00000         1.0000
        1.0000          0.00000

       -0.65201         1.0000          1.0000
       -0.64953        -0.65276         1.0000
        1.0880          0.99745         0.57228

        1.0000          0.00000         0.00000
        1.0000          1.0000          0.00000
        1.0000          1.0000          1.0000

        2.0000          0.00000         0.00000
        1.0000          2.0000          0.00000
        1.0000          1.0000          2.0000
```

shape

```
shape(const ma, const r, const c);
```
    ma   in: arithmetic type
    r   in: int
    c   in: int

Return value

Returns an $r \times c$ matrix, filled by column from vec(ma). If there are fewer than rc elements in ma, the value 0 is used for padding.

Description

Shapes a matrix. It runs through the columns of ma from left to right, and can be used e.g. to undo a vec operation. So shape puts the first r elements of ma in the first column of the return matrix, etc. To do the opposite, namely put the first c elements in the first row of the return matrx, use shape(ma, c, r)'.

Shape is closely related to vec: `v = shape(x, rows(x)*columns(x), 1)` is the same as `v = vec(x)`. `shape(v, rows(x), columns(x)` undoes the vectorization.

See also
> reshape, vec

Example

```
#include <oxstd.h>

main()
{
    print( shape(<0:5>, 2, 4) );
    print( shape(<0:5>, 4, 2)' );
}
```

produces

```
    0.00000         2.0000          4.0000          0.00000
    1.0000          3.0000          5.0000          0.00000

    0.00000         1.0000          2.0000          3.0000
    4.0000          5.0000          0.00000         0.00000
```

sin, sinh

```
sin(const ma);
```
> ma   in: arithmetic type

Return value
> sin returns the sine of ma, of double or matrix type.
> sinh returns the sine hyperbolicus of ma, of double or matrix type.

See also
> acos (for examples), asin, atan, cos, cosh, sinh, tan, tanh

sizeof

```
sizeof(const ma);
```

Description
> This function is identical to rows().

See also
> columns (for an example), rows

solveldl

```
solveldl(const ml, const md, const mb);
```
ml	in:	$m \times m$ lower diagonal matrix L, $LDL' = A$
md	in:	$1 \times m$ matrix with reciprocals of D
mb	in:	$m \times n$ matrix B, the right-hand side

Return value

Returns the $m \times n$ matrix X from solving $AX = B$.

Description

Solves $AX = B$ for X following a square root free Choleski decomposition of A using decldl (A is symmetric and positive definite).

See also

decldl (for an example), invertsym

solveldlband

```
solveldlband(const ml, const md, const mb);
```
ml	in:	$p \times m$ vector specifying the L^b matrix
md	in:	$1 \times m$ matrix with reciprocals of D
mb	in:	$m \times n$ matrix B, the right-hand side

Return value

Returns the $m \times n$ matrix X from solving $AX = B$.

Description

Solves $AX = B$ for X when A is a symmetric positive definite band matrix. The band form of A (A^b) must have been decomposed using decldlband first. See under decldlband for the storage format of A^b and examples to move between A^b and A.

See also

decldlband (for an example), solvetoeplitz

solvelu

```
solvelu(const ml, const mu, const mp, const mb);
```
ml	in:	$m \times m$ lower diagonal matrix L
mu	in:	$m \times m$ upper diagonal matrix U
mp	in:	$2 \times m$ matrix with interchange permutations in the second row
mb	in:	$m \times n$ matrix B, the right-hand side

Return value

Returns the $m \times n$ matrix X from solving $AX = B$.

Description

Solves $AX = B$ for X following a LU decomposition of A using declu.

See also

declu (for an example), invert

solvetoeplitz

```
solvetoeplitz(const mr, const cm, const mb);
solvetoeplitz(const mr, const cm, const mb, alogdet);
```
mr	in:	double, or $r \times 1$ or $1 \times r$ matrix, specifying the positive definite (band) Toeplitz matrix
cm	in:	dimension of complete Toeplitz matrix: $m \times m$, $m \geq r$
mb	in:	$m \times n$ matrix B, the right-hand side
alogdet	in:	(optional argument) address of variable
	out:	double, the *logarithm* of (the absolute value of) the determinant of A

Return value

Returns the $m \times n$ matrix X from solving $AX = B$, or 0 if the Toeplitz matrix is singular.

Description

Solves $AX = B$ for X when A is symmetric Toeplitz. A Toeplitz matrix has the same values along each diagonal (see under toeplitz). The algorithm is based on the Levinson algorithm in Golub and Van Loan (1989, algorithm 4.7.2, page 187).

The algorithm also accepts a non-positive (non-singular) Toeplitz matrix, but note that it computes $\log[\mathrm{abs}(|A|)]$ for the optional third argument. The exponent of that can only be computed for values $\leq$ DBL_MAX_E_EXP and $\geq$ DBL_MIN_E_EXP (see Ch. 9).

See also

toeplitz

Example

```
#include <oxstd.h>

main()
{
    decl ct = 10, mb, mt, mx;
```

```
mb = <2;3;4;5;6>;
mx = solvetoeplitz(<3,.5,.2,.1>, 5, mb);
print(mx');
mx = invertsym( toeplitz(<3,.5,.2,.1>,5) ) * mb;
print(mx');
}
```

produces

0.46189	0.63974	0.88536	1.1737	1.7240
0.46189	0.63974	0.88536	1.1737	1.7240

sortbyc, sortbyr

```
sortbyc(const ma, const icol);
sortbyr(const ma, const irow);
```

ma	in:	matrix
icol	in:	scalar: index of column to sort, or
		matrix: specifying the columns to sort by.
irow	in:	index of row to sort

Return value

The reordered (sorted in ascending order) matrix.

Description

The sortbyc function sorts the rows of a matrix according to the specified column; sortbyr sorts the columns of a matrix according to the specified row. Sorting is in ascending order using combsort (Lacey and Box, 1991).

If you want the sorting to be in descending order, you can use reversec after sortbyc, and reverser after sortbyr.

The sortbyc function can also sort on multiple columns. In that case specify a vector of columns on which to sort. The sorting is on the first specified column, within that on the second, etc. The elements in the icol argument when it is a matrix are processed by row, so corresponding to vecr(icol).

See also

reversec, reverser, sortc, sortr

Example

```
#include <oxstd.h>

main()
{
    decl m = <1,0,3;0,4,4;4,3,0>;
    print( sortbyc(m,0), sortbyr(m,0) );

    m = <1,3;1,2;3,4;3,5;2,3;2,2>;
```

```
        print("%4.1g", m ~ sortbyc(m, 0) ~ sortbyc(m, 0~1));
}
```
produces

```
    0.00000         4.0000          4.0000
    1.0000          0.00000         3.0000
    4.0000          3.0000          0.00000

    0.00000         1.0000          3.0000
    4.0000          0.00000         4.0000
    3.0000          4.0000          0.00000

    1    3    1    3    1    2
    1    2    1    2    1    3
    3    4    2    2    2    2
    3    5    2    3    2    3
    2    3    3    5    3    4
    2    2    3    4    3    5
```

sortc, sortr

```
sortc(const ma);
sortr(const ma);
```
       ma   in: arithmetic type

Return value

    If ma is a matrix, the return value is ma with each column (sortc) or row
    (sortr) sorted in ascending order. If ma is scalar the return type and value are
    that of ma. The sorting method used is combsort.

See also

    sortbyc, sortbyr

Example

```
#include <oxstd.h>

main()
{
    decl m = <1,0,3;0,4,4;4,3,0>;
    print( sortc(m), sortr(m) );
}
```
produces

```
    0.00000         0.00000         0.00000
    1.0000          3.0000          3.0000
    4.0000          4.0000          4.0000

    0.00000         1.0000          3.0000
    0.00000         4.0000          4.0000
    0.00000         3.0000          4.0000
```

spikes

```
spikes(const ma, const icol);
```
    ma   in: matrix

    icol   in: scalar: index of column to find spikes of.

Return value

Returns a $4 \times n$ matrix:

    1st row: low of each subsequent non-decreasing run,

    2nd row: high of each subsequent non-decreasing run,

    3rd row: row index of low,

    4th row: row index of high.

This is computed for the specified column.

Description

The spikes function runs through the specified column, which is seen as a sequence of non-decreasing runs (a sequence of trends). For each non-decreasing runs, it records the low and high, and the row index at which they occur. If the column is visualized as a saw tooth function, the function records its spikes.

The spikes function could be useful to inspect runs after sorting by multiple columns. An example would be a panel data set, where there is a time series of observations on many individuals. Once the data are sorted by individual by time, the spikes function can be used to find the start and end of each individual.

See also

    limits, sortbyc

Example

```
#include <oxstd.h>

main()
{
    decl m = <1,1;2,2;1,3;3,2;3,3;2,4;3,1;5,2;5,3>;

    print(m, spikes(m, 0), spikes(m, 1));
}
```

produces

```
    1.0000          1.0000
    2.0000          2.0000
    1.0000          3.0000
    3.0000          2.0000
    3.0000          3.0000
    2.0000          4.0000
    3.0000          1.0000
    5.0000          2.0000
    5.0000          3.0000
```

1.0000	1.0000	2.0000
2.0000	3.0000	5.0000
0.00000	2.0000	5.0000
1.0000	4.0000	8.0000
1.0000	2.0000	1.0000
3.0000	4.0000	3.0000
0.00000	3.0000	6.0000
2.0000	5.0000	8.0000

spline

```
spline(const my, const mx, const alpha);
spline(const my, const mx, const alpha, agcv);
```
   my   in: $T \times n$ matrix with variables (observations in columns) to
                    smooth
   mx   in: 0 for evenly spaced Y,

                    else $T \times m$ matrix with X (where $m = 1$: same X used for
                    all Ys, or $m = n$: corresponding X is used with Y)
   alpha   in: double, bandwidth α (also see below),

                    0: automatic bandwidth selection using GCV,

                    < 0: absolute value is bandwidth,

                    > 0: specifies equivalent number of parameters.
   agcv   in: (optional) address, returns GCV (generalized cross validation
                    score) and k_e (equivalent number of parameters)

Return value

   Returns a $T \times n$ matrix with the smooth from applying the natural cubic spline.
   The optional agcv argument is a $2 \times n$ matrix, with the generalized cross validation (GCV) score in the first row, and the equivalent number of parameters in the
   second.

Description

   The spline smoothes the cross plot of Y against time (mx argument is 0), or against
   an x variable. Consider a plot of y_t, against x_t, and sort the data according to x:
   $a < x_{[1]} < \ldots < x_{[T]} < b$. In a spline model, the sum of squared deviations
   from a function g is minimized, subject to a roughness penalty:

   $$\min \sum_{t=1}^{T} \left[y_t - g\left(x_{[t]} \right) \right]^2 + \alpha \int_a^b \left[g''\left(x \right) \right]^2 \, dx.$$

   Ox uses a *natural cubic spline*, which is cubic because the function g is chosen
   as a third degree polynomial, and natural because the smooth is a straight line

between a and $x_{[1]}$ and between $x_{[1]}$ and b. Two good references on splines and nonparametric regression are Green and Silverman (1994) and Hastie and Tibshirani (1994).

The α parameter is the bandwidth: the smaller α, the lower the roughness penalty, and hence the closer the smooth will track the actual data.

There are three ways of specifying the bandwidth α :

0 use automatic bandwidth selection based on GCV;

The GCV criterion is computed as:

$$GCV(\alpha) = T\left(\frac{RSS}{T - 1.25k_e + 0.5}\right).$$

A bracketing search algorithm is used to minimize GCV.

< 0 the absolute value is used for the bandwidth;

No iteration is required.

> 0 specifies the equivalent number of parameters k_e to be used.

A bracketing search algorithm is used to locate the specified k_e (k_e is approximately comparable to the number of regressors used in a linear regression)

The spline is evaluated at the data points, where missing y_t values (both in and outside sample) are estimated by the fit from the smooth. Observations where both y_t and x_t are missing are omitted in the calculations. The missing value used is -9999.99.

The spline procedure handles ties in the x variable. The algorithm used to compute the spline is of order T, and consists of the Reinsch algorithm combined with the Hutchinson-de Hooch algorithm for computing the GCV score (see Green and Silverman, 1994, Chs. 2 & 3).

Example

The following example first smoothes the four variables in the variable my using time as the X variable, and automatic bandwidth selection. The second observation of the first variable is set to a missing value.

The second spline smoothes the cross plot of the last three variables against the first, choosing the bandwidth as 12 equivalent parameters.

```
#include <oxstd.h>

main()
{    decl my, ms, gcv;

     my = loadmat("c:/ox/samples/database/data.in7");
     my[1][0] = -9999.99;
     ms = spline(my, 0, 0);
     print( "%c", {"CONS", "smooth"},
             my[:4][0] ~ ms[:4][0]);
```

```
        ms = spline(my[][1:], my[][0], 12, &gcv);
        print( "%r", {"GCV", "k_e"}, gcv);
}
```
produces

```
            CONS        smooth
          890.45        890.01
         -10000.        888.19
          886.33        886.58
          884.88        885.38
          885.25        884.66

GCV                     13.932      1.4645      24.309
k_e                     12.000      11.999      11.999
```

sprint

```
sprint(const a, ...);
    a           in:  any type
    ...         in:  any type
```

Return value

Returns a string containing the written text, or 0 if the sprint buffer was too small (see `sprintbuffer`).

Description

Each argument is printed to a string. See `print` for a description of formatting; the `"%m"`, `"%M"`, `"%#m"` and `"%#M"` formats may not be used in `sprint`. The maximum text length is 2048 characters by default. The `sprintbuffer` function can be used to enlarge the buffer size.

Error messages

sprint(): no string buffer

sprint(): string buffer length exceeded

See also

`eprint`, `print`, `sprintbuffer`

Example

```
#include <oxstd.h>

main()
{
    decl s = sprint("a", "_", "%0X", 10);

    print( s );
}
```

produces: a_A

sprintbuffer

```
sprintbuffer(const len);
    len         in:  int
```

Return value

Returns 0 of type int.

Description

Sets the size of the internal sprint buffer. The default is 2048 characters, and this function is only needed if texts of more than 2048 characters will be written using sprint.

See also

sprint

sqr, sqrt

```
sqr(const ma);
sqrt(const ma);
    ma          in:  arithmetic type
```

Return value

sqrt returns the square root of the elements of ma, of double or matrix type.
sqr returns the square of the elements of ma. If the input to sqr is a double or matrix, the return type is a double or matrix. If the input is an integer, the return type is integer unless the result would overflow in integer computation. In that case the return type is double in order to represent the result.

Example

```
#include <oxstd.h>

main()
{
    print( sqrt(<2,3>), <2,3> .^ 0.5 );
    print( sqr(<2,3>), <2,3> .^ 2 );

    print( sqr(2^15),
        isint(sqr(2^15)) ? "int" : "double", "\n");
    print( sqr(2^16),
        isint(sqr(2^16)) ? "int" : "double", "\n");
}
```

produces

```
      1.4142      1.7321

      1.4142      1.7321

      4.0000      9.0000

      4.0000      9.0000
1073741824int
4.29497e+009double
```

sscan

```
sscan(const string, const a, ...);
sscan(const astring, const a, ...);
```
> string   in: string to scan from
>
> astring   in: address of string to scan from, on return the scanned text has
>   been removed from the string
>
> a   in: any type
>
> ...   in: any type

Return value

> Returns the number of arguments successfully scanned and assigned. If s
> is a string, then sscan(s,...will leave the string unchanged, whereas ss-
> can(&s,...will remove the read characters from the string.

Description

> This function works as fscan, but reading from a string, not a file. See fscan
> for a description of formatting; the "%m", "%M", "%#m" and "%#M" formats may
> not be used in sscan.

See also

> fscan, fwrite, scan

Example

> The following example reads one input line at a time (leading spaces in each line
> are skipped, because of the starting space in " %z", and reads from that string
> using sscan. The * in "%*d" suppresses assignment, so the integer is skipped
> in the file.

```
#include <oxstd.h>

main()
{

    decl file, s, c;
    decl svar, address;
```

```
    file = fopen("../database/data.in7");
    if (!isfile(file))
    {
        print("failed to open file\n");
        exit(1);
    }

    do
    {   c = fscan(file, " %z", &s);
        if (c >= 0 && s[0] == '>')
        {
            sscan(&s, ">%s", &svar, "%*d", "%*d", "%*d",
                "%*d", "%*d", "%d", &address, " ");
            print("variable : ",
                svar, " address:", address, "\n");
            print("remainder: ", s, "\n");
        }
    } while (c >= 0);

    fclose(file);
}
```

If the .in7 file can be found, this program produces:

```
variable : CONS address:32
remainder: data 10-04-1992 13:20:38.33
variable : INC address:1336
remainder: data 10-04-1992 13:20:38.33
variable : INFLAT address:2640
remainder: data 10-04-1992 13:20:38.33
variable : OUTPUT address:3944
remainder: data 10-04-1992 13:20:38.33
```

standardize

```
standardize(const ma);
```
    ma   in: $T \times n$ matrix A

Return value

Returns a $T \times n$ matrix holding the standardized columns of ma. If any variance is $\leq 10^{-20}$, then the corresponding column is set to 0.

Description

Standardization implies subtracting the mean, and then dividing by the standard deviation. A standardized vector has mean zero and variance one.

See also

acf, standardize (for an example), meanc, meanr, varc, varr, variance

string

```
string(const ma);
```
         ma   in: arithmetic type

Return value
     Casts the argument to a string, see §12.7.2.3.

See also
```
     double
```

strfind

```
strfind(const as, const s);
```
         as   in: an array of strings
         s   in: the strings to find

Return value
     Returns an integer which is the index of the first occurrence of s in as. If the
     string is not found, the return value is -1. strfind is case sensitive.

Example

```
#include <oxstd.h>

main()
{
    print( strfind({"tinker", "tailor", "spy"}, "spy") );
}
```

     produces: 2 (remember that the first entry has index 0).

strlwr, strupr

```
strlwr(const s);
strupr(const s);
```
         s   in: the strings to convert

Return value
     Returns a copy of the string, which is converted to lower case (strlwr) or up-
     percase (strupr).

Example

```
#include <oxstd.h>

main()
{
    decl s = "A StrinG\n";
    print( strlwr(s), strupr(s), s);
}
```
produces
```
a string
A STRING
A StrinG
```

submat

```
submat(const ma, const r1, const r2, const c1, const c2);
    ma          in:  matrix
    r1,r2       in:  int
    c1,c2       in:  int
```

Return value

Returns the submatrix of ma from row indices r1 to r2 and column indices c1 to c2. This is equivalent to ma[r1:r2][c1:c2].

sumc, sumr

```
sumc(const ma);
sumr(const ma);
    ma              in:  $T \times n$ matrix $A$
```

Return value

The sumc function returns a $1 \times n$ matrix r which holds the sum of the column elements of ma.

The sumr function returns a $T \times 1$ matrix which holds the sum of the row elements of ma.

See also

meanc, meanr, prodc, prodr, sumsqrc, sumsqrr, varc, varr

Example

```
#include <oxstd.h>

main()
{
    print( sumc(<0:3;1:4;2:5>) );
    print( sumr(<0:3;1:4;2:5>) );
}
```

produces

```
3.0000          6.0000          9.0000          12.000

6.0000
10.000
14.000
```

sumsqrc, sumsqrr

```
sumsqrc(const ma);
sumsqrr(const ma);
    ma          in:  T × n matrix A
```

Return value

The sumsqrc function returns a $1 \times n$ matrix r which holds the sum of the squares of the column elements of ma.

The sumsqrr function returns a $T \times 1$ matrix which holds the sum of the squares of the row elements of ma.

See also

sumc, sumr, varc, varr

Example

```
#include <oxstd.h>

main()
{
    print( sumsqrc(<0:3;1:4;2:5>) );
    print( sumsqrr(<0:3;1:4;2:5>) );
}
```

produces

```
        5.0000          14.000          29.000          50.000

        14.000
        30.000
        54.000
```

tailchi, tailf, tailn, tailt

```
tailchi(const ma, const df);
tailf(const ma, const df1, const df2);
tailn(const ma);
tailt(const ma, const idf);
```

ma	in:	arithmetic type
df	in:	arithmetic type, degrees of freedom
df1	in:	arithmetic type, degrees of freedom in the numerator
df2	in:	arithmetic type, degrees of freedom in the denominator
idf	in:	int, degrees of freedom

Return value

Returns the requested tail probabilities at ma (the returned tail probabilities are between zero and one):

tailchi	tail probabilities from $\chi^2(df)$ distribution
tailf	tail probabilities from $F(df1, df2)$ distribution
tailn	one-sided standard normal tail probability
tailt	one-sided tail probabilities from student-$t(df)$ distribution

The tail probabilities are accurate to about 10 digits.

The return type is derived as follows:

returns	ma	degrees of freedom arguments
$m \times n$ matrix	$m \times n$ matrix	scalar (int for tailt)
$m \times n$ matrix	scalar	$m \times n$ matrix
$m \times n$ matrix	$m \times n$ matrix	$m \times n$ matrix
double	scalar	scalar (int for tailt)

See also

dens..., prob..., quan...

Example

```
#include <oxstd.h>

main()
{
    print("%r", {"chi(2):"}, tailchi(<0,4.61,5.99>, 2));
    print("%r", {"normal:"}, tailn(<-1.96, 0, 1.96>) );
    print("%r", {"t(4):"},   tailt(<-1.96, 0, 1.96>, 4) );
    print("%r", {"t(50):"},  tailt(<-1.96, 0, 1.96>, 50) );
}
```

produces

```
chi(2):          1.0000      0.099759    0.050037
normal:          0.97500     0.50000     0.024998
t(4):            0.93922     0.50000     0.060777
t(50):           0.97221     0.50000     0.027790
```

tan, tanh

```
tan(const ma);
tanh(const ma);
```

ma   in: arithmetic type

Return value

tan returns the tangent of ma, of double or matrix type.

tanh returns the tangent hyperbolicus of ma, of double or matrix type.

See also

acos (for examples), asin, atan, cos, cosh, sin, sinh, tanh

thinc, thinr

```
thinc(const ma,  const c);
thinr(const ma,  const r);
```
ma   in: $m \times n$ matrix A

c   in: int, desired number of columns to extract

r   in: int, desired number of rows to extract

Return value

The thinc function returns an $m \times$ c matrix consisting of a selection of columns of the original matrix.

The thinr function returns an r $\times n$ matrix consisting of a selection of rows of the original matrix.

Description

The thinc function selects columns as follows:

$$0, \ g, \ 2g, \ 3g, \ldots, \ (c-1)g,$$

$$\text{where} \quad g = 1 + \text{int}\left(\frac{n-c}{c-1}\right) \text{ if } c > 1.$$

The thinr function selects rows similarly.

The example below also indicates how to draw a random sample.

Example

Note in the example that, strictly speaking, it is not necessary to truncate the random indices in idx, as this is done automatically when using a matrix to index another matrix.

```
#include <oxstd.h>

main()
{
    decl m = rann(1000, 2), idx;
    print( thinr(m, 3) ~ m[<0,499,998>][] );
    print( thinc(m', 3)' ~ m[<0,499,998>][] );
```

```
                /* get three random indices in idx */
        idx = trunc(ranu(1,3) * rows(m));
        print(idx, m[idx][] ~ m[sortr(idx)][] );
    }
```

produces

```
    -0.65201        0.46053       -0.65201        0.46053
    -0.26963       -1.5278        -0.26963       -1.5278
    -0.88630       -0.98172       -0.88630       -0.98172

    -0.65201        0.46053       -0.65201        0.46053
    -0.26963       -1.5278        -0.26963       -1.5278
    -0.88630       -0.98172       -0.88630       -0.98172

     307.00        41.000         976.00

     1.0565         1.1471        -0.40231       -0.087221
    -0.40231       -0.087221       1.0565         1.1471
     0.28920       -1.1108         0.28920       -1.1108
```

time

```
time();
```

Return value

A string holding the current time.

See also

date (for an example)

timer, timespan

```
timer();
timespan(const time);
```

time   in: double, value from previous call to timer

Return value

The timer function returns a double representing the current time in one 100th of a second. The timespan function returns a string holding the time lapsed since the time argument.

Example

```
#include <oxstd.h>

main()
{
```

```
        decl i, time, m = rann(100,10), m2;

        time = timer();

        for (i = 0; i < 1000; ++i)
            m2 = m'm;

        print("time lapsed: ", timespan(time), "\n");
        print("or in seconds: ", (timer() - time) / 100, "\n");
    }
```

prints the time it took to do the for loop.

toeplitz

```
toeplitz(const ma);
toeplitz(const ma, const cm);
```

ma	in:	double, or $r \times 1$ or $1 \times r$ matrix
cm	in:	(optional argument) m: dimension of matrix to be created, $m \geq r$; if the argument is missing, $m = r$ is used.

Return value

Returns a symmetric Toeplitz matrix.

Description

Creates a symmetric Toeplitz matrix using the supplied argument. A Toeplitz matrix has the same values along each diagonal. Here we allow for a banded Toeplitz matrix, e.g. when $r = 3$ and $m = 5$:

$$\begin{pmatrix} a_0 & a_1 & a_2 & 0 & 0 \\ a_1 & a_0 & a_1 & a_2 & 0 \\ a_2 & a_1 & a_0 & a_1 & a_2 \\ 0 & a_2 & a_1 & a_0 & a_1 \\ 0 & 0 & a_2 & a_1 & a_0 \end{pmatrix}$$

See also

diag, solvetoeplitz (for an example)

trace

```
trace(const ma);
```

ma	in:	arithmetic type

Return value

Returns the trace of ma (the sum of its diagonal elements). Return type is double.

See also
      determinant

Example

```
#include <oxstd.h>

main()
{
    print( trace(<2,1;1,4>) );
}
```

produces: 6

trunc, truncf

```
trunc(const ma);
truncf(const ma);
      ma              in:   arithmetic type
```

Return value

trunc returns the truncated elements of ma, of double or matrix type.
truncf is fuzzy truncation.

Description

Truncation is rounding towards zero, however, the result remains a double value.
Note that conversion to an integer also results in truncation, but that in that case
the result is undefined if the real number is too big to be represented as an integer.
truncf multiplies positive numbers by one plus the current fuzziness (one minus
fuzziness for negative numbers) before truncation.

See also
      ceil, floor, fuzziness, round,

Example

```
#include <oxstd.h>

main()
{
    print( trunc(<-2.0-1e-15, -2.0+1e-15,
                   2.0-1e-15,  2.0+1e-15>) );
    print(truncf(<-2.0-1e-15, -2.0+1e-15,
                   2.0-1e-15,  2.0+1e-15>) );
}
```

produces

```
      -2.0000       -1.0000       1.0000       2.0000
      -1.0000       -1.0000       2.0000       2.0000
```

unit

```
unit(const rc);
      rc           in:   int
```

Return value

Returns an `rc` by `rc` identity matrix.

See also

`constant`, `unit`, `zeros`

Example

```
#include <oxstd.h>

main()
{
    print( unit(2) );
}
```

produces

```
    1.0000      0.00000
    0.00000     1.0000
```

upper

```
upper(const ma);
      ma           in:   m × n matrix
```

Return value

Returns the upper diagonal (including the diagonal) of a matrix; the strict lower diagonal elements are set to zero.

See also

`lower` (for an example), `setdiagonal`, `setlower`, `setupper`

va_arglist

```
va_arglist();
```

Return value

Returns an array holding the arguments starting with the first variable in the variable argument list.

Description

See §12.5.5.1.

Example

See §12.5.5.1.

varc, varr

```
varc(const ma);
varr(const ma);
    ma          in:  T × n matrix A
```

Return value

The varc function returns a $1 \times n$ matrix holding the variances of the columns of ma.

The varr function returns a $T \times 1$ matrix holding the variances of the rows of ma.

See also

meanc, meanr, sumc, sumr, variance

Example

```
#include <oxstd.h>

main()
{
    decl m1 = rann(100,2), m2;

    print( variance(m1), varc(m1), varr(m1') );
}
```

produces

```
    0.89027        0.097436
    0.097436       0.93015

    0.89027        0.93015

    0.89027
    0.93015
```

variance

```
variance(const ma);
    ma          in:  T × n matrix A
```

Return value

Returns an $n \times n$ matrix holding variance-covariance matrix of ma.

Description

Computes the variance-covariance matrix of a $T \times n$ matrix $A = (a_0, a_1, \ldots, a_{n-1})$:

$$T^{-1} \breve{A}' \breve{A}, \quad \text{where } \breve{A} = (a_0 - \bar{a}_0, a_1 - \bar{a}_1, \ldots a_{n-1} - \bar{a}_{n-1}),$$

and

$$\bar{a}_i = \frac{1}{T} \sum_{t=0}^{T-1} a_{it}.$$

See also

    `acf`, `correlation`, `meanc`, `meanr`, `standardize`, `varc`, `varr`

Example

```
#include <oxstd.h>

main()
{
    decl m1 = rann(100,2), m2;

    m2 = m1 - meanc(m1);
    print( variance(m1), m2'm2/rows(m2) );
}
```

produces

```
      0.89027        0.097436
      0.097436       0.93015

      0.89027        0.097436
      0.097436       0.93015
```

vec

`vec(const ma);`

    `ma`   in: arithmetic type

Return value

    If ma is an $m \times n$ matrix, the return value is an $mn \times 1$ matrix consisting of the stacked columns of ma. If ma is scalar, the return value is an 1×1 matrix consisting of the value ma.

Description

    Vectorizes a matrix by stacking columns.

See also

    `shape`, `vech`, `vecr`

Example

```
#include <oxstd.h>

main()
{
    print( vec(<0,1;2,3>) );
}
```

produces

```
0.00000
2.0000
1.0000
3.0000
```

vech

```
vech(const ma);
```
    ma   in: arithmetic type

Return value

If ma is an $m \times n$ matrix, the return value is an $(m(m+1)/2 - j(j+1)/2) \times 1$ matrix, where $j = \max(m - n, 0)$, consisting of the stacked columns of the lower diagonal of ma. If ma is scalar, the return value is a 1×1 matrix consisting of the value ma.

Description

Vectorizes the lower diagonal of a matrix by stacking columns.

See also

vec, vecr

Example

```
#include <oxstd.h>

main()
{
    print( vech(<0,1;2,3>) );
}
```

produces

```
0.00000
2.0000
3.0000
```

vecindex

```
vecindex(const ma);
```
    ma   in: matrix

Return value

Returns a $p \times 1$ matrix holding the row index of the non-zero elements of vec(ma), where p is the number of non-zero elements in ma. If there is no non-zero element, the function returns the integer -1.

Description

Creates a matrix holding the row index of the non-zero elements of vec(ma).

See also

shape, vec

Example

```
#include <oxstd.h>

main()
{
    print( vecindex( <0,1,2;0,2,0> ) );
}
```

produces

```
    2.0000
    3.0000
    4.0000
```

vecr

```
vecr(const ma);
    ma              in:   arithmetic type
```

Return value

If ma is an $m \times n$ matrix, the return value is an $mn \times 1$ matrix consisting of the stacked rows of ma. If ma is scalar, the return value is a 1×1 matrix consisting of the value ma.

Description

Vectorizes a matrix by stacking rows into a column vector.

See also

shape, vech, vecr

Example

```
#include <oxstd.h>

main()
{
    print( vecr(<0,1;2,3>) );
}
```

produces

```
    0.00000
    1.0000
    2.0000
    3.0000
```

zeros

```
zeros(const r, const c);
     r           in:  int
     c           in:  int
```

Return value

Returns an r by c matrix filled with zeros.

See also

ones, unit, zeros, new

Example

```
#include <oxstd.h>

main()
{
    print( zeros(2, 2) );
}
```

produces

```
0.00000     0.00000
0.00000     0.00000
```

Chapter 9

Predefined Constants

oxstd.h

FALSE	0
TRUE	1

oxfloat.h

M_PI	π
M_2PI	2π
M_PI_2	$\pi/2$
M_1_PI	$1/\pi$
M_E	$e = \exp(1)$
M_EULER	Euler's constant, γ
DBL_DIG	number of decimal digits of precision
DBL_EPSILON	machine precision ϵ_m, smallest number such that $1.0 + \epsilon_m\ ! = 1.0$
DBL_MANT_DIG	number of bits in mantissa
DBL_MAX	maximum double value
DBL_MIN	minimum positive double value
DBL_MIN_EXP	minimum 2 exponent
DBL_MAX_EXP	maximum 2 exponent
DBL_MIN_E_EXP	minimum e exponent
DBL_MAX_E_EXP	maximum e exponent
DBL_MIN_10_EXP	minimum 10 exponent
DBL_MAX_10_EXP	maximum 10 exponent
INT_MAX	maximum integer value
INT_MIN	minimum integer value

The following constants are predefined by the Ox compiler:

`OX_BIG_ENDIAN`	only on a big-endian machine (MS-DOS, Windows)
`OX_Windows`	when running `oxlw` or `oxrun`
`OX_MSDOS`	when running `oxl`
`OX_Solaris`	when running `oxsol`
`OX_SunOs`	when running `oxsun`
`OX_Linux`	when running `oxlinux`
`OX_HPUX`	when running `oxhp`
`OX_Irix`	when running `oxsgi`

Chapter 10

Graphics function reference

Graphs in Ox are drawn on a graphics worksheet, consisting of 15 000 by 10 000 pixels, with (0,0) in the bottom left corner:

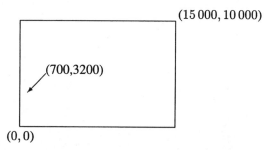

Positions can be specified in pixel coordinates, as for example $(p_x, p_y) = (70, 3200)$. More often it is convenient to use real world coordinates. This is done by specifying an area on the graphics worksheet, and attaching real world coordinates to it. These areas are allowed to overlap, but need not:

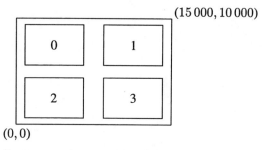

Suppose we have set up all areas as being from $(x, y) = (0.0, 0.0)$ to $(x, y) = (1.0, 1.0)$ (again within each area the origin is the lower left corner). Then we can draw a line through area 2 in two ways:

(1) in real coordinates within an area

        step 1: select area 2;

step 2: move to (0.0, 0.0);

step 3: draw a line to (1.0,1.0).

(2) using pixel coordinates on the worksheet

step 1: move to pixel coordinates (600,600);

step 2: draw a line to pixel coordinates (3600, 3600),

where we assume that (600,600) to (3600,3600) are the pixel coordinates chosen for area 2. Drawing in real world coordinates has the advantage that it corresponds more closely to our data.

In general we use high level drawing functions. These select an area, and a type of graph, and give the data to plot. Note that the supplied matrix must have the data in *rows* (unlike, for example,. the Database, where it is in columns). The functions documented below expect an $m \times T$ matrix for T observations on m variables. The header file to be included for graphics is oxdraw.h.

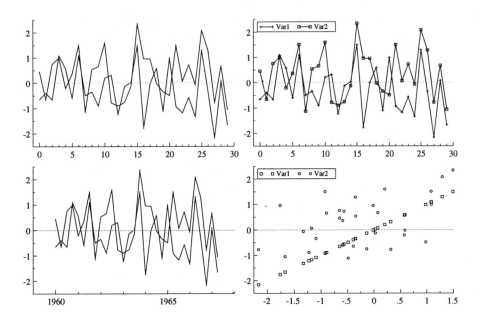

Figure 10.1   draw1.eps.

Example

```
#include <oxstd.h>
#include <oxdraw.h>

main()
{
    decl m = rann(30,2);

    Draw(0, m', 0, 1);
    DrawMatrix(1, m', {"Var1", "Var2"}, 0, 1, 2);
    DrawT(2, m', 1960, 1, 4);
    DrawXMatrix(3, m', {"Var1", "Var2"},
        m', "Var1", 1, 3);

    SetDrawWindow("draw1");
    ShowDrawWindow();
//  SaveDrawWindow("draw1.eps");
}
```

The file `draw1.eps` produces Fig. 10.1. The `SetDrawWindow` function is only relevant when you use *OxRun* to run the program. Then it may be used to specify the name of the graphics window in *GiveWin*.

Example

```
#include <oxstd.h>
#include <oxdraw.h>

main()
{
    decl m = rann(100,2);

    DrawCorrelogram(0, m', "var", 9);
                                // (only uses first row)
    DrawDensity(1, m', "var", TRUE, TRUE, TRUE);
    DrawQQ(2, m', "var", QQ_N, 0, 0);
    DrawQQ(3, m', "var", QQ_U, 0, 0);

    ShowDrawWindow();
//  SaveDrawWindow("draw2.eps");
}
```

The file `draw2.eps` produces Fig. 10.2.

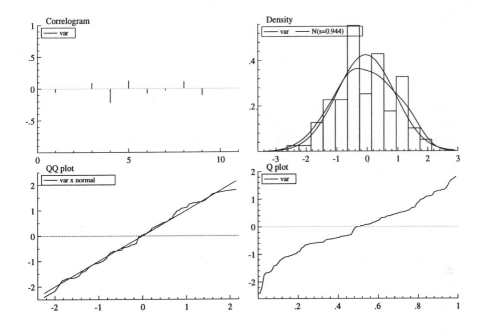

Figure 10.2   draw2.eps.

CloseDrawWindow

```
CloseDrawWindow();
```
No return value.

Description
    Closes the draw window. On many platforms nothing will happen, e.g. when the graphs appear in *GiveWin*, the graph will remain active there. Under MS-DOS, however, the screen will switch back from graphics mode to text mode.

Draw

```
Draw(const iArea, const mYt, const dXfirst,const dXstep);
```
iArea	in:	int, area index
mYt	in:	int, $m \times T$ matrix with m rows of data
dXfirst	in:	double, X-value of first observation, x
dXstep	in:	double, gap between X-values, d_x

No return value.

Description

> This function draws m variables against an X variable, where the X variable consists of evenly spaced observations $x, x + d_x, x + 2d_x, x + 3d_x, \ldots$. Each variable is drawn by linking up the points. The first line index is 2.

DrawCorrelogram

```
DrawCorrelogram(const iArea, const vY, const sY,
    const cLag);
    iArea    in:   int, area index
    vY       in:   int, 1 × T matrix, only one row will be used
    sY       in:   string, variable name
    cLag     in:   int, highest lag to be used in correlogram
```
No return value.

Description

> Draws a correlogram which plots the autocorrelation function. The autocorrelation at lag zero is always one, and not included in the graph. The y-axis is $[0, 1]$ if all autocorrelations are positive, $[-1, 1]$ otherwise. The acf is computed differently from that in the $\mathtt{acf()}$ library function (see equation (8.1) on page 53). The difference is that $\mathtt{DrawCorrelogram}$ uses the running mean:

$$\hat{r}_j^* = \frac{\sum_{t=j+1}^{T} (x_t - \bar{x}_0)(x_{t-j} - \bar{x}_j)}{\sqrt{\sum_{t=j+1}^{T} (x_t - \bar{x}_0)^2 \sum_{t=j+1}^{T} (x_{t-j} - \bar{x}_j)^2}}.$$

> Here $\bar{x}_0 = \frac{1}{T-j} \sum_{t=j+1}^{T} x_t$ is the sample mean of x_t, $t = j+1, \ldots, T$, and $\bar{x}_j = \frac{1}{T-j} \sum_{t=j+1}^{T} x_{t-j}$ is the sample mean of x_{t-j}, so that $\hat{r}_j^*$ corresponds to a proper sample correlation coefficient. The difference with the definition of the sample autocorrelations in (8.1) tends to be small, and vanishes asymptotically.

DrawDensity

```
DrawDensity(const iArea, const vY, const sY, const fDens,
    const fHist, const fNormal);
    iArea     in:   int, area index
    vY        in:   int, 1 × T matrix, only one row will be used
    sY        in:   string, variable name
    fDens     in:   int, TRUE: draw estimated density
    fHist     in:   int, TRUE: draw histogram
    fNormal   in:   int, TRUE: add normal density for reference
```
No return value.

Description

Draws the histogram and/or density of the data in the specified area. When fNormal is TRUE, a normal density with the same mean and variance as the data will be drawn.

The density estimate is based on a kernel density estimation, with Gaussian kernel, and optimal bandwidth (if the data are indeed from a normal density) of $1.06\hat{\sigma}T^{-0.2}$. The density is estimated at 128 points using the fast Fourier transform due to B.W. Silverman (see Silverman, 1986) and Applied Statistics algorithm AS 176). Also see the *GiveWin* book.

DrawMatrix

```
DrawMatrix(const iArea, const mYt, const asY,
    const dXfirst, const dXstep);
DrawMatrix(const iArea, const mYt, const asY,
    const dXfirst, const dXstep, iSymbol);
DrawMatrix(const iArea, const mYt, const asY,
    const dXfirst, const dXstep, iSymbol, iFirstIndex);
```

iArea	in:	int, area index
mYt	in:	int, $m \times T$ matrix with m rows of data
asY	in:	array of strings (holds variable names), or 0 (no names)
dXfirst	in:	double, X-value of first observation, x
dXstep	in:	double, gap between X-values, d_x
iSymbol	in:	int, 0: draw line, 1: draw symbols, 2: draw both (optional argument, default is 0).
iFirstIndex	in:	int, line index for first row (see below), (optional argument, default is 2). Each subsequent row will have the next index.

No return value.

Description

This is a more flexible version of the Draw() function. DrawMatrix draws the m variables in the rows of mYt. The X variable consists of evenly spaced observations $x, x + d_x, x + 2d_x, x + 3d_x, \ldots$.

The following table gives the default settings for each line index. Note that index 0 is the background colour, and 1 the foreground colour.

index	color	line type	width	symbol	size
0	white	solid	10	plus	80
1	black	solid	6	plus	80
2	red	solid	10	plus	80
3	blue	solid	10	box	80
4	blue/green	solid	10	circle	80
5	purple	dotted	10	plus	80
6	green	dotted	10	plus	80
7	brown/yellow	long dash	10	plus	80
8	dark purple	long dash	10	plus	80
9	pastel yellow	dotted	10	plus	80
10	pastel green	dotted	10	plus	80
11	pastel blue	solid	10	plus	80
12		solid	10	plus	80
13	light grey	solid	10	plus	80
14	grey	solid	10	plus	80
15	light grey	solid	10	plus	80

DrawQQ

```
DrawQQ(const iArea, const vY, const sY, const iDens,
    const df1, const df2);
```

iArea	in:	int, area index
vY	in:	int, $1 \times T$ matrix, only one row will be used
sY	in:	string, variable name
iDens	in:	int, one of: QQ_CHI, QQ_F, QQ_N, QQ_T, QQ_U
df1	in:	int, first parameter for distribution
df2	in:	int, second parameter for distribution

No return value.

Description

Draws a QQ plot. The first row of vY would normally hold critical values which are hypothesized to come from a certain distribution. This function then draws a cross plot of these observed values (sorted), against the theoretical quantiles. The $45°$ line is drawn for reference (the closer the cross plot to this line, the better the match).

The following distributions are supported:

QQ_CHI	$\chi^2(df1)$,
QQ_F	$F(df1, df2)$,
QQ_N	$N(0, 1)$,
QQ_T	$t(df1)$,
QQ_U	Uniform$(0, 1)$, resulting in a quantile plot.

DrawSpectrum

```
DrawSpectrum(const iArea, const vY, const sY,
    const iOrder);
    iArea      in:  int, area index
    vY         in:  int, 1 × T matrix, only one row will be used
    sY         in:  string, variable name
    iOrder     in:  int, lag truncation parameter m
```
No return value.

Description

Draws the estimated spectral density, which is a smoothed function of the autocor-relations r_j. The graph corresponds to the results computed with the period-ogram library function using imode = 2, and cpoints = 128. Note that the horizontal axis in the graph is scaled by π, thus transforming the scale from $[0, \pi]$ to $[0, 1]$.

Example

```
#include <oxstd.h>
#include <oxfloat.h>
#include <oxdraw.h>

main()
{
    decl m = rann(100,1), cp = 128;

    DrawSpectrum(0, m', "var", 10);
    Draw(1, periodogram(m,10, cp,2)', 0, M_PI / (cp-1));
    Draw(2, periodogram(m,100,cp,0)', 0, M_PI / (cp-1));
    Draw(3, periodogram(m,100,cp,1)', 0, M_PI / (cp-1));
    ShowDrawWindow();
}
```

produces a graph like Fig. 10.3.

DrawT

```
DrawT(const iArea, const mYt, const mnYear,
    const mnPeriod, const iFreq);
    iArea          in:  int, area index
    mYt            in:  int, m × T matrix with m y variables
    mnYear         in:  int, year of first observation
    mnPeriod       in:  int, period of first observation
    iFreq          in:  int, frequency of observations
```
No return value.

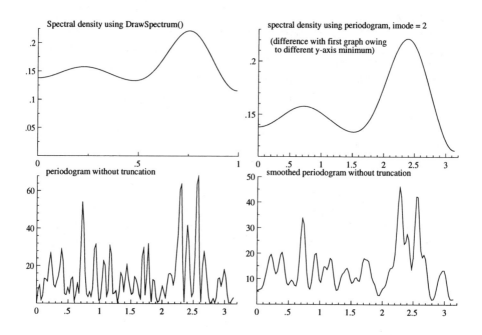

Figure 10.3   Periodograms and spectral density estimates.

Description

Draws *m* variables in the specified area against time. Each variable is drawn by linking up the points. The first line index is 2.

DrawTMatrix

```
DrawTMatrix(const iArea, const mYt, const asY,
    const mnYear, const mnPeriod, const iFreq);
DrawTMatrix(const iArea, const mYt, const asY,
    const mnYear, const mnPeriod, const iFreq, iSymbol);
DrawTMatrix(const iArea, const mYt, const asY,
    const mnYear, const mnPeriod, const iFreq, iSymbol,
    iFirstIndex);
```

iArea	in:	int, area index
mYt	in:	int, $m \times T$ matrix with m y variables
asY	in:	array of strings (holds variable names), or 0 (no names)
mnYear	in:	int, year of first observation
mnPeriod	in:	int, period of first observation
iFreq	in:	int, frequency of observations
iSymbol	in:	int, 0: draw line, 1: draw symbols, 2: draw both (optional argument, default is 0).
iFirstIndex	in:	int, line index for first row (see below), (optional argument, default is 2). Each subsequent row will have the next index.

No return value.

Description

This is a more flexible version of the DrawT() function. Draws m variables in the specified area against time. See under DrawMatrix for the default settings for each line index.

DrawX

```
DrawX(const iArea, const mYt, const vX);
    iArea    in:  int, area index
    mYt      in:  int, $m \times T$ matrix with $m$ $y$ variables
    vX       in:  int, $1 \times T$ matrix with $x$ variable
```

No return value.

Description

Draws m y variables in the specified area against an x variable. Each point is marked, but the points are not linked, resulting in a cross plot. The first line index is 2.

DrawXMatrix

```
DrawXMatrix(const iArea, const mYt, const asY, const vX,
    const sX);
DrawXMatrix(const iArea, const mYt, const asY, const vX,
    const sX, iSymbol);
DrawXMatrix(const iArea, const mYt, const asY, const vX,
    const sX, iSymbol, iFirstIndex);
```

iArea	in:	int, area index
vX	in:	int, $1 \times T$ matrix with x variable
iSymbol	in:	int, 0: draw line, 1: draw symbols, 2: draw both (optional argument, default is 0).
iFirstIndex	in:	int, line index for first row (see below), (optional argument, default is 2). Each subsequent row will have the next index.

No return value.

Description

This is a more flexible version of the DrawX() function. Draws m variables in the specified area against an x variable See under DrawMatrix for the default settings for each line index.

SaveDrawWindow

```
SaveDrawWindow(const sFilename);
```
sFilename	in:	valid file name

No return value.

Description

Saves the current graph to the specified file. The file format for saving is derived from the extension. The following formats are supported:

extension	format
.eps	Encapsulated PostScript
.gwg	*GiveWin* graphics file
.ps	PostScript

See the *GiveWin* book for a description of these formats.

SetDrawWindow

```
SetDrawWindow(const sTitle);
```
sTitle	in:	string, name of window

No return value.

Description

This function is only relevant when interacting with *GiveWin* otherwise it does nothing. It sets the name of the *GiveWin* window in which the graphs of the Ox program appear to sTitle.

SetTextWindow

```
SetTextWindow(const sTitle);
```
     sTitle   in: string, name of window

No return value.

Description

    This function is only relevant when interacting with *GiveWin* otherwise it does nothing. It sets the name of the *GiveWin* window in which the output (from the print() function) of the Ox program appears to sTitle.

ShowDrawWindow

```
ShowDrawWindow();
```

No return value.

Description

    Shows the drawing. Note that in some implementations the graphs cannot be displayed. Then a message is printed (SaveDrawWindow() will still work in that case!).

    A call to ShowDrawWindow also clears the drawing buffer, so that subsequent graphing starts from an empty sheet.

Chapter 11

Class reference

11.1 Database class

The `Database` class stores a matrix of data, together with the sample period (the class derives from the `Sample` class, see §11.4), and the names of the variables. Functions to create a database from disk files (ASCII, *GiveWin* and spreadsheet formats) are provided. A sample period for selection can be set, variables are selected by name, optionally with a lag length. This selection can then be extracted from the database. The selected sample is always adjusted so as not to include missing values (−9999.99). Some examples follow (don't forget to link in the database code when using this class, and include `data-base.h`).

Example

```
#include <oxstd.h>
#include <database.h>
#pragma link("database.oxo")

main()
{   decl dbase, y, dy, names;

    dbase = new Database();
    dbase->LoadXls("data.xls");

    dbase->Info();

    dbase->Select(0, { "CONS", 0, 0, "INC", 0, 0 } );
    dbase->Select(1, { "CONS", 1, 1, "INC", 1, 1 } );
    dbase->SetSample(1953, 1, 1992, 3);

    y = dbase->GetGroup(0);
    dy  = y - dbase->GetGroup(1);

    names = {"CONS", "INC", "DCONS", "DINC"};
    print("\nsample variance over ",
          dbase->GetSelSample(),
          "%r", names, "%c", names, variance(y ~ dy) );
```

```
      delete dbase;
}
```

produces

```
Database information
4 variables, 159 observations

name           sample period       min    mean     max   stddev
CONS     1953 (1) 1992 (3)       853.5  875.94  896.83   13.497
INC      1953 (1) 1992 (3)      870.22  891.69  911.38   10.725
INFLAT   1953 (1) 1992 (3)     -0.6298  1.7997  6.4976   1.2862
OUTPUT   1953 (1) 1992 (3)      1165.9  1191.1  1213.3   10.974

sample variance over 1953 (2) - 1992 (3)
                      CONS        INC       DCONS        DINC
CONS                181.97     135.71      2.9314      3.7989
INC                 135.71     114.01      1.9820      5.4127
DCONS               2.9314     1.9820      4.8536      5.5060
DINC                3.7989     5.4127      5.5060      11.183
```

Database::Append

```
Database::Append(const mNew, const asNew, const iT1);
```
mNew	in:	$T \times k$ matrix with the new variables
asNew	in:	array with k variable names of the new variables
iT1	in:	starting observation index in database

No return value.

Description

Appends the k new variables to the database, storing the observations and variable names. The first observation has database index iT1 (use 0 if the variables start at the same sample point as the database), the last is the end of the database sample, or the end of mNew, whichever comes first.

Example

The following example shows how you could load a matrix file into a database, assuming that that matrix file contains a $T \times 2$ matrix:

```
decl dbase, mx;

dbase = new Database();

mx = loadmat("./mydata.mat");
dbase->Create(1,1,1,rows(mx),1);
dbase->Append(mx, {"Y1", "Y2"}, 0);
```

Here the database is created with frequency 1 (annual data), and first observation year 1, period 1. We give the two variables the names "Y1" and "Y2", and match the first observation of mx to the first in the database (which has index 0).

Database::Create

```
Create(const iFreq, const iYear1, const iPeriod1,
    const iYear2, const iPeriod2);
    iFreq              in:  int, frequency
    iYear1             in:  int, start year
    iPeriod1           in:  int, start period
    iYear2             in:  int, end year
    iPeriod2           in:  int, end period
```
No return value.

Description
> Creates a database. Use this when the database is not to be loaded from disk. The Append member function allows adding data to the database.

Database::Database

```
Database::Database();
```
No return value.

Description
> Constructor.

Database::DeSelect

```
Database::DeSelect();
```
No return value.

Description
> Clears the current selection.

Database::Deterministic

```
Database::Deterministic(const fCseason);
    fCseason           in:  if TRUE: create centred seasonals
```
No return value.

Description
> Appends constant, trend and seasonals to the database. These variables are named Constant, Trend and Season Season_1, ..., Season_x, where x is the frequency.
> Season has a 1 in quarter 1 (for quarterly data), and zeros elsewhere, Season_1 has a 1 in quarter 2, etc.

If fCseason is TRUE, the seasonals are centred (with quarterly observations, for quarter 1: 0.75, −0.25, −0.25, −0.25, ...), in which case the names are CSeason, CSeason_1, ..., CSeason_x.

Database::FindSelection

```
Database::FindSelection(const sVar, const iLag);
```
    sVar   in: string, variable name
    iLag   in: int, lag length

Return value

Returns the selection index of the specified variable with the specified lag, or −1 if it is not selected.

Database::GetAll

```
Database::GetAll();
```

Return value

GetAll returns the whole database matrix.

Database::GetGroup, Database::GetGroupLag

```
Database::GetGroup(const iGroup);
Database::GetGroupLag(const iGroup, const iLag1,
    const iLag2);
```
    iGroup   in: int, group number
    iLag1   in: int, first lag
    iLag2   in: int, last lag

Return value

GetGroup returns a $T \times n$ matrix with all selected variables of group iGroup. GetGroupLag returns only those with the specified lag length. If no database sample has been selected yet, the return value is a 0.

Description

GetGroup extracts all selected variables of group iGroup.
GetGroupLag extracts all selected variables of group iGroup which have a lag in iLag1 ...iLag2. The selection sample period must have been set.

Database::GetGroupLagNames

```
Database::GetGroupLag(const iGroup, const iLag1,
    const iLag2, aasNames);
    iGroup              in:  int, group number
    iLag1               in:  int, first lag
    iLag2               in:  int, last lag
    aasNames            in:  array
                        out: will hold an array of strings with the names of the
                             variables with specified group and lag
```
No return value.

Description

GetGroupLag gets the names of all selected variables of group iGroup which have a lag in iLag1 ... iLag2. The selection sample period must have been set. The following code section gets all names of X_VAR variables and prints them.

```
decl as, i;

GetGroupLag(X_VAR, 0, 10000, &as);

for (i = 0; i < columns(as); ++i)
    print(as[i], "\n");
```

Database::GetMaxGroupLag, GetMaxLag

```
Database::GetMaxLag();
Database::GetMaxGroupLag(iGroup);
    iGroup     in:  int, group number
```

Return value

GetMaxLag returns the highest lag in all selected variables.
GetMaxGroupLag returns the highest lag in selected variables of the specified group.

Description

Gets lag information on the selection.

Database::GetSelEnd, Database::GetSelStart

```
Database::GetSelStart();
Database::GetSelEnd();
```

Return value
>　GetSelStart returns the database index of the first observation of the selected
>　sample.
>　GetSelEnd returns the database index of the last observation of the selected
>　sample.

Database::GetSelSample

```
Database::GetSelSample();
```

Return value
>　GetSelSample returns a string with the selected sample text, e.g. "1980 (1)
>　- 1984 (2)".

Database::GetVar

```
Database::GetVar(const sName);
    sName      in:   string, variable name
```

Return value
>　GetVar returns the specified variable, or 0 if the variable cannot be found.

Database::Info

```
Database::Info();
```
No return value.

Description
>　Prints information on the contents of the database.

Database::LoadDht

```
Database::LoadDht(const sFilename, const iYear1,
    const iPeriod1, const iFreq);
    sFilename          in:   string, filename
    iYear1             in:   int, start year
    iPeriod1           in:   int, start period
    iFreq              in:   int, frequency
```
No return value.

Description
>　LoadDht creates the database and loads the specified *Gauss* data file from disk.

Such files come in pairs: the .dht is a binary file which specifies the number of columns, the corresponding .dat file (with the same base name) is a binary file with the data.

Database::LoadFmtVar, Database::LoadIn7

```
Database::LoadFmtVar(const sFilename);
Database::LoadIn7(const sFilename);
    sFilename              in:   string, filename
```
No return value.

Description

LoadIn7 creates the database and loads the specified *GiveWin* file (which is the same as a PcGive 7 data file) from disk.

LoadFmtVar creates the database and loads the ASCII file with formatting information from disk. In *GiveWin* this is called 'Data with load info'. Such a file is human-readable, with the data ordered by variable, and each variable preceded by a line of the type:

> *name year1 period1 year2 period2 frequency.*

For example:

```
>CONS 1953 1 1955 4 4
      890       886       886       884
      885       884       884       884
      887       889       890       894
```

Database::LoadObs, Database::LoadVar

```
Database::LoadObs(const sFilename, const cVar,const cObs,
    const iYear1, const iPeriod1, const iFreq,
    const fOffendMis);
Database::LoadVar(const sFilename, const cVar,const cObs,
    const iYear1, const iPeriod1, const iFreq,
    const fOffendMis);
    sFilename         in:   string, filename
    cVar              in:   int, number of variables
    cObs              in:   int, number of observations
    iYear1            in:   int, start year
    iPeriod1          in:   int, start period
    iFreq             in:   int, frequency
    fOffendMis        in:   int, TRUE:offending text treated as missing value
                            FALSE: offending text skipped
```
No return value.

Description

Creates the database and loads the specified human-readable data file from disk. The data is ordered by observation (LoadObs), or by variable. Since there is no information on the sample or the variable names in these files, the sample must be provided as function arguments. The variable names are set to Var1, Var2, etc., use Rename to rename the variables.

As the name suggests, a human-readable (or ASCII) data file is a file that can be read using a file viewer or editor. (A binary file cannot be read in this way.) The default extension is .DAT.

Each variable must have the same number of observations. So variables that have too short a sample have to be padded by missing values (−9999.99). Text following ; or // up to the end of the line is considered to be comment, and skipped. Data files can be ordered by observation (first observation on all variables, second observation on all variables, etc.) or by variable (all observations of first variable, all observations of second variable, etc.). Examples are:

// by variable	//by observation
// cons	891 2.8 //1953 (1)
883 884 885	883 2.7 //1953 (2)
889 891 900	884 3.5 // etc.
// inflat	891 2.8
2.7 3.5 3.9	885 3.9
2.6 2.8 3.4	889 2.6
	891 2.8

The fOffendMis argument gives additional flexibility in reading human- readable files, by giving the option to treat offending words as missing values, or to skip them. The former can be used to read files with a . or a word for missing values, the latter for comma-separated files. Treating offending words or symbols as missing values (fOffendMis is TRUE) can be visualized as:

10 M 30	read as →	10 −9999.99 30
20 . 40		20 −9999.99 40

When read by observation (LoadObs), the second variable will be removed (consisting of missing values only), and the database variables will be labelled Var1 and Var3.

And for a comma separated example using the skip option (fOffendMis is FALSE):

10,5,30,	read as →	10 5 30
20,6,40,		20 6 40

Database::LoadWks, Database::LoadXls

```
Database::LoadWks(const sFilename);
Database::LoadXls(const sFilename);
    sFilename            in:   string, filename
```

No return value.

Description

Creates the database and loads the specified spreadsheet file from disk. A .wks or .wk1 file is a Lotus file, an .xls file is an Excel worksheet (up to version 4). The Database class can read and write the following spreadsheet files:

- Excel: .xls files;
- Lotus: .wks, .wk1 files;

provided the following convention is adopted:

- Ordered by observation (that is, variables are in columns).
- Columns with variables are labelled.
- There is an unlabelled column with the dates (as a string), in the form year–period (the – can actually be any single character), for example, 1980–1 (or: 1980Q1 1980P1 1980:1 etc.). This doesn't have to be the first column.
- The data form a contiguous sample (non-numeric fields are converted to missing values, so you can leave gaps for missing observations).

Database class can read the following types of Excel file:

- Excel 2.1;
- Excel 3.0;
- Excel 4.0 (called 'normal' inside Excel 4).

When saving an Excel file, it is written in Excel 2.1 format.

For example, the format for writing is (this is also the optimal format for reading):

	A	B	C	D
1		CONS	INFL	DUM
2	1980-1	883	2.7	3
3	1980-2	884	3.5	5
4	1980-3	885	3.9	1
5	1980-4	889	2.6	9
6	1981-1	900	3.4	2

If these conventions are not adopted the file can still be read, but you will have to check the final result.

Database::Remove

```
Database::Remove(const sName);
```
     sName   in: string, variable name

No return value.

Description
     Removes the named variable from the database.

Database::Rename

```
Database::Rename(const sNewName, const sOldName);
```
     sNewName   in: new name
     sOldName   in: name of database variable to rename

No return value.

Description
     Renames a database variable.

Database::Renew

```
Database::Renew(const mNew, const sName, const iT1);
```
     mNew   in: $T \times 1$ matrix
     sName   in: variable names
     iT1   in: first observation

No return value.

Description
     Renews the observations on the named variable. The first new observation has
     database index iT1, the last is the end of the database sample, or the end of mNew,
     whichever comes first.

Database::SaveFmtVar, Database::SaveIn7

```
Database::SaveIn7(const sFilename);
Database::SaveFmtVar(const sFilename);
```
     sFilename   in: string, filename

No return value.

Description
     SaveIn7 saves the database as a *GiveWin* file.
     SaveFmtVar saves the database as a formatted ASCII file. Also see under
     LoadFmtVar.

Database::SaveObs, Database::SaveVar

```
Database::SaveObs(const sFilename);
Database::SaveVar(const sFilename);
    sFilename           in:   string, filename
```
No return value.

Description

Saves the database as a human-readable data file, ordered by observation, or by variable. Also see under `LoadObs`, `LoadVar`.

Database::SaveWks, Database::SaveXls

```
Database::SaveWks(const sFilename);
Database::SaveXls(const sFilename);
    sFilename           in:   string, filename
```
No return value.

Description

Saves the database as a Lotus or Excel spreadsheet file. Also see under `LoadWks`, `LoadXls`.

Database::Select

```
Database::Select(const iGroup, const aSel);
    iGroup      in:   int, group number
    aSel        in:   array, specifying name, start lag, end lag
```
No return value.

Description

Selects variables by name and with specified lags, and assigns the `iGroup` number to the selection. The `aSel` argument is an array consisting of sequences of three values: name, start lag, end lag. For example:

```
Select(0, {"CONS", 0, 0});    // select CONS as group 0
                                   // from lag 0 to 0
Select(0, {"INC", 0, 0}); // also select INC as group 0
Select(1, {"CONS", 1, 1, "INC", 1, 1});
            // the first lag of CONS and INC as group 1
```

After a sample period is set, the selection can be extracted from the database.

Database::SetSample

```
Database::SetSample(const iYear1, const iPeriod1,
    const iYear2, const iPeriod2);
```

iYear1	in:	int, start year of selection, use −1 for earliest year and period
iPeriod1	in:	int, start period of selection
iYear2	in:	int, end year of selection, use −1 for latest year and period
iPeriod2	in:	int, end period of selection

No return value.

Description

Selects a sample for the variables previously selected with the Select function. The actually selected sample will be the largest starting from the specified starting date (but not exceeding the specified end date) without any missing values. Use DeSelect to deselect the current sample and variables.

Database data members

m_mData	data matrix ($T \times k$)
m_asNames	variable names (array with k strings)
m_mVarsel	variable selection ($1 \times s$ matrix with selection) the selection consists of indices in m_mData and m_asNames
m_mLagsel	lag length of each entry in m_mVarsel ($1 \times s$ matrix)
m_mSelgroup	group number of each entry in m_mVarsel ($1 \times s$ matrix)
m_iT1sel	row index in m_mData of first selected observation (int)
m_iT2sel	row index in m_mData of last selected observation (int)

11.2 PcFiml class

The PcFiml class provides part of the advanced computations available in the menu
driven computer program *PcFiml*, see Doornik and Hendry (1994). The class is derived
from the Database class, and provides model formulation using variable names.

The class allows for estimating a Vector Autoregression (VAR), cointegration analysis ('Johansen procedure'), and multivariate regression model (such as an unrestricted
reduced form, URF), as well as a simultaneous equations model (2SLS, 3SLS, FIML).
No identities equations are currently possible. Mis-specification tests include: vector
autoregression, vector normality, vector heteroscedasticity, vector portmanteau, as well
as a Chow test.

The documentation here is rather cursory, the actual source code (pcfiml.ox)
gives more documentation. The required header file is pcfiml.h.

Example

```
#include <oxstd.h>
#include <pcfiml.h>

#pragma   link("maximize.oxo")
#pragma   link("nortest.oxo")
#pragma   link("database.oxo")
#pragma   link("pcfiml.oxo")

main()
{
    decl system;

    system = new PcFiml();

    system->LoadIn7("../database/data.in7");
    system->Deterministic(FALSE);
                                    // formulate the system
    system->Select(Y_VAR, { "CONS", 0, 2, "INC", 0, 2 } );
    system->Select(X_VAR, { "INFLAT", 0, 0 } );
    system->Select(U_VAR, { "Constant", 0, 0 } );

    system->SetSample(1953, 1, 1992, 3);
    system->Estimate();            // estimate the system (VAR)
    system->Cointegration();       // cointegration analysis

    system->Chow(1980, 2);                      // some tests
    system->Portmanteau(12);
    system->NormalityTest();
    system->ArTest(1, 5);
    system->HeteroTest(FALSE, FALSE);
    system->HeteroTest(FALSE, TRUE);

    delete system;
}
```

produces

```
---- System estimation by OLS ----
The estimation sample is 1953 (3) 1992 (3)
CONS        lag 0 status Y
CONS        lag 1 status Y
CONS        lag 2 status Y
INC         lag 0 status Y
INC         lag 1 status Y
INC         lag 2 status Y
INFLAT      lag 0 status X
Constant    lag 0 status U

coefficients
                       CONS            INC
CONS _1             0.90553       0.083906
CONS _2            0.039957        0.17361
INC _1             0.060179        0.73816
INC _2            -0.033528      -0.089942
INFLAT            -0.95629       0.0023221
Constant            25.505         87.920

coefficient standard errors
                       CONS            INC
CONS _1             0.13261        0.21549
CONS _2             0.12260        0.19923
INC _1             0.086063        0.13986
INC _2             0.075989        0.12349
INFLAT              0.17341        0.28179
Constant            15.216         24.727

equation standard errors
           CONS          INC
         1.9275       3.1323

residual covariance
                       CONS            INC
CONS                 3.7152         4.9906
INC                  4.9906         9.8111

log-likelihood=-185.911118 det-omega=10.6792 T=157

Cointegration analysis
eigenvalues
       0.40306       0.12502 -1.3878e-017

beta
CONS                0.22102        0.17651
INC                -0.24747       -0.25253
INFLAT              1.0903        -0.22638

alpha
CONS               -0.74698        0.62647
```

```
INC                    0.24209        1.1558


standardized beta
CONS                   1.0000        -0.69898
INC                   -1.1197         1.0000
INFLAT                 4.9332         0.89643


standardized alpha
CONS                  -0.16510       -0.15820
INC                    0.053507      -0.29187


long run matrix
                          CONS            INC           INFLAT
CONS                  -0.054518       0.026651       -0.95629
INC                    0.25752       -0.35178         0.0023221


Chow tests for break on or after 1980 (2)
F(50,101):
        1.2555         1.0588
Vector Chow test:      F(100,200)=1.18617 [0.155744]
Vector portmanteau:    Chi(38)=45.8927 [0.177574]
Vector normality:      Chi(4)=3.49129 [0.479204]
Vector AR 1-5 test:    F(20,280)=1.74601 [0.0264711]
                       Chi(20)=34.6453 [0.0220766]
Vector hetero test:    F(30,405)=0.977499 [0.502996]
                       Chi(30)=30.8847 [0.421091]
Vector hetero-X test:F(60,382)=1.07614 [0.335742]
                       Chi(60)=67.4407 [0.237818]
```

The next example involves simultaneous equations estimation.

```
#include <oxstd.h>
#include <pcfiml.h>

#pragma   link("maximize.oxo")
#pragma   link("nortest.oxo")
#pragma   link("database.oxo")
#pragma   link("pcfiml.oxo")

main()
{
    decl system;

    system = new PcFiml();

    system->LoadIn7("../database/data.in7");
    system->Deterministic(FALSE);
                                    // formulate the system
    system->Select(Y_VAR, { "CONS", 0, 2, "INC", 0, 2 } );
    system->Select(X_VAR, { "INFLAT", 0, 0 } );
    system->Select(U_VAR, { "Constant", 0, 0 } );

    system->SetSample(1953, 1, 1992, 3);
    system->SetPrint(FALSE);        // don't print URF results
    system->Estimate();                        // estimate URF

    system->SetPrintUrf(FALSE);
    system->SetPrint(TRUE);         // but print model output
                                    // formulate a model
    system->SetEquation("CONS", {"CONS",1,2, "INC",0,0 });
    system->SetEquation("INC",  {"INC", 1,2 } );

    system->Fiml();                 // estimate the model by FIML
    system->Portmanteau(12);                    // do some tests
    system->EgeArTest(1, 1);
    system->EgeArTest(1, 5);
    system->NormalityTest();
    system->HeteroTest(FALSE, FALSE);
    system->HeteroTest(FALSE, TRUE);

    delete system;                  // done with the system
}
```

produces

```
---- Model estimation by FIML ----
The estimation sample is 1953 (3) 1992 (3)

coefficients
                        CONS            INC
CONS                 -1.0000        0.00000
INC               -0.0024749        -1.0000
```

```
CONS _1                  1.2238        0.00000
CONS _2                 -0.24947       0.00000
INC _1                   0.00000       0.99702
INC _2                   0.00000      -0.044049
INFLAT                   0.00000       0.00000
Constant                24.528        41.796
```

coefficient standard errors

	CONS	INC
CONS	0.00000	0.00000
INC	0.035193	0.00000
CONS _1	0.063435	0.00000
CONS _2	0.062315	0.00000
INC _1	0.00000	0.065539
INC _2	0.00000	0.063625
INFLAT	0.00000	0.00000
Constant	16.305	22.300

equation standard errors

```
          CONS          INC
        2.1822        3.3125
```

residual covariance

	CONS	INC
CONS	4.7620	5.5795
INC	5.5795	10.973

log-likelihood=-236.414419 det-omega=20.3209 T=157
FIML estimation: Strong convergence

```
Vector portmanteau:    Chi(43)=77.2491 [0.00104276]
Vector EGE-AR 1-1 test:F(4,302)=1.53533 [0.191821]
                       Chi(4)=6.21487 [0.183666]
Vector EGE-AR 1-5 test:F(20,286)=2.23428 [0.00217042]
                       Chi(20)=41.6164 [0.00310201]
Vector normality:      Chi(4)=4.07129 [0.396443]
Vector hetero test:    F(30,405)=2.10418 [0.000766605]
                       Chi(30)=59.4064 [0.00108575]
Vector hetero-X test:  F(60,382)=2.67076 [8.39093e-009]
                       Chi(60)=133.127 [1.81737e-007]
```

PcFiml function members

ArTest(const iAr1, const iAr2);
    System vector AR test for lags iAr1...iAr2.
Chow(const iYear, const iPeriod);
    Forecast Chow tests for break on or after iYear (iPeriod).
Cointegration();
    Estimate cointegrating space.
EgeArTest(const iAr1, const iAr2);
    Model vector AR test for lags iAr1...iAr2.
Estimate();
    Estimate the system (NB: use ->SetSample() first).
EstimateAcc();
    SVD based estimation of the system (NB: use ->SetSample() first).
Fiml();
    Do FIML estimation.
GetOmega();
    Returns $n \times n$ matrix of URF/RRF residual variance $\mathbf{V'V}/(T-k)$.
GetPi();
    Returns $n \times k$ matrix of URF/RRF coefficients.
GetResiduals();
    Returns $T \times n$ matrix $\mathbf{V}$ of URF/RRF residuals.
GetResult();
    Returns results from FIML estimation (return code from MaxBFGS).
GetVarPi();
    Returns $n \times k$ matrix with variances of RRF/URF coefficients.
GetVarTheta();
    System: returns full $nk \times nk$ variance-covariance matrix of URF coefficients;
    Model: returns full $np \times np$ variance-covariance matrix of model coefficients.
HeteroTest(const fStand, const fCross);
    Vector heteroscedasticity test.
NormalityTest();
    Vector normality test.
Output(const fSys, const fCoint);
    Print System and/or Cointegration results.
PcFiml();
    Constructor.
Portmanteau(const iLag);
    Vector portmanteau test up to lag iLag.
SetEquation(const sEquation, const aModel);
    Delete or add variable from model.

```
SetPrint(fPrint);
```
Toggles print switch.
```
SetPrintUrf(fPrintUrf);
```
Toggles URF print switch.
```
ThreeSLS();
```
Do 3SLS estimation.
```
TwoSLS();
```
Do 2SLS estimation.

11.3 PcNaiveDgp class

The PcNaiveDgp class is a data generation process (DGP), designed for use in dynamic econometric Monte Carlo experiments. The class is used through the header file pcnaive.h. The design is an n-variate version of the DGP used in Hendry, Neale and Ericsson (1991). The form of the DGP in mathematical formulation is:

$$
\begin{aligned}
\mathbf{y}_t &= \mathbf{A}_0 \mathbf{y}_t + \mathbf{A}_1 \mathbf{y}_{t-1} + \mathbf{A}_2 \mathbf{z}_t + \mathbf{a}_3 + \mathbf{u}_t, \\
\mathbf{u}_t &= \mathbf{B}_0 \mathbf{u}_{t-1} + \mathbf{e}_t + \mathbf{B}_1 \mathbf{e}_{t-1}, \\
\mathbf{z}_t &= \mathbf{C}_0 \mathbf{z}_{t-1} + \mathbf{c}_1 + \mathbf{c}_2 t + \mathbf{v}_t.
\end{aligned}
\tag{11.1}
$$

The vectors $\mathbf{y}_t, \mathbf{u}_t, \mathbf{e}_t$ are $n \times 1$, so that the coefficient matrices $\mathbf{A}_0, \mathbf{A}_1, \mathbf{B}_0, \mathbf{B}_1$ are $n \times n$, and $\mathbf{a}_3$ is $n \times 1$. The $\mathbf{z}_t$ vector is $q \times 1$, making $\mathbf{a}_2$ $n \times q$, $\mathbf{C}_0$ $q \times q$, and $\mathbf{c}_1, \mathbf{c}_2$ $q \times 1$. The zs can be kept fixed between experiments, or regenerated for the experiment. A distribution for $\mathbf{e}_t$ and $\mathbf{v}_t$ can be specified.

Example

```
#include <oxstd.h>
#include <pcnaive.h>

#pragma link("pcnaive.oxo")

main()
{
    decl dgp;

    dgp = new PcNaiveDgp(3,3);

    dgp->SetYParameter(zeros(3,3), unit(3), zeros(3,3),
        zeros(3,1));
    dgp->SetDistribution(U_DGP, MVNORMAL, zeros(3,1),
        ones(3,3)/10 + unit(3)/5);

    dgp->Print();

    delete dgp;
}
```

produces (all non specified parameters are zero by default):

```
----PcNaive DGP ----
y is (3 x 1), z is (3 x 1) and fixed.

y[t] = e[t] + a1 y[t-1]
a1 =
        1.0000        0.00000        0.00000
        0.00000        1.0000        0.00000
        0.00000        0.00000        1.0000

e ~ MVN(0,sigma)
```

```
sigma=
          0.30000        0.10000        0.10000
          0.10000        0.30000        0.10000
          0.10000        0.10000        0.30000
```

PcNaiveDgp::Asymp

```
PcNaiveDgp::Asymp();
```
No return value.

Description
    Prints an asymptotic analysis (companion matrix with eigenvalues) of the current DGP.

PcNaiveDgp::DiscardZ

```
PcNaiveDgp::DiscardZ();
```
No return value.

Description
    Discards the current z_t; the next call to Generate() will generate new observations on z_t.

PcNaiveDgp::Generate

```
PcNaiveDgp::Generate(const cT);
     cT            in:  int, sample size T
```

Return value
    Returns generated $\mathbf{Y} = (\mathbf{y}_0 \ldots \mathbf{y}_T)'$, as a $T \times n$ matrix.

Description
    Generates cT observation of the current DGP.

PcNaiveDgp::GetU, GetY, GetZ

```
PcNaiveDgp::GetU();
PcNaiveDgp::GetY();
PcNaiveDgp::GetZ();
```

Return value
    GetU returns current $\mathbf{U} = (\mathbf{u}_0 \ldots \mathbf{u}_{t-1})'$, as a $T \times n$ matrix.
    GetY returns current $\mathbf{Y} = (\mathbf{y}_0 \ldots \mathbf{y}_{t-1})'$, as a $T \times n$ matrix (as does Generate).
    GetZ returns current $\mathbf{Z} = (\mathbf{z}_0 \ldots \mathbf{z}_{t-1})'$, as a $T \times q$ matrix.

PcNaiveDgp::PcNaiveDgp

```
PcNaiveDgp::PcNaiveDgp(const cY, const cZ);
```
    cY   in: int, n, dimension of $\mathbf{y}_t$

    cZ   in: int, q, dimension of $\mathbf{z}_t$

No return value.

Description

    Constructor.

PcNaiveDgp::Print

```
PcNaiveDgp::Print();
```

No return value.

Description

    Prints the setup of the current DGP.

PcNaiveDgp::SetDistribution

```
PcNaiveDgp::SetDistribution(const iEqn, const iDist,
    mPar1, mPar2);
```
    iEqn   in: one of: U_DGP, Z_DGP

    iDist   in: one   of: NO_DIST,   NOR-
                        MAL, MVNORMAL, LOGNORMAL, T_DIST, F_DIST, EXPO-
                        NENTIAL, MVNARCH, MVNHETERO

    mPar1   in: first parameter of distribution, α

                      MVNARCH, MVNHETERO: $n \times n$ for $\mathbf{y}_t, \mathbf{u}_t$; $q \times q$ for $\mathbf{z}_t$

                      others: $n \times 1$ for $\mathbf{y}_t, \mathbf{u}_t$; $q \times 1$ for $\mathbf{z}_t$

    mPar2   in: second parameter of distribution, β

                      MVNORMAL, MVNARCH, MVNHETERO: $n \times n$ for $\mathbf{y}_t, \mathbf{u}_t$; $q \times q$
                      for $\mathbf{z}_t$

                      others: $n \times 1$ for $\mathbf{y}_t, \mathbf{u}_t$; $q \times 1$ for $\mathbf{z}_t$

No return value.

Description

    Specifies the distribution for the **u**, or **z** equation in (11.1). The first argument indicates the equation, the second the distribution. The last two arguments parameterize the distribution.

    Write ϵ_t for either $\mathbf{e}_t$ or $\mathbf{v}_t$, then:

argument	distribution
NO_DIST	0 (no distribution)
NORMAL	$\epsilon_{it} \sim N(\alpha_i, \beta_i) = N(0,1) \times \sqrt{\beta_i} + \alpha_i$
MVNORMAL	$\epsilon_t \sim N_n(\alpha, \beta)$
LOGNORMAL	$\epsilon_{it} \sim \Lambda(\alpha_i, \beta_i) = \exp\{N(0,1)\} \times \sqrt{\alpha_i} + \beta_i$
T_DIST	$\epsilon_{it} \sim t(\alpha_i)$
F_DIST	$\epsilon_{it} \sim F(\alpha_i, \beta_i)$
EXPONENTIAL	$\epsilon_{it} \sim \exp(\alpha_i)$
MVNARCH	$\epsilon_t \sim N_n(0, \alpha + \beta\epsilon_{t-1}\epsilon'_{t-1}\beta')$
MVNHETERO	$e_t \sim N_n(0, \alpha + \beta y_{t-1}y'_{t-i}\beta')$

PcNaiveDgp::SetFixedZ

PcNaiveDgp::SetFixedZ(const fSetting);
    fSetting   in: 0: z_t is fixed, 1: z_t not fixed

No return value.

Description
    Specifies whether z_t is fixed or not. Fixed z_t is only generated once, until a call to DiscardZ or SetFixedZ is made.

PcNaiveDgp::SetMixing

PcNaiveDgp::SetMixing(const iEqn, const iDist,
    mPar1, mPar2, const iT1, const iT2,
    const mMixParIn, const mMixParOut);

No return value.

Description
    Not yet implemented

PcNaiveDgp::SetUParameter

PcNaiveDgp::SetUParameter(const mLagAr, const mLagMa);
    mLagAr   in: $n \times n$ matrix B_0
    mLagMa   in: $n \times n$ matrix B_1

No return value.

Description
    Sets the parameters for the e_t equation.

PcNaiveDgp::SetYParameter

```
PcNaiveDgp::SetYParameter(const mLevel, const mLag,
    const mZpar, const vConst);
```
mLevel	in:	$n \times n$ matrix $\mathbf{A}_0$ *must have zeros on the diagonal*
mLag	in:	$n \times n$ matrix $\mathbf{A}_1$
mZpar	in:	$n \times q$ matrix $\mathbf{A}_2$
vConst	in:	$n \times 1$ matrix $\mathbf{a}_3$

No return value.

Description

Sets the parameters for the $\mathbf{y}_t$ equation.

PcNaiveDgp::SetZParameter

```
PcNaiveDgp::SetZParameter(const mLag, const vConst,
    const vTrend);
```
mLag	in:	$q \times q$ matrix $\mathbf{C}_0$
vConst	in:	$q \times 1$ matrix $\mathbf{c}_1$
vTrend	in:	$q \times 1$ matrix $\mathbf{c}_2$

No return value.

Description

Sets the parameters for the $\mathbf{z}_t$ equation.

PcNaiveDgp data members

m_cY	n, dimension of $\mathbf{y}_t$,
m_cZ	q, dimension of $\mathbf{z}_t$,
m_mZ	generated $\mathbf{Z}$, $T \times q$,
m_mY	generated $\mathbf{Y}$, $T \times n$,
m_mU	generated $\mathbf{U}$, $T \times n$,
m_mUlag	$\mathbf{B}_0'$, error AR parameters, $n \times n$,
m_mElag	$\mathbf{B}_1'$, error MA parameters, $n \times n$,
m_iEdist	error distribution,
m_mEdistPar1	error distribution parameter 1,
m_mEdistPar2	error distribution parameter 2,
m_iEmix	error mixing distribution,
m_mEmixPar1	mixing distribution parameters, $1 \times n$,
m_mEmixPar2	mixing distribution parameters, $1 \times n$,
m_iEmixT1	first observation over which to mix,
m_iEmixT2	last observation over which to mix,
m_mEmixParIn	error mixing parameter inside sample, $1 \times n$,

m_mEmixParOut	error mixing parameter outside sample, $1 \times n$,
m_mZlag	$\mathbf{C}_0'$, coefficients on $\mathbf{z}_{t-1}$, $q \times q$,
m_mZconst	$\mathbf{c}_1'$, coefficients on constant, $1 \times q$,
m_mZtrend	$\mathbf{c}_2'$, coefficients on trend, $1 \times q$,
m_iZdist	$\mathbf{z}$ distribution,
m_mZdistPar1	$\mathbf{z}$ distribution parameters 1,
m_mZdistPar2	$\mathbf{z}$ distribution parameter 2,
m_iZmix	$\mathbf{z}$ mixing distribution,
m_mZmixPar1	$\mathbf{z}$ mixing distribution parameters, $1 \times q$,
m_mZmixPar2	$\mathbf{z}$ mixing distribution parameters, $1 \times q$,
m_iZmixT1	first observation over which to mix $\mathbf{z}$,
m_iZmixT2	last observation over which to mix $\mathbf{z}$,
m_mZmixParIn	$\mathbf{z}$ mixing parameter inside sample, $1 \times n$,
m_mZmixParOut	$\mathbf{z}$ mixing parameter outside sample, $1 \times n$,
m_fFixedZ	TRUE for fixed $\mathbf{z}_t$,
m_mYlevel	$\mathbf{A}_0$ structural coefficients on $\mathbf{y}_t$, $n \times n$,
m_mYlag	$\mathbf{A}_1$ structural coefficients on $\mathbf{y}_{t-1}$, $n \times n$,
m_mYparZ	$\mathbf{A}_2$ structural coefficients on $\mathbf{z}_t$, $n \times q$,
m_mYconst	$\mathbf{a}_3$ structural coefficients on constant, $n \times 1$,
m_mY0inv	$\mathbf{D}^{-1}$, $\mathbf{D} = (\mathbf{I} - \mathbf{A}_0)'$,
m_mYlagRf	$\mathbf{A}_1'\mathbf{D}^{-1}$ reduced form coefficients on $\mathbf{y}_{t-1}$,
m_mYparZRf	$\mathbf{A}_2'\mathbf{D}^{-1}$ reduced form coefficients on $\mathbf{z}_t$,
m_mYconstRf	$\mathbf{a}_3'\mathbf{D}^{-1}$ reduced form coefficients on constant.

11.4 Sample class

The Sample class stores a time interval, and the frequency, e.g. 1980 (1) – 1990 (1), with frequency 4 (i.e. quarterly observations). Although we talk about year and period to denote a point in time, the year denotes the major time period, and the period the minor, so that, for example, 20 (3) could be day 3 in week 20, when the frequency is 7 (daily data). The member functions of Sample return information about the sample. Use frequency 1 for cross-section data.

The Sample class is only used to derive from, and has no constructor function, as the example shows (don't forget to link in the database code, and include database.h):

Example

```
#include <oxstd.h>
#include <database.h>

#pragma link("database.oxo")

class MySample : Sample     // derive to provide constructor
{
    MySample(const iFreq,                        // constructor
        const iYear1, const iPeriod1,
        const iYear2, const iPeriod2);
};
MySample::MySample(const iFreq, const iYear1,
    const iPeriod1, const iYear2, const iPeriod2)
{
    m_iFreq = iFreq;
    m_iYear1 = iYear1;  m_iPeriod1 = iPeriod1;
    m_iYear2 = iYear2;  m_iPeriod2 = iPeriod2;
}


main()
{
    decl sam = new MySample(4, 1980, 1, 1990, 1);

    print("\nnumber of observations:  ", sam->GetSize());
    print("\nperiod of observation 9: ", sam->ObsYear(9),
        " (", sam->ObsPeriod(9), ")");
    print("\nindex of 1985 (4) date:  ",
        sam->GetIndex(1985, 4));

    delete sam;
}
```

produces

```
number of observations:  41
period of observation 9: 1982 (2)
index of 1985 (4) date:  23
```

Sample::GetYear1

```
Sample::GetYear1();
```

Return value
> The year of the first observation.

Sample::GetPeriod1

```
Sample::GetPeriod1();
```

Return value
> The period of the first observation.

Sample::GetYear2

```
Sample::GetYear2();
```

Return value
> The year of the last observation.

Sample::GetPeriod2

```
Sample::GetPeriod2();
```

Return value
> The period of the last observation.

Sample::GetSize

```
Sample::GetSize();
```

Return value
> The number of observations in the sample.

Sample::GetIndex

```
Sample::GetIndex(const iYear, const iPeriod);
   iYear      in:   int, year
   iPeriod   in:   int, period
```

Return value
> The index of the specified time point.

Sample::ObsYear

```
Sample::ObsYear(iObs);
```
   iObs   in: int, observation index

Return value
      The year of the observation index.

Sample::ObsPeriod

```
Sample::ObsPeriod(iObs);
```
   iObs   in: int, observation index

Return value
      The period of the observation index.

Sample data members

m_iFreq	data frequency (int)
m_iYear1	year of first observation (int)
m_iPeriod1	period of first observation (int)
m_iYear2	year of last observation (int)
m_iPeriod2	period of last observation (int)

11.5 Simulation class

The Simulation class can be used to set up Monte Carlo experiments. Derive your own simulation experimentation class from this, overriding the virtual functions. Simulation will handle the replications and storage, and print the final results. The type of data it can handle are coefficients, test statistics and p-values of test statistics. The class is used through the header file simula.h.

An extensive example, using the PcFiml class for estimation, is given in the file samples/simula/artest.ox. An example more in line with the one here is samples/simula/simnor.ox. This program compares the small sample size of two tests for normality. When run in *OxRun*, it will plot the distribution of the test statistics as the Monte Carlo experiment proceeds.

The example discussed here generates data from a standard normal distribution, and estimates the mean and variance. It also tests whether the mean is different from zero. The properties of the estimated coefficients and test statistic are studied by repeating the experiment M times, and averaging the outcome of the M experiments. So the data generation process is:

$$y_t = \mu + \epsilon_t \text{ with } \epsilon_t \sim N(0, \sigma^2),$$

together with $\mu = 0$ and $\sigma^2 = 1$. We estimate the parameters from a sample of size T by:

$$\hat{\mu} = T^{-1} \sum_{t=0}^{T-1} y_t, \quad \hat{\sigma}^2 = (T)^{-1} \sum_{t=0}^{T-1} (y_t - \hat{\mu})^2,$$

and

$$\hat{s} = \left\{ (T-1)^{-1} \sum_{t=0}^{T-1} (y_t - \hat{\mu})^2 \right\}^{\frac{1}{2}} = \left\{ \frac{T}{T-1} \hat{\sigma}^2 \right\}^{\frac{1}{2}}.$$

The *t*-test which tests the hypothesis H_0: $\hat{\mu} = 0$ is:

$$T^{\frac{1}{2}} \frac{\hat{\mu}}{\hat{s}}.$$

The code for this Monte Carlo experiment is in simtest.ox (remember that the simula code needs to be linked in):

Example

```
#include <oxstd.h>
#include <simula.h>

#pragma link("simula.oxo")


/*--------------- SimNormal : Simulation ---------------*/
class SimNormal : Simulation     // inherit from simulation
{
```

```
    decl m_mCoef;                                // coefficient
    decl m_mTest;                                // test statistic
    decl m_mPval;                                // p-value of t-test

    SimNormal();                                 // constructor
    Generate(const iRep, const cT, const mxT);
                                         // generate replication
    GetCoefficients();             // return coefficient values
    GetPvalues();                     // return p-values of tests
    GetTestStatistics();            // return test statistics
};
SimNormal::SimNormal()
{
    this->Simulation(<50>, 100, 1000, TRUE, ranseed(-1),
        <0.2,0.1,0.05,0.01>,       // p-values to investigate
        <0,1>);                     // true coefs: mean=0, sd=1
    this->SetTestNames({"t-value"});
    this->SetCoefNames({"constant", "std.dev"});
}
SimNormal::Generate(const iRep, const cT, const mxT)
{
    decl my, sdevy, meany;

    my = rann(cT, 1);                            // generate data

    meany = meanc(my);                           // mean of y
    sdevy = sqrt(cT * varc(my) / (cT-1));    // std.dev of y

    m_mCoef = meany | sdevy;                    // mean,sdev of y
    m_mTest = meany / (sdevy / sqrt(cT));//t-value on mean
    m_mPval = tailt(m_mTest, cT-1);   // t(T-1) distributed

return 1;
}
SimNormal::GetCoefficients()
{
    return m_mCoef;
}
SimNormal::GetPvalues()
{
    return m_mPval;
}
SimNormal::GetTestStatistics()
{
    return m_mTest;
}
/*------------ END SimNormal : Simulation --------------*/

main()
{
    decl experiment = new SimNormal();    // create object

    experiment->Simulate();                // do simulations
```

```
        delete experiment;                          // remove object
    }
produces

T=50, M=1000, seed=198195252 (common)

critical values
                          20%          10%           5%            1%
    t-value            0.80563       1.2758        1.6512        2.2456

rejection frequencies
                          20%          10%           5%            1%
    t-value            0.18500      0.097000      0.049000      0.0050000

coefficients
                    mean    std.dev    mean bias  se mn bias    rmse
    constant   -0.0074297   0.14044   -0.0074297  0.0044412  0.14064
    std.dev     0.99471     0.10130   -0.0052933  0.0032035  0.10144
```

The sample size is $T = 50$, with $M = 1000$ experiments. Setting the seed enables us to obtain exactly the same results when rerunning the program. The first table gives the empirical critical values for the test statistic, at the p-values we provided. These should correspond to the theoretical distribution, namely t(49). The value 0.82216 is the 800th number in the 1000 t-values after sorting the t values. The empirical rejection frequencies give the percentage of experiments which were rejected at the specified probability points, based on the p-values returned by GetPvalues. The final table gives the results for the coefficients. If $\hat{\mu}_m$ is the estimated mean for experiment m, and μ the true parameter then:

mean $\qquad \bar{\hat{\mu}} = M^{-1} \sum_{m=0}^{M-1} \hat{\mu}_m,$

std.dev $\qquad \hat{\sigma}_{\hat{\mu}} = \left\{ M^{-1} \sum_{m=0}^{M-1} (\hat{\mu}_m - \bar{\hat{\mu}})^2 \right\}^{\frac{1}{2}},$

mean bias $\qquad \bar{\hat{\mu}} - \mu,$

se mean bias $\qquad \hat{\sigma}_{\bar{\hat{\mu}}} = M^{-\frac{1}{2}} \hat{\sigma}_{\hat{\mu}},$

rmse $\qquad \left\{ M^{-1} \sum_{m=0}^{M-1} (\hat{\mu}_m - \mu)^2 \right\}^{\frac{1}{2}} = \left\{ (\text{std.dev})^2 + (\text{mean bias})^2 \right\}^{\frac{1}{2}},$

where rmse is the root of the mean squared error.

Simulation::Generate

```
virtual Simulation::Generate(const iRep, const cT,
    const mxT);
    iRep       in:  int, index of current replication (0 is first)
    cT         in:  int, sample size to be used for replication
    mxT        in:  int, maximum sample size to be used for replication (this is
                    only relevant when using common random numbers)
```

Return value

The functions should return 1 if successful, 0 if the replications failed. If the call to the Generate function fails, it is retried until a successful return (*so always returning 0, or not returning a value could result in an infinite loop*). The number of rejected replications is reported in the output.

Description

Virtual function which the derived class must override. It is called for every replication, and must perform the actual replication. The results from this replication are obtained by the simula class by calling GetCoefficients, GetPvalues and GetTestStatistics.

Simulation::GetCoefficients, GetPvalues, GetTestStatistics

```
virtual Simulation::GetCoefficients();
virtual Simulation::GetPvalues();
virtual Simulation::GetTestStatistics();
```

Return value

The functions return 0 if the information is not generated, otherwise:

GetCoefficients	$s_c \times 1$ matrix with the observed coefficients
GetPvalues	$s_p \times 1$ matrix with observed p-values of the tests
GetTestStatistics	$s_t \times 1$ matrix with the observed test statistics

Description

Virtual functions which the derived class must override.

Simulation::SetCoefNames, Simulation::SetTestNames

```
Simulation::SetCoefNames(const asNames)
Simulation::SetTestNames(const asNames)
      asNames    in:   array with names:
                       SetCoefNames: array with $s_c$ names
                       SetTestNames: array with $s_t$ names
```

No return value.

Description

Installs the names of tests statistics and coefficients, to make the report more readable.

Simulation::Simulate

```
Simulation::Simulate()
```

No return value.

Description

   This is the core function. It runs the Monte Carlo experiment, and prints the results.

Simulation::Simulation

```
Simulation::Simulation(const mT, const mxT,
    const cRep, const fCommon, const dSeed,
    const mPvalue, const mTrueParam);
```

mT	in:	$1 \times r$ matrix of sample sizes
mxT	in:	int, maximum sample size
cRep	in:	int, number of replications
fCommon	in:	1: reset seed for each experiment; else 0
dSeed	in:	double, resets seed to dSeed if fCommon == TRUE
mPvalue	in:	$1 \times s_p$ matrix with p-values to test at, only used if GetPvalues returns p-values
mTrueParam	in:	$1 \times s_c$ matrix with true parameters, only used if GetCoefficients returns coefficients

No return value.

Description

   Constructor function.

Simula data members

`m_mT`	sample size matrix
`m_mxT`	maximum sample size
`m_cRep`	number of replications
`m_cRejected`	number of replications rejected
`m_mPvalue`	row vector with p-values for tests
`m_asPvalue`	array with names of p-values
`m_asTest`	array with names of tests
`m_asCoef`	array with names of coefficients
`m_mTrueParam`	actual parameter values for coeffs
`m_fCommon`	TRUE if same seed for each experiment
`m_dSeed`	reset to dSeed if fCommon==TRUE
`m_mCoefMean`	mean of coefficients
`m_mCoefMeanSq`	mean of squares of coefficients
`m_mReject`	rejection frequencies
`m_mTestVal`	sorted test values for last sample size
`m_mCritVal`	critical values corresponding to mPvalue

Chapter 12

Language reference

12.1 Introduction

The Ox syntax is formalized in a fashion similar to Kernighan and Ritchie (1988) and Stroustrup (1988). These two books describe the C and C++ languages on which the Ox language is modelled.

As an example, consider the syntax of enum declaration statements:

enum { *enumerator-list* } ;

enumerator-list:
    enumerator
    enumerator-list , enumerator

enumerator:
    identifier
    identifier = int-constant-expression

Symbols which have to be typed literally are given in `typewriter` font; these are called terminal symbols. *Italic* symbols are non-terminal, and require further definition. Ultimately, the whole syntax can be reduced to terminal statements. The subscript $_{opt}$ denotes an optional element. In this example, *identifier* and *int-constant-expression* remain as yet undefined. An *enumerator-list* is defined recursively: consisting of one or more enumerators, separated by columns. This can be visualized as follows:

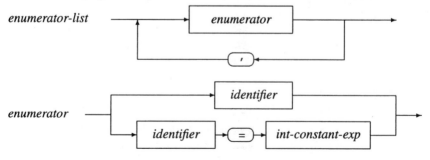

12.2 Lexical conventions

12.2.1 Tokens

The first action of a compiler is to divide the source code into units it can understand, so-called tokens. There are four kinds of tokens: identifiers, keywords, constants (also called literals) and operators. White space (newlines, formfeeds, tabs, comments) is ignored, but can serve to separate tokens.

12.2.2 Comment

Anything between /* and */ is considered comment. This comment *can* be nested (unlike C and C++). Everything following // up to the end of the line is also comment, but is ignored inside /* ... */ type comment. So nested comment is possible:

```
one = cons + 1;    // comment
/* two = cons + 1;    // comment
*/
```

This is also legal:

```
two = cons + 1;    /* comment /* nested comment */ */
```

Note that code can also be removed using preprocessor statements, see §12.8.2.

12.3 Identifiers

Identifiers are made up of letters and digits. The first character must be a letter. Underscores (_) count as a letter. Valid names are CONS, cons, cons_1, _a_1_b, etc. Invalid are #CONS, 1_CONS, log(X), etc. Ox is case sensitive, so CONS and cons are different identifiers. It is better not to use identifiers with a leading underscore, as several compilers use these for internal names. The maximum length of an identifier is 60 characters; additional characters are ignored.

12.3.1 Keywords

The following keywords are reserved:

    keyword: one of

array	decl	extern	new	this
break	default	for	operator	virtual
case	delete	goto	return	while
char	do	if	short	
class	double	inline	static	
const	else	int	string	
continue	enum	matrix	switch	

12.3.2 Constants

Arithmetic types, string type and array type (see §12.4.1) have corresponding constants.

> *constant:*
> > *scalar-constant:*
> > > *int-constant*
> > > *double-constant*
> > *vector-constant:*
> > > *matrix-constant*
> > *string-constant*
> > *array-constant*

12.3.2.1 Integer constants

A sequence of digits is an integer constant. A hexadecimal constant is a sequence of digits and the letters A to F or a to f, prefixed by 0x or 0X. Examples are:

```
1236
0x1a          (26 decimal)
0xFF          (255 decimal)
0xffffffff    (–1 decimal using 32 bit integers)
```

12.3.2.2 Character constants

Character constants are interpreted as an integer constant. A character constant is an integer constant consisting of a single character enclosed in single quotes (e.g. 'a' and '0') or an escape sequence enclosed in single quotes.

> *escape-sequence:* one of

\"	double quote (")
\'	single quote (')
\0	null character
\\	backslash (\)
\a	alert (bel)
\b	backspace
\f	formfeed
\n	newline
\r	carriage return
\t	horizontal tab
\v	vertical tab
\x*hh*	hexadecimal number (*hh*)

So '\n' is the integer constant corresponding to the newline character. On most systems the newline character has decimal value 10, and in that case could also be written as '\x0A' or '\x0a', but not '\X0a'.

12.3.2.3 Double constants

A double constant consists of an integer part, a decimal point, a fraction part, an e, E, d or D and an optionally signed integer exponent. Either the integer or the fraction part may be missing (not both); either the decimal point or the full exponent may be missing (not both). A hexadecimal double constant is written as 0x.*hhhhhhhhhhhhhhh*. The format used is an 8 byte IEEE real. The hexadecimal string is written with the most significant byte first (the sign and exponent are on the left). If any hexadecimal digits are missing, the string is left padded with 0's. Examples of correct double constants are:

```
0.
1.2
.5
-.5e-10
2.1E-112
1D-1                      (0.1)
1E1                       (10.0)
0x.7FF0000000000000    (infinity)
0x.3ff0000000000000       (1)
0x.3fb999999999999a      (-0.1)
```

The last example shows that most numbers which can be expressed exactly in decimal notation, cannot be represented exactly on the computer.

12.3.2.4 Matrix constants

A matrix constant lists within < and > the elements of the matrix, row by row. Each row is delimited by a semicolon, successive elements in a row are separated by a comma. For example:

```
< 00, 01, 02; 10, 11, 12 >
< 0.0, 0.1, 0.2 >
< 1100 >
```

which are respectively a 2×3 matrix, a 1×3 matrix and a 1×1 matrix:

$$\begin{pmatrix} 00 & 01 & 02 \\ 10 & 11 & 12 \end{pmatrix} \quad \begin{pmatrix} 0.0 & 0.1 & 0.2 \end{pmatrix} \quad \begin{pmatrix} 1100 \end{pmatrix}$$

Elements in a matrix constant can be specified as:

matrix element:
>   *constant-expression*
>   *constant-expression* : *constant-expression*
>   *constant-expression* : [*constant-expression*]
>   *constant-expression*
>   [*constant-expression*] [*constant-expression*] =
>   *constant-expression*
>   [*constant-expression*] *
>   *constant-expression*

The constant expressions must evaluate to an integer or a double. The index of each row is one higher than the previous row. Within each row, the column index of an element is one higher than that created with the previous element in the same row.

We have seen examples of the first element type. The second specifies an integer range, e.g. 2 : 5 corresponds to 2 , 3 , 4 , 5. The range may decrease, so that 5 . 3 : 2 . 8 corresponds to 5 . 3 , 4 . 3 , 3 . 3. It is also possible to specify a stepsize as in 2 : [2] 8, which gives 2 , 4 , 6 , 8. The third form sets a specific element in the matrix (which overrides the location implicit in the position of the element in the matrix constant). Note that the top left element is [0] [0], the second element in the first row [0] [1], etc. Consider for example:

$$\begin{pmatrix} 1 & 2 & 3 \\ 4 & 5 & 6 \\ 7 & 8 & 9 \end{pmatrix} \quad \text{indexed as} \quad \begin{matrix} [0][0] & [0][1] & [0][2] \\ [1][0] & [1][1] & [1][2] \\ [2][0] & [2][1] & [2][2] \end{matrix}$$

Finally, it is possible to specify a number of identical elements, e.g. [3] * 0 corresponds to 0 , 0 , 0. Unspecified elements are set to zero.

As an example involving all types, consider:

```
<  [4]*1,2;  10,11,14-2;  1:4;  [3][4]=99,2;8:[-2-1]2  >
```

The 2 in the first row will be in column 4, as columns 3 was the last created previously. The 2 in the penultimate row gets column 5. The last specified row is equivalent to 8 : [-3] 2. The result is:

$$\begin{pmatrix} 1 & 1 & 1 & 1 & 2 & 0 \\ 10 & 11 & 12 & 0 & 0 & 0 \\ 1 & 2 & 3 & 4 & 0 & 0 \\ 0 & 0 & 0 & 0 & 99 & 2 \\ 8 & 5 & 2 & 0 & 0 & 0 \end{pmatrix}$$

Further examples are given in §12.5.3.

12.3.2.5 String constants

A string constant is a text enclosed in double quotes. Adjacent string constants are concatenated. A null character is always appended to indicate the end of a string. The maximum length of a string constant is 1024 characters. Escape sequences can be used to represent special characters, as in §12.3.2.2. At least one and at most two hexadecimal digits must be given for the hexadecimal escape sequence. A single quote need not be escaped. Some examples of string constants:

```
"a simple string"
"two strings" " joined together"
"with double quote \" and a newline character:\n"
"three ways to include a tab: \t, \x9 and \x09"
"use \\ to include a backslash,e.g. c:\\ox\\include"
```

12.3.2.6 Array constants

An array constant is a list of constants in braces, separated by a comma. This is a recursive definition, because the constant can itself be an array constant. The terminating level consists of non-array constants. Each level of array constants creates an array of pointers. For example:

```
{ "tinker", "tailor", "soldier" }
{{ "tinker", "tailor"}, {"soldier"} }
```

The first creates an array of three pointers to strings, the second an array of two pointers, the first points to an array of two pointers to strings, the second to an array of one pointer to the word soldier:

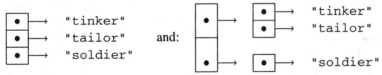

Remember that { "tinker" "tailor" "soldier" } is identical to an array consisting of one string: { "tinkertailorsoldier" }.

12.4 Objects

12.4.1 Types

Variables in Ox are implicitly typed, and can change type during their lifetime. The life of a variable corresponds to the level of its declaration. Its scope is the section of the program in which it can be seen. Scope and life do not have to coincide.

There are three basic types and four derived types. The integer type int is a signed integer. The double precision floating point type is called double. A matrix is a two-dimensional array of doubles which can be manipulated as a whole. A string-type holds a string, while an array-type is an array of pointers.

arithmetic-type:
>   int
>   double
>   matrix

string-type:
>   string

scalar-type:
>   int
>   double

vector-type:
>   string
>   matrix

derived-type:
>   array
>   function
>   class
>   pointer to class object

12.4.1.1 Type conversion

When a double is converted to an int, the fractional part is discarded; if the resulting value cannot be represented, the behaviour is undefined. When an int is converted to a double, the nearest representation will be used. For example, conversion to int of 1.3 and 1.7 will be 1 on both occasions.

A single element of a string (a character) is of type int. An int or double can be assigned to a string element, which first results in conversion to int, and then to a single byte character.

Explicit type conversion is discussed in §12.7.2.3.

12.4.2 Lvalue

An lvalue is an object to which an assignment can be made.

12.4.3 Scope

Variables declared at the start of a statement block have scope and life restricted to the block. These variables are called automatic: they are created and initialized whenever the block is entered, and removed as soon as the block is exited. Variables declared outside any statement block have global scope and life; these are called static. Note that Ox assignment of arithmetic types and string type implies copying over the contents from the right-hand side to the left-hand side. Automatic variables of any type can be assigned to variables with broader scope.

12.5 External declarations

> *external-declaration:*
> > enum { *enumerator-list* } ;
> > *specifier*$_{opt}$ const$_{opt}$ decl *ext-variable-decl-list* ;
> > *specifier*$_{opt}$ *function-declaration* ;
> > *specifier*$_{opt}$ *function-definition*
> > inline$_{opt}$ *function-definition*
> > inline$_{opt}$ *member-function-definition*
> > *class-specifier* ;

An Ox program consists of a sequence of external declarations. These either reserve storage for an object, or serve to inform of the existence of objects created elsewhere. Each program must define one function called main, where execution of the program will start.

12.5.1 Enumerations

> enum { *enumerator-list* } ;
>
> *enumerator-list:*
> > *enumerator*
> > *enumerator-list* , *enumerator*
>
> *enumerator:*
> > *identifier*
> > *identifier* = *int-constant-expression*

An enumeration defines a list of integer constants. They do not reserve storage space, but provide a convenient way of centralizing parameters which have a constant value. Members of an enumeration cannot be assigned to, but can occur in a constant expression. By default, the first member will have value 0, and each successive member will have a value of one plus that of the previous member. The value of a member can be set by assigning it a constant integer value. The names of enumerators cannot coincide with names of other objects in the same scope. Enumerator names only exist in the file in which they occur. Enumerations should be placed in header files if they need to be shared between several source files.

Here are some examples with corresponding values:

```
enum { C_FIRST, C_SECOND, C_THIRD };                    // 0,1,2
enum { T_INT, T_DBL=2, T_STR, T_MAT=C_THIRD };   // 0,2,3,2
enum { FLAG0,FLAG1, FLAG2=FLAG1*2, FLAG3=FLAG2*2};//0,1,2,4
enum { T_ERR = 1.0 } ;                                  // error
```

12.5.2 Specifiers

specifier: one of
static
extern

The static specifier restricts the scope of the declared object to the remainder of the file. Although it will exist throughout the program's life, it cannot be seen from other files. In classes (§12.5.6), the static keyword is used with a different meaning. The extern specifier informs the remainder of the file that the object can be accessed, although defined (created) in another file. The extern and static specifiers are mutually exclusive. External declarations are most conveniently placed in header files.

12.5.3 External variable declarations

specifier~opt~ const*~opt~* decl *ext-variable-decl-list* ;

ext-variable-decl-list:
 ext-init-declarator
 ext-variable-decl-list , ext-init-declarator

ext-init-declarator:
 identifier
 identifier = constant-expression
 mat-identifier
 mat-identifier = int-constant-expression

mat-identifier:
 identifier [int-constant-expression] [int-constant-expression]

The static or extern specifier and the const qualifier preceding an external variable declaration list applies to all variables in the list. Each identifier creates space for an object with global lifetime, unless declared extern or const.

A const object must be initialized (unless declared extern) but its value may not be changed thereafter. Unless declared extern, a const object cannot be accessed from other files. If of scalar type (see §12.4.1), a const can appear in a constant-expression.

At the external level of declarations, as treated here, it is possible to specify a matrix size, and initialize that matrix to zero. If an external variable is created without explicit value and without dimensions, it will default to an int with value 0. Here are some examples:

```
decl a, b;                        // default to type int, value 0
enum { AAP, NOOT, MIES, WIM };
const decl ia = NOOT, ib = NOOT + WIM;          // type: int
const decl ma = < NOOT, AAP; 0, 1 >;            // type: matrix
const decl aa = {"tinker", "tailor"};           // type: array
```

```
decl id = ia * (WIM - 1) * MIES + ib;          // type: int
decl da = ia + 0.;                             // type: double
decl mb = <0:3; 4:7; 8:11>;                    // type: matrix
decl ab = { ma, ma};                           // type: array
extern decl elsewhere;              // defined in other file

decl mc[3][3] = 1.5;         // 3 x 3 matrix with values 1.5
decl md[2][1];               // 3 x 1 matrix of zeros

enum { ZUS = id };           // error: id is not const
decl ih = id;                // error: id is not const
decl ia;                     // error: already defined
```

12.5.4 Function declarations

*specifier*_{opt} *function-declaration ;*

extern *string-constant function-declaration ;*

function-declaration:
　　identifier (*argument-type-list*$_{opt}$)

argument-type-list:
　　argument-list , . . .

argument-list:
　　argument
　　argument-list , argument

argument:
　　const$_{opt}$ *identifier*

A function declaration communicates the number of arguments and their types to a
file, so that the function can be called correctly from that file. The actual creation of
the function is done through a function definition (which at the same time declares the
function). A function can be declared many times, but type and number of arguments
must always be identical:

```
test0();                     // function takes no arguments
test1(const a1);                    // one const argument
test2(const a2, a3);       // two arguments, first is const
static test3(a1);         // cannot be used outside this file
extern test4(a1);        // function defined outside this file
print(a1, ...);                 // variable number of arguments
test1(a1);       // error: previous declaration was different
```

The second form, which uses extern *string-constant*, provides dynamic linking
of extension functions (which could be written in C, Pascal, etc.). This feature is not
available on all platforms, and implementation is platform dependent. In the following
example, test5 corresponds to the external function MyCFunc(), located in the dynamic library mydll. If this feature is supported, mydll will be automatically loaded,

and the function imported.

```
extern "mydll,MyCFunc" test5(a1);
```

12.5.5 Function definitions

> *specifier*_{opt} *function-definition*
> `inline`_{opt} *function-definition*
>
> *function-definition:*
> > *identifier* (*argument-type-list*_{opt}) *compound-statement*

A function definition specifies the function header and body, and declares the function so that it can be used in the remainder of the file. A function can be declared many times, but defined only once. Arguments declared `const` cannot be changed inside the function. If the argument is a `const` pointer, the pointer cannot be changed, but what it points to can. An empty argument list indicates that the function takes no arguments at all. The . . . indicates a variable number of arguments; it must have the last position in the header, but cannot be the first.

```
test1(const a1);                        // declaration of test1
print(a1, ...);              // variable number of arguments
test2(const a1, a2)                     // definition of test2
{
    test1(a2);                          // call function test1
    print(a1, 1, 2, "\n");          // at least one argument
    test1(a2, 1);          // error: wrong number of arguments
    a2 = 1;                             // a2 may be changed
    a1 = 1;                             // error: a1 is const
    /* ... */
}
```

All function arguments are passed by value. This means that a copy of the actual object is made. For int, double, matrix and string types the whole object is copied. Any changes to the copy are lost as soon as the function returns. Derived types (see §12.4.1) are accessed through a pointer, and that pointer is passed by value. However, what is pointed to may be changed, and that change will remain in effect after function return. So passing pointers allows a function to make a permanent change to a variable, for examples see §12.7.2.2. It is good practice to label an argument `const` if a function doesn't change the variable. This increases program clarity and enables the compiler to generate more efficient code.

All functions may have a return value, but this return value need not be used by the caller. *If a function does not return a value, its actual return value is undefined.*

12.5.5.1 Variable length argument list

A special library function `va_arglist()` is used to access arguments in the variable argument list. It returns the arguments supplied for the ellipse as an array. An example illustrates:

```
test(const a, ...)
{
    decl i, args = va_arglist();

    for (i = 0; i < sizeof(args); i++)
        print (" vararg ", i, ": ", args[i]);
}
main()
{
    test("tinker", "tailor", "soldier");
}
```

which prints `vararg 0:   tailor vararg 1:   soldier`.

12.5.5.2 Inline function definitions

A function can be defined as `inline`. This instructs the compiler to expand the function body wherever it is called, and tends to be used for very small functions. The compiler may ignore the `inline` instruction. Inline functions can only be defined, not declared. If an inline function is to be shared accross several files, the whole definition must be put in a header file.

12.5.6 Classes

> *class-specifier* ;
>
> *class-specifier:*
> > `class` *identifier base-class$_{opt}$* { *member-list* }
>
> *base-class:*
> > : *identifier*
>
> *member-list:*
> > *member*
> > *member-list member*
>
> *member:*
> > `static`$_{opt}$ `decl` *member-variable-decl-list* ;
> > `static`$_{opt}$ *function-declaration* ;
> > `virtual`$_{opt}$ *function-declaration* ;
>
> *member-variable-decl-list:*
> > *identifier*
> > *member-variable-decl-list* , *identifier*

A class is a collection of data objects combined with functions operating on those objects. Access to data members from outside the class is through member functions:

only member functions can access data directly. All data members are private, and all
function members public, using C++ parlance.

Consider a simple line class, which supports drawing lines from the current cursor
position to the next, and moving the cursor:

```
class Line                          // Line is the class name
{
    decl x, y;                          // two data members
    const decl origin;                  // const data member
    static decl cLines;             // static data member
    Line(const orig);                       // constructor
    moveto(const x, const y);               // move cursor
    lineto(const x, const y);   // draw line and move cursor
    static getcLines();                 // static function
    static setcLines(c);                // static function
};                                  // don't forget the ;
```

All member names within a class must be unique. A class declaration introduces a
type, and can be shared between source files through inclusion in header files. Ox accesses an object through a pointer to the object which is created using the new operator.
Data members cannot be initialized in the class, but can in the constructor function, see
§12.5.7.1.

12.5.7 Member function definitions

inline_{opt} *member-function-definition*

member-function-definition:
    identifier : : *identifier* (*argument-type-list_{opt}*) *compound-statement*

A member function provides access to data members of an object. It is defined as its
class name, followed by : : and the function name. The function name must have been
declared in the class. Member functions cannot be declared outside a class; the class
declaration contains the member function declaration. Only a member function can use
data members of its own class directly.

Here are the definitions of the member functions of class Line:

```
Line::Line(const orig)
{
    x = y = orig;                   // set cursor at the origin
    origin = orig;                  // only allowed in constructor
    cLines++;                       // count number of Line objects
}
Line::moveto(const ax, const ay)
{
    x = ax;   y = ay;
    print("moved to ", ax, " ", ay, "\n");
    return this;
}
Line::lineto(const ax, const ay)
{
```

```
                    // draw the line from (x,y) to (ax,ay) ...
    x = ax;   y = ay;
    print("line to ", ax, " ", ay, "\n");
    return this;
}
```

The new operator creates an object of the specified class, calls the constructor function, and returns a pointer to it. A member function is called through a member reference. For example:

```
decl lineobj;
lineobj = new Line(0);                      // create object and
                                            // set cursor to (0,0)
lineobj->lineto(10, 10);                 // draw line to (10, 10)
lineobj->Line::lineto(10, 10);                  // same call
lineobj::lineto(10, 10);                     // error, needs ->

    delete lineobj;      // delete object from memory when done
```

Since lineobj is of class Line, both calls to lineto are to the same function. The only difference is one of efficiency. Ox has implicit typing, so can only know the class of lineobj at run time. In the second case the class is specified, and the function address can be resolved at compile time.

12.5.7.1 Constructor and destructor functions

The member function with the same name as the class is called the constructor, and is automatically invoked when creating an object of the class. If the constructor function is absent, a default constructor function will be assumed which takes no arguments. A constructor may not be static. A constructor always returns a pointer to the object for which it was called and may not specify a return value. Only the constructor function may set const data members. In the Line class, the origin is only set during construction, and not thereafter. However, each Line object has its own origin (unless origin is made static).

A destructor is called after a request to delete an object, and before the object is actually removed. It may be used to clear up any allocated objects inside the object to be deleted. A destructor function has the same name as the class, is prefixed by ~, and may neither take arguments, nor return a value. It does however receive the this pointer.

```
class Line
{   /* ... */
    Line(const orig);                           // constructor
    ~Line();                                    // destructor
    /* ... */
};
test()
{
    decl lineobj;

    lineobj = new Line(0);//create object, call constructor
```

```
        delete lineobj;         // call destructor, delete object
    }
```

12.5.7.2 The this pointer and member scope

All non-static member functions receive a hidden argument called this, which points
to the object for which the function is called. So the constructor function Line obtains
in this a pointer to the newly created object. The assignment to x and y refer to the
members of the this object. When accessing a variable in a member function, it is
determined first whether the function is a local variable or an argument. Next it is considered as a member of this. If all these fail, it is considered as a global variable. So
local variables and arguments hide members, together these hide global variables. The
following example shows how the scope resolution operator : : may be used to resolve
conflicts:

```
    decl x, y;                          // global variables
    extern moveto(x, y);                // external function

    Line::moveto(const x, const y)
    {
        ::x = x;            // assign arguments to global variables
        ::y = y;
        this->x = x;           // assign arguments to data members
        this->y = y;

        ::moveto(x, y);             // call non-member function
        moveto(x, y);           // error: call to itself will
    }                                   // cause infinite loop
```

12.5.7.3 Static members

There is only one copy of a static member, shared by all objects of a class. A static
member may not have the same name as the class it is in. A static member function
can only make direct access to static data members.

```
    Line::getcLines()
    {   return cLines;
    }
    Line::setcLines(c)
    {   cLines = c;
        x = 0;                  // error: must be static member
        lineto(1, 1);           // error: must be static member
    }
```

A static member function can be called directly, and indirectly:

```
    Line::setcLines(0);                 // no Line objects yet
    lineobj = new Line(0);                  // create object
    lineobj2 = new Line(3);             // create another object
    i = Line::getcLines();                      // i = 2
    i = lineobj->getcLines();                   // i = 2
```

```
i = lineobj2->getcLines();                              // i = 2
Line::moveto(0, 0);           // error: function is not static
Line->getcLines();                            // error, needs ::
```

Since there is only one instance of the static function, in all cases the same `getcLines` function is called (assuming both `lineobj` and `lineobj2` are an object of class `Line`).

12.5.7.4 Derived classes

A class may derive from a previously declared class. A derived class will inherit all members from its base class, and can access these inherited members as its own members. However, if the derived class has members with the same name as members of the base class, the former take precedence. In this way, a class can redefine functionality of its base class. If a function is redefined, the base class name followed by : : may be used to refer to the base class function.

Deriving from the `Line` class:

```
class Angle : Line              // Line is the base class
{
    Angle();                                    // constructor
    lineto(const x, const y);    // draw dash, move cursor
};
Angle::Angle()
{
    Line(0);                                    // starts at zero
}
Angle::lineto(const ax, const ay)
{
    Line::lineto(ax, y);                        // horizontal line
    Line::lineto(ax, ay);                       // vertical line
    print("is angle to ", ax, " ", ay, "\n");
    moveto(ax, ay);
}
```

`Angle`'s constructor just calls the base class constructor, as the body may be read as `this->Line(0);`. Note that the base class constructor and destructor functions are *not* called automatically (unlike in C++). In the new `lineto` object, `Line::lineto` is used to make sure that we call the correct function (otherwise it would make a recursive call). For the `moveto` that is no problem, `moveto` calls the base function, as it was not redefined in the `Angle` class. Non-static member functions may be declared as virtual (that is, they can be redefined by a derived class), this is discussed in the next section.

New classes may be derived from a class which is itself derived, but Ox only supports single inheritance: a class can only derive from one other class at a time.

12.5.7.5 Virtual functions

Virtual functions allow a derived class to supply a new version of the virtual function in the derived class, replacing the version of the base class. When the base class calls the virtual function, it will actually use the function of the derived class. For a virtual function, the call can only be resolved at run time. Then, the object type is known, and the called function is the one first found in the object, when moving from the highest class towards the base class. The effect of using virtual functions is most easily explained by the following example.

```
#include <oxstd.h>

class Base
{
    basefunc();
    virtual vfunc();
};
Base::basefunc()
{
    vfunc();                            // call the virtual function
}
Base::vfunc()
{   print("Base vfunc()\n");
}

class Derived : Base
{
    derfunc();
    vfunc();
};
Derived::derfunc()
{
    this->Base::basefunc();
    Base::basefunc();
    basefunc();                         // three equivalent calls
}
Derived::vfunc()
{   print("Derived vfunc()\n");
}

main()
{
    decl obj = new Derived();
    obj->basefunc();
    obj->derfunc();
}
```

The output is:

```
Derived vfunc()
Derived vfunc()
Derived vfunc()
Derived vfunc()
```

Even though Base has its own vfunc(), the derived class provides a new version of this function. This is used whenever Basefunc() is called for an object of class Derived. Were we to remove the virtual keyword, the output would be four times `Base vfunc()`. If we replace `vfunc()` with `Base::vfunc()` inside `Base::basefunc`, the result would also be four times `vfunc()` from `Base`.

12.6 Statements

statement-list:
> *statement*
> *statement-list statement*

statement:
> *labelled-statement*
> *expression-statement*
> *compound-statement*
> *selection-statement*
> *iteration-statement*
> *jump-statement*
> *declaration-statement*

expression-statement:
> *expression$_{opt}$* ;

compound-statement:
> { statement-list$_{opt}$ }

labelled-statement:
> : *label statement*

The executable part of a program consists of a sequence of statements. Expression statements are expressions or function calls. It can be a do-nothing expression, as in:

```
for (i = 0; i < 10; i++)
    ;
```

A compound statement groups statements together in a block, e.g.:

```
for (i = 0; i < 10; i++)
{
    a = test(b);
    b = b + 10;
}
```

A statement can be prefixed by a label as in:

```
:L001
    for (i = 0; i < 10; i++)
        ;
```

Labels are the targets of `goto` statements (see §12.6.3); labels are local to a function and have separate name spaces (which means that variables and labels may have the same name). Note that labels are defined in a non-standard way: the colon is prefixed, rather than suffixed as in C or C++.

12.6.1 Selection statements

> *selection-statement:*
> > if (*expression*) *statement*
> > if (*expression*) *statement* else *statement*

The conditional expression in an if statement is evaluated, and if it is nonzero (*for a matrix: no element is zero*), the statement is executed. The conditional expression may not be a declaration statement. Some examples for the if statement:

```
if (i == 0)
    i++;                                // do only if i equals 0

if (i >= 0)
    i = 1;                              // do only if i >= 0
else
    i = 0;                              // set negative i to 0

if (i == 0)
    if (k > 0)
        j = 1;                          // do only if i != 0 and k > 0
    else                        // this else matches the inner if
        j = -1;                 // do only if i != 0 and k <= 0

if (i == 0)
{   if (k > 0)
        j = 1;                          // do only if i != 0 and k > 0
}
else                            // this else matches the outer if
    j = -1;                             // do only if i != 0
```

Each else part matches the closest previous if, but this can be changed by using braces. When coding nested ifs, it is advisable to use braces to make the program more readable and avoid potential mistakes.

Further examples involving matrices are given in §12.7.9.

12.6.2 Iteration statements

> *iteration-statement:*
> > while (*expression*) *statement*
> > do *statement* while (*expression*) ;
> > for (*expression*$_{opt}$; *expression*$_{opt}$; *expression*$_{opt}$) *statement*

The while statement excutes the substatement as long as the test expression is nonzero (for a matrix: at least one element is nonzero). The test is performed before the substatement is executed.

The do statement excutes the substatement, then repeats this as long as the test expression is nonzero (for a matrix: at least one element is nonzero). The test is performed after the substatement is executed. So for the do statement the substatement is executed one or more times, whereas for the while statement this is zero or more times.

The while and do statements can be envisaged respectively as:

```
:startwhile                          :startdo
    if (expression)                      statement
    {                                    if (expression)
        statement                            goto startdo;
        goto startwhile;
    }
```

The for expression:

```
for (init_expr; test_expr ; increment_expr) statement
```

corresponds to:

```
init_expr;
while (test_expr )
{
    statement
    increment_expr;
}
```

Note that, unlike C++, the *init_expr* cannot be preceded by a declaration.

12.6.3 Jump statements

jump-statement:
        break ;
        continue ;
        goto *label;*

A continue statement may only appear within an iteration statement and causes control to pass to the loop-continuation portion of the smallest enclosing iteration statement.

The use of goto should be kept to a minimum, but could be useful to jump out of a nested loop, jump to the end of a routine or when converting Fortran code. It is always possible to rewrite the code such that no gotos are required.

A break statement may only appear within an iteration statement and terminates the smallest enclosing iteration statement.

Two examples:

```
for (i = 0; i < 10; i++)
{
    if (test1(i))
        continue;
    test2();                  // only done if test1(i) returns 0
}
for (i = 0; i < 10; i++)
{
    if (test1(i) == 0)
```

```
            break;      // jump out of loop if test1(i) returns 0
        test2();
    }
```

12.6.4 Declaration statements

> *declaration-statement:*
>   decl *declaration-list* ;
>
> *declaration-list:*
>   *init-declaration*
>   *declaration-list* , *init-declaration*
>
> *declaration-list:*
>   *identifier*
>   *identifier = expression*

Declarations at the external level were discussed in §12.5. Here we treat declaration within a block. Declaration statements create a variable for further manipulation as long as it stays within scope. The created object is removed as soon as the block in which it was created is exited. Variables can be intitialized in a declaration statement. Variables in Ox are implicitly typed, and their type can change during program execution. Non-externally declared variables must be initialized before they can be used in an expression. It is not possible to specify matrix dimension as can be done at the external level, so instead of decl ma[3][3] = 1.5 write decl ma = constant(1.5,3,3). Unlike C, declaration statements do not have to occur at the start of a block. Consider for example:

```
test1(arg0)
{
    decl k, a = arg0;
    decl ident = <1, 0; 0, 1>;
    decl identsq = ident * ident;

    print("test\n");

    decl i, j;
    for (i = 0; i < 10; i++)
    {
        test2(i);
        test3(j);                   // error: j has no value
    }
```

Variables declared in an inner block hide variables in the outer block:

```
decl i = 3;                         // external declaration

test2(a)
{
    print(i, "\n");                 // 3
```

```
{   decl i = 0;
    print(i, "\n");                          // 0
    if (i == 0)                         // is true
    {
        decl i = 1;
        print(i, "\n");                      // 1
        print(::i, "\n");                    // 3
    }
    decl a;            // error: conflict with argument
}
```

12.7 Expressions

Table 12.1   Ox operator precedence.

Category	operators	associativity
primary	( ) ::	left to right
postfix	-> ( ) [] ++ -- '	left to right
unary	++ -- + - ! & new delete	right to left
power	^ .^	left to right
multiplicative	** * .* / ./	left to right
additive	+ -	left to right
horizontal concatenation	~	left to right
vertical concatenation	|	left to right
relational	< > <= >= .< .> .<= .>=	left to right
equality	== != .== .!=	left to right
logical dot-and	.&&	left to right
logical-and	&&	left to right
logical dot-or	.||	left to right
logical-or	||	left to right
conditional	? : .? .:	right to left
assignment	= *= /= += -= ~= |=	right to left
comma	,	left to right

Table 12.1 gives a summary if the operators available in Ox, together with their precedence (in order of decreasing precedence) and associativity. The precedence is in decreasing order. Operators on the same line have the same precedence, in which case the associativity gives the order of the operators. Note that the order of evaluation of expressions is not fully specified. In:

```
i = a() + b();
```
it is unknown whether a or b is called first.

Subsections below give a more comprehensive discussion. Several operators require an *lvalue*, which is a region of memory to which an assignment can be made. Note that an object which was declared const is not an lvalue. Many operators require operands of arithmetic type, that is int, double or matrix.

The most common operators are *dot-operators* (operating element-by-element) and relational operators (operating element by element, but returning a single boolean value). The resulting value is given Tables 12.2 and 12.3 respectively. In addition, there are special matrix operations, such as matrix multiplication and division; the result from these operators is explained below.

Table 12.2   Result from dot operators.

left a	operator	right b	result	computes
int	*op*	int	int	a *op* b
int/double	*op*	double	double	a *op* b
double	*op*	int/double	double	a *op* b
int/double	*op*	matrix $m \times n$	matrix $m \times n$	a *op* b_{ij}
matrix $m \times n$	*op*	int/double	matrix $m \times n$	a_{ij} *op* b
matrix $m \times n$	*op*	matrix $m \times n$	matrix $m \times n$	a_{ij} *op* b_{ij}
matrix $m \times n$	*op*	matrix $m \times 1$	matrix $m \times n$	a_{ij} *op* b_{i0}
matrix $m \times n$	*op*	matrix $1 \times n$	matrix $m \times n$	a_{ij} *op* b_{0j}
matrix $m \times 1$	*op*	matrix $m \times n$	matrix $m \times n$	a_{i0} *op* b_{ij}
matrix $1 \times n$	*op*	matrix $m \times n$	matrix $m \times n$	a_{0j} *op* b_{ij}
matrix $m \times 1$	*op*	matrix $1 \times n$	matrix $m \times n$	a_{i0} *op* b_{0j}
matrix $1 \times n$	*op*	matrix $m \times 1$	matrix $m \times n$	a_{0j} *op* b_{i0}
matrix $m \times n$	*op*	matrix 1×1	matrix $m \times n$	a_{ij} *op* b_{00}
matrix 1×1	*op*	matrix $m \times n$	matrix $m \times n$	a_{00} *op* b_{ij}

12.7.1 Primary expressions

> *primary-expression:*
>   (*expression*)
>   *constant*
>   *identifier*
>   : : *identifier*
>   *class-name* : : *identifier*
>   `this`

Table 12.3   Result from relational operators.

left a	operator	right b	result	computes
int	*op*	int	int	a *op* b
int/double	*op*	double	int	a *op* b
double	*op*	int/double	int	a *op* b
int/double	*op*	matrix $m \times n$	int	a *op* b_{ij}
matrix $m \times n$	*op*	int/double	int	a_{ij} *op* b
matrix $m \times n$	*op*	matrix $m \times n$	int	a_{ij} *op* b_{ij}
matrix $m \times n$	*op*	matrix $m \times 1$	int	a_{ij} *op* b_{i0}
matrix $m \times n$	*op*	matrix $1 \times n$	int	a_{ij} *op* b_{0j}
matrix $m \times 1$	*op*	matrix $m \times n$	int	a_{i0} *op* b_{ij}
matrix $1 \times n$	*op*	matrix $m \times n$	int	a_{0j} *op* b_{ij}
string	*op*	string	int	a *op* b

An expression in parenthesis is a primary expression. Its main use is to change the order of evaluation, or clarify the expression.

All types of constants discussed in §12.3.2 form a primary expression.

The operator : : followed by an identifier references a variable declared externally (see §12.5). Section 12.5.7.2 gives examples. A class name followed by : : and a function member of that class references a static function member, or any function member if preceded by an object pointer, see sections 12.5.7.3 and 12.5.7.

The this pointer is only available inside non-static class member functions, and points to the object for which the function was called.

12.7.2 Postfix expressions

postfix-expression:
  primary-expression
  postfix-expression ->
  postfix-expression (*expression-list$_{opt}$*)
  postfix-expression [*index-expression$_{opt}$*]
  postfix-expression ++
  postfix-expression − −
  postfix-expression '

expression-list:
  assignment-expression
  expression-list , *assignment-expression*

12.7.2.1 Member reference

The -> operator selects a member from an object pointer. The left-hand expression must evaluate to a pointer to an object, the right-hand expression must result in a member of that object. See section 12.5.6.

12.7.2.2 Function calls

A function call is a postfix expression consisting of the function name, followed in parenthesis by a possibly empty, comma-separated list of assignment expressions. All argument passing is by value, but when an array is passed, its contents may be changed by the function (unless they are const). The order of evaluation of the arguments is unspecified; all arguments are evaluated before the function is entered. Recursive function calls are allowed. A function must be declared before it can be called, and the number of arguments in the call must coincide with the number in the declaration, unless the declaration has . . . as the last argument, see §12.5.4.

Some examples:

```
func1(a0, a1, a2, a3)
{    print("func1(", a0, ",", a1, ",", a2, ",", a3, ")\n");
}
func2()
{    return 0;
}
func3(a0)
{    a0[0] = 1;
}
test1()
{    decl a, b;

     a = 1;
     func1(a, b = 10, func2(), a != 0);    // func1(1,10,0,1)
     a = func2();                           // a = 0
     func3(&a);                             // a = 1
     func3(a);                              // error
}
```

In the latter example a will have been changed by func3. Function arguments are passed by giving the name of the function:

```
func4(a0, a1)
{    a1(a0);                               // make function call
}
func5(a0)
{    print("func5(", a0, ")\n");
}
test2()
{    decl a = func5;

     func4(1, func5);                      // prints "func5(1)"
     func4(1, a);                          // prints "func5(1)"
```

```
    func4(1, func5(a));          // error: requires function
    func4(1, func2);             // error: func2 takes incorrect
}                                //            number of arguments
```

Note that the parentheses in `func5()` indicate that it is a function call, whereas lack of brackets just passes the function itself.

12.7.2.3 Explicit type conversion

Explicit type conversion has the same syntax as a function call, using types `int`, `double`, `matrix` and `string`:

	int	double	matrix	string
	v=0;	v=0.6;	v=<0.6,1>;	v="tinker";
matrix(v)	< 0 >	< 0.6 >	v	< 97 >
double(v)	0.0	v	0.6	see below
int(v)	v	0	0	97

Use `double("tinker")` to store the string in a double value. Since a double is 8 bytes, the string is truncated at 8 characters (or padded by null characters). Conversely, `string(dbl)` extracts the string from a double value `dbl` (a null character is automatically appended). Storing strings in doubles or matrix elements is better avoided: more flexibility is offered by the string type.

12.7.2.4 Indexing vector and array types

Vector types (that is, string or matrix) and array types are indexed by postfixing square brackets. A matrix must always have two indexes, a string only one. For an array type it depends on the level of indirection. *Note that indexing always starts at zero.*[1] So a 2 × 3 matrix has elements:

```
[0][0]   [0][1]   [0][2]
[1][0]   [1][1]   [1][2]
```

Three ways of indexing are distinguished:

indexing type	matrix, string	array	example
scalar	√	√	m[0][0]
matrix	√		m[0][<0,1,2>]
range	√		m[][1:]

In the first indexing case (allowed for all non-scalar types), the expression inside square brackets must have scalar type, whereby double is converted to integer.

Vector types may also be indexed by a matrix or have a range expression inside the brackets. In a matrix index to a string the first *column* of the matrix specifies the selected elements of the string.

---

[1] But see §12.8.3 for the option to change that.

If a matrix is used as an index to a matrix, then each element (row by row, i.e. the vecr of the argument) is used as an index. As a consequence, indexing by a column vector or its transpose (a row vector) have the same effect. A matrix in the first index selects rows, a matrix in the second index selects columns. The resulting matrix is the intersection of those rows and columns.

A range index has the form *start-index* : *end-index*. Either the start-index or the end-index may be missing, which results in the lower-bound or upper-bound being used respectively. An empty index selects all elements. The resulting type from a range or empty index is always a vector type.

Some examples:

```
decl mat = < 0:3; 10:13 >, d, m;
decl str = "tinkertailor", s;
decl arr = { "tinker", "tailor", "soldier" };

                                // mat = <0,1,2,3; 10,11,12,13>
d = mat[0][0];                                        // d = 0
d = mat[1][2];                                        // d = 12
m = mat[1][];                              // m = <10,11,12,13>
m = mat[][2];                                    // m = <2; 12>
m = mat[][];                              // same as: m = mat;
m = mat[0][<1:3>];    // matrix indexes columns: m = <1,2,3>
m = mat[<1,0,1>][<1,3>];        // m = < 11,13; 1,3; 11,13 >
mat[0][1:3] = 9;                     // range indexes columns:
                                // mat = <0,9,9,9; 10,11,12,13>
s = str[6:11];                                 // s = "tailor"
str[6:11] = 'a';                       // str = "tinkeraaaaaa"
s = arr[1];                                    // s = "tailor"
arr[1][0] = 'a';                          // arr[1] = "aailor"
```

12.7.2.5 Postfix incrementation

A postfix expression followed by ++ or -- leads to the value of the expression being evaluated and then incremented or decremented by 1. The operand must be an lvalue and must have arithmetic type. For a matrix the operator is applied to each element separately. The result of the expression is the value prior to the increment/decrement operation.

```
decl mat = < 0:3; 10:13 >, m, i, j;
decl str = "tinkertailor", s;

j = 0;
i = j++;                                       // i = 0, j = 1
m = mat++;                  // mat = <1,2,3,4; 11,12,13,14>
                           // m   = <0,1,2,3; 10,11,12,13>
str[0]++;                          // str = "uinkertailor"
str++;                                              // error
```

12.7.2.6 Transpose

The postfix operator ′ takes the transpose of a matrix. It has no effect on other arithmetic types of operands. Note the following translations:

′ *identifier*	into	′	* *identifier*
′ (	into	′	* (
′ this	into	′	* this

Some care is required when using variable names consisting of one character, in case the expression can be interpreted as a character constant:

```
mat = m' * a';
mat = m' a';                    // interpreted as m' * a'
mat = m'';                      // two '' cancel out
mat = m'a';  // error: 'a' is character constant, use m' a'
```

12.7.3 Unary expressions

> *unary-expression:*
>> *postfix-expression*
>> ++ *unary-expression*
>> −− *unary-expression*
>> + *unary-expression*
>> − *unary-expression*
>> ! *unary-expression*
>> & *unary-expression*
>> new *class-name* (*expression-list*)
>> new matrix [*expression-list*] [*expression-list*]
>> new string [*expression-list*]
>> new array [*expression-list*]
>> delete *unary-expression*

12.7.3.1 Prefix incrementation

A prefix expression preceded by ++ or −− leads to the lvalue being incremented or decremented by 1. This new value is the result of the operation. The operand must be an lvalue and must have arithmetic type. For a matrix the operator is applied to each element separately.

```
j = 0;
i = ++j;                              // i = 1, j = 1
```

12.7.3.2 Unary minus and plus

The operand of the unary minus operator must have arithmetic type, and the result is the negative of the operand. For a matrix each element is set to its negative. Unary plus is ignored.

12.7.3.3 Logical negation

The operand of the logical negation operator must have arithmetic type, and the result is
1 if the operand is equal to 0 and 0 otherwise. For a matrix, logical negation is applied
to each element.

```
j = 0;   k = 10;
i = !j;                                          // i = 1
i = !k;                                          // i = 0
```

12.7.3.4 Address operator

The operand of the address operator & must be an lvalue. In addition, it must be an object: it is possible to take the address of a class object or a function, but not of an array
element, or matrix element. The result is an array of one element, pointing to the region
of space occupied by the lvalue. Ox's limited pointer support works through arrays, the
C indirection operator * is not supported.

```
test5(const arrstring)
{
    arrstring[0][0] = 'x';
}
test6(astring)
{
    astring[0] = 'a';
}
test4()
{
    decl a, str = "spy";

    a = &str;
    a[0][0]--;                                   // str="rpy"
    test5(&str);                                 // str="xpy"
    test6(str);                                  // str unchanged
}
```

12.7.3.5 New and delete

The new operator can be used to create an object of a class, or to create a matrix, string
or array. The delete operator removes an object created by new. Note that matrices,
strings and arrays are automatically removed when they go out of scope. Only one array
level at a time can be created by new; however, delete removes all sublevels. A string
created by new consists of null characters, a matrix will have all elements zero.

```
decl i, m1, a1;

m1 = new matrix[2][2];                           // m1 = <0,0; 0,0>
```

```
m1[0][0] = 1;

delete m1;
a1 = m1[0][0];                    // error: contents of m1 deleted

a1 = new array[3];

for (i = 0; i < sizeof(a1); i++)
{
    a1[i] = new string[3];
    a1[i][0] = 'a' + i;
    a1[i][1] = '0' + i;
}
```

The a1 variable has the following structure:

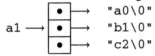

al $\longrightarrow$ "a0\0"
         "b1\0"
         "c2\0"

Examples involving objects of classes are given in §12.5.6.

12.7.4 Power expressions

> *power-expression:*
> > *unary-expression*
> > *power-expression ^ unary-expression*
> > *power-expression . ^ unary-expression*

The operands of the power operator must have arithmetic type, and the result is given in the table. If the first operand is not a matrix . ^ and ^ are the same.

left a	operator		right b	result	computes
int	^	. ^	int or double	int	a^b
int/double	^	. ^	double	double	a^b
double	^	. ^	int/double	double	a^b
int/double	^	. ^	matrix $m \times n$	matrix $m \times n$	$a^{b_{ij}}$
matrix $m \times n$		. ^	int/double	matrix $m \times n$	a_{ij}^b
matrix $m \times n$		. ^	matrix $m \times n$	matrix $m \times n$	$a_{ij}^{b_{ij}}$
matrix $m \times m$	^		int/double	matrix $m \times m$	a^b

When a and b are integers, then a ^ b is an integer if $b \geq 0$ and if the result can be represented as a 32 bit signed integer. If $b < 0$ and $a! = 0$ or the integer result would lead to overflow, the return type is double, giving the outcome of the floating point power operation.

The second line in the example shows that unary minus has higher precedence than the power operator:

```
i = 1 - 2 ^ 3;                                        // i = -7
i = 1 - - 2 ^ 3;                                      // i = 9
decl r, m1 = <1,2; 2,1>, m2 = <2,3; 3,2>;
r = m1 .^ 3;                                  // <1,8; 8,1>
r = m1 .^ 3.7;                        // <1,12.996; 12.996,1>
r = 3 .^ m1;                                  // <3,9; 9,3>
r = 3 ^  m1;                                  // <3,9; 9,3>
r = m1 .^ m2;                                 // <1,8; 8,1>
r = m1 ^  3;                              // <13,14; 14,13>
r = m1 ^  3.7;                            // <13,14; 14,13>
r = m1 ^  -3;              // equivalent to: r = (1 / m1) ^ 3;
r = m1 ^  m2;                                    // error
```

The following code prints 14 zero matrices of dimension 2×2:

```
decl i, ma, m1 = <1,2; 2,1>;

for (i = 0, ma = <1,0; 0,1>; i <= 13; i++, ma *= m1)
    print("i = ", i, ma - m1^i);
```

12.7.5 Multiplicative expressions

> *multiplicative-expression:*
> > *power-expression*
> > *multiplicative-expression* * * *power-expression*
> > *multiplicative-expression* * *power-expression*
> > *multiplicative-expression* . * *power-expression*
> > *multiplicative-expression* / *power-expression*
> > *multiplicative-expression* . / *power-expression*

The operators **, *, .*, /, and ./ group left-to-right and require operands of arithmetic type. These operators conform to Table 12.2, except for:

left a	operator	right b	result	computes
matrix $m \times n$	*	matrix $n \times p$	matrix $m \times p$	$a_{i.}b_{.k}$
matrix $m \times n$	**	matrix $p \times q$	matrix $mn \times nq$	$a_{ij}b$
matrix $m \times n$	/	matrix $p \times n$	matrix $p \times m$	$a_{i.}b_{.k}^+$
int/double	/	matrix $m \times n$	matrix $n \times m$	ab_{ij}^+
int/double	/ ./	int/double	double	a/b

This implies that * ** are the same as .* when one or both arguments are scalar, and similarly for / and verb./ when the right-hand operand is not a matrix.

Kronecker product is denoted by **. If neither operand is a matrix, this is identical to normal multiplication.

The binary * operator denotes multiplication. If both operands are a matrix, this is matrix multiplication and the number of columns of the first operand has to be identical to the number of rows of the second operand. The .* operator defines element by element multiplication. It is only different from * if both operands are a matrix (these must have identical dimensions). The product of two integers remains an integer. This means that overflow could occur (when it would not occur in operations where one of the argument is a double). For example 5000 * 50000 fits in an integer and yields 250 000 000, but 50000 * 50000 overflows, yielding −1.794 967 296. When using double arithmetic: 50000.0 * 50000 = 2500 000 000.0.

The binary / operator denotes division. If the second operand is a matrix, this is identical to post-multiplication by the inverse (if the matrix is square the matrix is inverted using the invert() library function; if that fails, or the matrix is non-square, the generalized inverse is used, see §12.7.5.1). The ./ operator defines element by element division. If either argument is not a matrix, this is identical to normal division. It is only different from / if both operands are a matrix (these must have identical dimensions).

Note that / does not support integer division (such as e.g. 3/2 resulting in 1). In Ox, the result of dividing two integers is a double (3/2 gives 1.5). Integer division can be performed using the idiv library function. The remainder operator (% in C and C++) is supported through the library function imod. Multiplication of two integers returns an integer.

Some examples of multiplication and division involving matrices:

```
decl m1 = <1,2; 2,1>, m2 = <2,3; 3,2>;

r = m1 * 2.;                                      // <2,4; 4,2>
r = 2. * m2;                                      // <4,6; 6,4>
r = m1 * m2;                                      // <8,7; 7,8>
r = m1 .* m2;                                     // <2,6; 6,2>
r = m1 .* <2,3>;                                  // <2,6;6,2>
r = m1 ** m2;      // <2,3,4,6; 3,2,6,4; 4,6,2,3; 6,4,3,2>
r = 2 / 3;                                        // 0.666667
r = 2 / 3.;                                       // 0.666667
r = m1 / 2.;                             // <0.5,1; 1,0.5>
r = m1 ./ <2;3>;                // <0.5,1; 0.666667,0.333333>
r = 2./ m2;                       // <0.8,1.2; 1.2,-0.8>
r = 2 ./ m2;                  // <1,0.666667; 0.666667,1>
r = m2 / m2;                  // <1,-2.22045e-016; 0,1>

r = 1/<1;2>;                                      // <0.2,0.4>
r = 1/<1,2>;                                      // <0.2; 0.4>
r = 1/<0,0;0,0>;                                  // <0,0; 0,0>
```

Notice the difference between 2./ m2 and 2 ./ m2. In the first case, the dot is interpreted as part of the real number 2., whereas in the second case it is part of the ./ dot-division operator. The white space is used here to change the syntax (as in the example in §12.7.2.6); it would be more clear to write the second case as 2.0 ./ m2. The same difference applies for dot-multiplication, but note that 2.0*m2 and 2.0.*m2 give the same result.

12.7.5.1 Generalized inverse

The $n \times m$ generalized inverse A^+ of an $m \times n$ matrix A is determined using the singular value decomposition:

$$A = UWV',$$

with:

U is $m \times n$ and $U'U = I_n$,
W is $r \times n$ and diagonal, with non-negative diagonal elements w_i,
V is $n \times n$ and $V'V = I_n$.

The generalized inverse A^+ is computed as:

$$A^+ = VW^+U',$$

where the diagonal elements of W^+ are given by:

$$w_i^{-1} = \begin{cases} 1/w_i & \text{if } w_i > 10\epsilon_{inv}||A||_\infty, \\ 0 & \text{otherwise.} \end{cases}$$

The rank of A is the number of non-zero w_i. The inversion epsilon, ϵ_{inv}, is set by the inverteps function. By default $\epsilon_{inv} = 1000\epsilon_m$, where ϵ_m is the machine precision for doubles ($\approx 2 \times 10^{-16}$) and

$$||A||_\infty = \max_{0 \le i < m} \sum_{j=0}^{n-1} |a_{ij}|.$$

When $n > m$ the singular value decomposition is applied to A' to avoid a large V matrix:

$$A^+ = UW^+V',$$

where U and V derive from $A' = UWV'$.

Note that the generalized inverse of a square non-singular matrix corresponds to the normal inverse. The generalized inverse of a matrix consisting of zeros only is a matrix of zeros. This follows from the four Moore-Penrose conditions for A^+:

$$AA^+A = A, \; A^+AA^+ = A^+, \; \left(AA^+\right)' = AA^+, \; \left(A^+A\right)' = A^+A.$$

12.7.6 Additive expressions

additive-expression:
    multiplicative-expression
    additive-expression + multiplicative-expression
    additive-expression – multiplicative-expression

The additive operators + and − are dot-operators, conforming to Table 12.2. Both operators group left-to-right. They respectively return the sum and the difference of the operands, which must both have arithmetic type. Matrices must be conformant in both dimensions, and the operator is applied element by element. For example:

```
decl m1 = <1,2; 2,1>, m2 = <2,3; 3,2>;

r = 2 - m2;                                      // <0,-1; -1,0>
r = m1 - m2;                                     // <-1,-1; -1,-1>
```

12.7.7 Concatenation expressions

horizontal-concatenation-expression:
    additive-expression
    horizontal-concatenation-expression ˜ additive-expression

vertical-concat-expression:
    horizontal-concatenation-expression
    vertical-concat-expression | horizontal-concatenation-expression

left	operator	right	result
int/double	˜	int/double	matrix 1×2
int/double	˜	matrix $m \times n$	matrix $m \times (1 + n)$
matrix $m \times n$	˜	int/double	matrix $m \times (n + 1)$
matrix $m \times n$	˜	matrix $p \times q$	matrix $\max(m, p) \times (n + q)$
int/double			int/double	matrix 2×1
int/double			matrix $m \times n$	matrix $(1 + m) \times n$
matrix $m \times n$			int/double	matrix $(m + 1) \times n$
matrix $m \times n$			matrix $p \times q$	matrix $(m + p) \times \max(n, q)$
int	˜			string	string
string	˜			int	string
string	˜			string	string
array	˜			array	array

If both operands have arithmetic type, the concatenation operators are used to create a larger matrix out of the operands. If both operands are scalar the result is a row vector (for ˜) or a column vector (for |). If one operand is scalar, and the other a matrix, an extra column (˜) or row (|) is pre/appended. If both operands are a matrix, the matrices are joined. Note that the dimensions need not match: missing elements are set to zero. Horizontal concatenation has higher precedence than vertical concatenation.

Two strings or an integer and a string can be concatenated, resulting in a longer string. Both horizontal and vertical concatenation yield the same result.

The result is most easily demonstrated by examples:

```
print(1 ~ 2 ~ 3 | 4 ~ 5 ~ 6);              // <1,2,3; 4,5,6>
print("tinker" ~ '&' ~ "tailor" );         // "tinker&tailor"
print(<1,0; 0,1> ~ 2);                      // <1,0,2; 0,1,2>
print(2 | <1,0; 0,1>);                      // <2,2; 1,0; 0,1>
print(<2> ~ <1,0; 0,1>);                    // <2,1,0; 0,0,1>
```

The first two lines could have been written as:

```
print(<1,2,3; 4,5,6>);
print("tinker" "&" "tailor" );
```

In the latter case, the matrix and string are created at compile time, whereas in the former case this is done at run time. Clearly, the compile time evaluation is more efficient. However, only the concatenation expressions can involve non-constant variables:

```
decl  i1 = 1, i2 = 2, s1 = "tinke";

print(i1 ~ i2);                             // <1,2>
print(s1 ~ 'r');                            // "tinker"
```

Array concatenation results in an array with combined size, with assignment of each member of both arrays to the new array.

```
decl  i, a1 = {"tinker", "tailor"}, a2 = {"soldier"};

a1 ~= a2;
for (i = 0; i < sizeof(a1); i++)
    print(a1[i]);
```

prints `tinkertailorsoldier`.

12.7.8 Relational expressions

> *relational-expression:*
>> *vertical-concat-expression*
>> *relational-expression < vertical-concat-expression*
>> *relational-expression > vertical-concat-expression*
>> *relational-expression <= vertical-concat-expression*
>> *relational-expression >= vertical-concat-expression*
>> *relational-expression . < vertical-concat-expression*
>> *relational-expression . > vertical-concat-expression*
>> *relational-expression . <= vertical-concat-expression*
>> *relational-expression . >= vertical-concat-expression*

The relational operators are <, <=, >, >=, standing for 'less', 'less or equal', 'greater', 'greater or equal'. They all yield 0 if the specified relation is false, and 1 if it is true. The type of the result is always an integer, see Table 12.3. If both operands are a matrix, the return value is true if the relation holds for each element where it is false. If one of the operands is of scalar-type, and the other of matrix-type, each element in the matrix is compared to the scalar, and the result is true if each comparison is true.

The dot relational operators are . <, . <=, . >, . >=, standing for 'dot less', 'dot less or equal', 'dot greater', 'dot greater or equal'. They conform to Table 12.2, except when both arguments are a string, in which case the result is as for the non-dotted versions.

If both arguments are scalar, the result type inherits the higher type, so 1 >= 1.5 yields a double with value 0.0. If both operands are a matrix the return value is a matrix with a 1 in each position where the relation is true and zero where it is false. If one of the operands is of scalar-type, and the other of matrix-type, each element in the matrix is compared to the scalar returning a matrix with 1 at each position where the relation holds.

String-type operands can be compared in a similar way. If both operands are a string, the results is int with value 1 or 0, depending on the case sensitive string comparison.

Examples are given in the next section.

12.7.9 Equality expressions

> *equality-expression:*
> > *relational-expression*
> > *equality-expression* == *relational-expression*
> > *equality-expression* ! = *relational-expression*
> > *equality-expression* . == *relational-expression*
> > *equality-expression* . ! = *relational-expression*

The == (is equal to), ! = (is not equal to), . == (is dot equal to) and . ! = (is not dot equal to) are analogous to the relational operators, but have lower precedence.

The non-dotted versions conform to Table 12.3. The dotted versions conform to Table 12.2, except when both arguments are a string, in which case the result is as for the non-dotted versions.

For example:

```
decl m1 = <1,2; 2,1>, m2 = <2,3; 3,2>, s1 = "tinke";

print(m1 == 1);                        // 0
print(m1 != 1);                        // 0
print(!(m1 == 1));                     // 1
print(m1 > m2);                        // 0
print(m1 < m2);                        // 1
print(s1 <= "tinker");                 // 1
print(s1 <= "tink"  );                 // 0
print(s1 == "tinker");                 // 0
print(s1 >= "tinker");                 // 0
print(s1 == "Tinke");                  // 0

print(m1 .== 1);                       // <1,0; 0,1>
print(m1 .!= 1);                       // <0,1; 1,0>
print(m1 .> m2);                       // <0,0; 0,0>
print(m1 .< m2);                       // <1,1; 1,1>
```

The non-dotted versions only return true if the relation holds for each element. In the first two examples neither m1 == 1 nor m1 != 1 is true for each element, hence the return value 0. The third example shows how to test if a matrix is not equal to a value. The parenthesis are necessary, because ! has higher precedence than ==, and !m1 == 1 results in <0,0; 0,0> == 1 which is false.

The last four examples use dot-relational expressions, resulting in a matrix of zeros and ones. In if statements, it is possible to use such matrices. Remember that a matrix is true if all elements are true (i.e. no element is zero). In the example below, both if (m1 .== 1) and if (m1 .!= 1) result in the else part being executed:

	evaluates to	leads to
if (m1 .== 1)	if (<1,0;0,1>)	else part
if (m1 .!= 1)	if (<0,1;1,0>)	else part
if (m1 == 1)	if (0)	else part
if (m1 != 1)	if (0)	else part

and both have at least one zero, so that both test statements are false. Consider a few more examples, using the matrix m2 = <2 2;2 2>:

	evaluates to	leads to
if (m2 .== 2)	if (<1,1;1,1>)	if part
if (m2 .!= 2)	if (<0,0;0,0>)	else part
if (m1 .== <1,2; 2,1>)	if (<1,1;1,1>)	if part
if (m1 - 1)	if (<0,1;1,0>)	else part
if (m1 .>= 1)	if (<1,1;1,1>)	if part
if (m1 .> 1)	if (<0,1;1,0>)	else part
if (m2 == 2)	if (1)	if part
if (m2 != 2)	if (0)	else part
if (m1 >= 1)	if (1)	if part
if (m1 > 1)	if (0)	else part

The any library function evaluates to TRUE if any element is TRUE, e.g.

	evaluates to	leads to
if (any(m1 .== 1))	if (any(<1,0;0,1>))	if part
if (any(m1 .!= 1))	if (any(<0,1;1,0>))	if part
if (m1 == 1)	if (0)	else part
if (m1 != 1)	if (0)	else part

12.7.10 Logical dot-AND expressions

> *logical-dot-and-expression:*
>   *equality-expression*
>   *logical-dot-and-expression* .&& *equality-expression*

The . && operator groups left-to-right. It returns 1 if both of its operands compare unequal to 0, 0 otherwise. Both operands must have arithmetic type. Handling of matrix-type is as for dot-relational operators: if one or both operands is a matrix, the result is a matrix of zeros and ones. Unlike the non-dotted version, both operands will always be executed. For example, in the expression func1() .&& func2() the second function is called, regardless of the return value of func1().

12.7.11 Logical-AND expressions

> *logical-and-expression:*
> > *logical-dot-and-expression*
> > *logical-and-expression* && *logical-dot-and-expression*

The && operator groups left-to-right.

It returns the integer 1 if both of its operands compare unequal to 0, and the integer 0 otherwise. Both operands must have arithmetic type. First the left operand is evaluated, if it is false (for a matrix: there is at least one zero element), the result is false, and the right operand will not be evaluated. So in the expression func1() && func2() the second function will *not* be called if the first function returned false.

12.7.12 Logical dot-OR expressions

> *logical-dot-or-expression:*
> > *logical-and-expression*
> > *logical-dot-or-expression* . || *logical-and-expression*

The . || operator groups left-to-right. It returns 1 if either of its operands compares unequal to 0, 0 otherwise. Both operands must have arithmetic type. Handling of matrix-type is as for dot-relational operators: if one or both operands is a matrix, the result is a matrix of zeros and ones. Unlike the non-dotted version, both operands will always be executed. For example, in the expression func1() . || func2() the second function is called, regardless of the return value of func1().

12.7.13 Logical-OR expressions

> *logical-or-expression:*
> > *logical-dot-or-expression*
> > *logical-or-expression* || *logical-dot-or-expression*

The || operator groups left-to-right. It returns the integer 1 if either of its operands compares unequal to 0, integer value 0 otherwise. Both operands must have arithmetic type. First the left operand is evaluated, if it is true (for a matrix: no element is zero), the result is true, and the right operand will not be evaluated. So in the expression func1() . || func2() the second function will *not* be called if the first function returned true.

12.7.14 Conditional expression

conditional-expression:
  logical-or-expression
  logical-or-expression ? *expression* : *conditional-expression*
  logical-or-expression . ? *expression* . : *conditional-expression*

Both the conditional and the dot-conditional expression are ternary expressions. For the conditional expression, the first expression (before the ?) is evaluated. If it is unequal to 0, the result is the second expression, otherwise the third expression.

The dot-conditional expression only differs from the conditional expression if the first expression evaluates to a matrix, here called the test matrix. In that case the result is a matrix of the same size as the test matrix, and the test matrix can be seen as a filter: non zero elements get a value corresponding to the second expression, zero elements corresponding to the third expression. If the second or third expression is scalar, each matrix element will get the appropriate scalar value. If it is a matrix, the corresponding matrix element will be used, unless the matrix is too small, in which case the value 0. will be used. *Note that in the dot-conditional expression both parts are executed, whereas in the conditional expression only one of the two parts is executed.*

```
decl r, m2;

r = <1,0; 0,1> ? 4 : 5;        // 4, <1,0; 0,1> has not all 0s
r = <1,0; 0,1> .? 4 .: 5;                     // <4,5; 5,4>
m2 = <1>;
r = r .== 4 .? m2 .: 0;                       // <1,0; 0,0>
```

12.7.15 Assignment expressions

assignment-expression:
  conditional-expression
  unary-expression assignment-operator assignment-expression

assignment-operator: one of
  =   *=   /=   +=   -=   ~= |=

The assignment operators are the =   *=   /=   +=   -=   ~= |= symbols. An lvalue is required as the left operand. The type of an assignment is that of its left operand. The combined assignment *l op= r* is equivalent to *l = l op (r)*.

The following code:

```
decl i, k;
for (i = 0, k = 1; i < 5; i += 2)
    k *= 2, print("i = ", i, " k = ", k, "\n");
```

writes:

```
i = 0 k = 2
i = 2 k = 4
i = 4 k = 8
```

12.7.16 Comma expression

> *expression:*
>   *assignment-expression*
>   *expression , assignment-expression*

A pair of expressions separated by a comma is evaluated left to right, and the value of the left expression is discarded. The result will have type and value corresponding to the right operand. The example in the previous section has two instances of the comma operator. The second could be omitted as follows:

```
for (i = 0, k = 1; i < 5; i += 2)
{   k *= 2;
    print("i = ", i, " k = ", k, "\n");
}
```

or as:

```
for (i = 0, k = 1; i < 5; i += 2)
    print("i = ", i, " k = ", k *= 2, "\n");
```

12.7.17 Constant expressions

An expression that evaluates to a constant is required in initializers and certain preprocessor expressions. A constant expression can have the operators `* / + -`, but only if the operands have scalar type. Some examples were given in sections 12.5.1 and 12.5.3.

12.8 Preprocessing

Preprocessing in Ox is primarily used for inclusion of files and conditional compilation of code. As such it is more restricted than the options available in C or C++. Escape sequences in strings literals are interpreted when used in preprocessor statements.

12.8.1 File inclusion

A line of the form
    `#include "`*filename*`"`
will insert the contents of the specified file at that position. The file is searched for as follows:

(1) in the directory containing the source file (if just a filename, or a filename with a relative path is specified), or in the specified directory (if the filename has an absolute path);
(2) the directories specified on the compiler command line (if any);
(3) the directories specified in the INCLUDE environment string (if any).
(4) in the current directory.

A line of the form

```
#include <filename>
```

will skip the first step, and search as follows:

(1) the directories specified on the compiler command line (if any);
(2) the directories specified in the INCLUDE environment string (if any);
(3) in the current directory.

The quoted form is primarily for inclusion of user created header or code files, whereas the second form will be mainly for system and library files. Note that escape sequences *are* interpreted in the include string, but not in the version which uses <...> (so in #include "dir\nheader.h", the \n is replaced by a newline character). Both forward and backslashes are allowed (use #include "dir/nheader.h", to avoid the newline character).

12.8.2 Conditional compilation

The first step in conditional compilation is to define (or undefine) identifiers:

```
#define identifier
#undef identifier
```

Identifiers so defined only exist during the scanning process of the input file, and can subsequently be used by #ifdef and #ifndef preprocessor statements:

```
#ifdef identifier
#ifndef identifier
#else
#endif
```

As an example, consider the following header file:

```
#ifndef OXSTD_INCLUDED
#define OXSTD_INCLUDED

// header statements

#endif
```

Now multiple inclusion of the header file into a source code file will only once include the actual header statements; on second inclusion, OXSTD_INCLUDED will be defined, and the code skipped.

Another example uses some predefined constants (see Ch. 9):

```
#include <oxstd.h>

main()
{
#ifdef OX_BIG_ENDIAN
```

```
    print("This is a big endian machine.\n");
#else
    print("This is a little endian machine.\n");
#endif

#ifdef OX_Windows
    print("This program is running under Windows.\n");
#endif
}
```

12.8.3 Pragmas

Pragmas influence the parsing process of the Ox compiler. Pragmas may only occur at the level of external declarations. Defined are:

```
#pragma array_base(integer)
#pragma link("filename")
```

As discussed at various points, indices in matrices, arrays and strings always start at 0. This is the C and C++convention. Ox, however, allows circumventing this convention by using the `array_base` pragma. *It is strongly recommended to adopt the zero-based convention, and not use the* `array_base` *pragma.* The following example shows the difference:

```
#include <oxstd.h>

base0(const m)
{   decl i;
    i = m[0][0];           // first row, first element: i = 0
    i = m[][1:2];                                     // i = <1,2>
}
#pragma array_base(1)
base1(const m)
{   decl i;
    i = m[1][1];           // first row, first element: i = 0
    i = m[][1:2];                                     // i = <0,1>
    i = m[0][0];                                     // error
}
#pragma array_base(0)                      // reset to base 0

main()
{   decl m = <0,1,2,3>;

    base0(m);
    base1(m);
}
```

More useful is the link pragma, which leads to inclusion of the named file (which should be compiled source code, with default extension `.oxo`) at the point of the pragma. This provides an alternative to specifying the link files on the command line. The search machanism is the same as for `#include` *"filename"*. Link pragmas will normally occur in the same file as the `main` function; multiple linking of the same file will lead to errors:

```
#include <oxstd.h>
#pragma  link("test.oxo")

main()
{                                                  // main code
}
```

12.9 Difference with ANSI C and C++

This section lists some of the differences between Ox and C/C++ which might cause confusion:

- /* */ type comments can be nested in Ox.
- `sizeof` is a function in Ox, not an operator (and not a reserved word).
- Labels (targets of `goto` statements) have the colon prefixed, rather than suffixed.
- Unlike C++, the *init_expr* of a `for` loop cannot be preceded by a declaration.
- All data members of a class are private, all function members public.
- The base class constructor and destructor functions are *not* called automatically.
- Integer division is not used, so `1 / 2` yields 0.5, instead of 0. Use `idiv(1, 2)` for integer division of 1 by 2.
- The preprocessor does not allow: `#define XXX value`, for integer constants, enums could be used, but more convenient is: `const decl XXX = value;`.

Part III

Appendices

Appendix A1

Packages

Packages implement a specific set of techniques in Ox or are ports of existing code to Ox. Often part of the code is available through a Dynamic Link Library (DLL) with accompanying header file.

A1.1 Arfima package

The Arfima package has a class for estimation and forecasting of ARFIMA(p, d, q) and ARMA(p, q) models. The available estimation methods are maximum likelihood and nonlinear least squares. The Arfima class derives from the database class to give easy loading of data sets and sample selection. An additional simulation class allows Monte Carlo experimentation of the facilities in the estimation class. Extensive documentation is supplied in a PostScript file. Check the online documentation for availability.

A1.2 QuadPack

QuadPack (documented in Piessens, de Donker-Kapenga, Überhuber and Kahaner, 1983) is a Fortran library for univariate numerical integration ('quadrature') using adaptive rules. Five functions are exported to Ox from quadpk.dll, using the header file quadpack.h. At the end of this section is a sample program using these functions.

QNG, QAG, QAGS, QAGP, QAGI

```
QNG (const func, const a, const b, const aresult,
     const aabserr);
QAG (const func, const a, const b, const key,
     const aresult, const aabserr);
QAGS(const func, const a, const b, const aresult,
     const aabserr);
QAGP(const func, const a, const b, const vpoints,
     const aresult, const aabserr);
QAGI(const func, const bound, const inf, const aresult,
```

```
const aabserr);
```

func	in:	function to integrate; func must be a function of one argument (a double), returning a double
a	in:	double, lower limit of integration
b	in:	double, upper limit of integration
key	in:	int, key for choice of local integration rule, which determines the number of points in the Gauss-Kronrod pair: ≤ 1 (7–15 points), 2 (10–21 points), 3 (15–31 points), 4 (20–41 points), 5 (25–51 points), ≥ 6 (30–61 points).
vpoints	in:	row vector with singularities of integrand
bound	in:	double, lower bound (key == 1) or upper bound (key == −1)
key	in:	int, $1 : \int_{b}^{\infty}, -1 : \int_{-\infty}^{b}, 2 : \int_{-\infty}^{\infty}$
aresult	in:	address of variable
	out:	double, approximation to the integral
aabserr	in:	address of variable
	out:	double, estimate of the modulus of the absolute error

Return value

Result of the QuadPack routine:

0	normal and reliable termination of routine;
1	maximum number of steps has been executed;
2	roundoff error prevents reaching the desired tolerance;
3	extremely bad integrand behaviour prevents reaching tolerance;
4	algorithm does not converge;
5	integral is probably convergent or slowly divergent;
6	invalid input;
10	not enough memory;

An error message greater than 0 is reported to stderr.

Description

QNG: simple non-adaptive automatic integrator for a smooth integrand.

QAG: simple globally adaptive Gauss-Kronrod-based integrator, with choice of formulae.

QAGS: globally adaptive integrator with extrapolation, which can handle integrand singularities of several types.

QAGP: as QAGS, but allows the user to specify singularities, discontinuities and other difficulties of the integrand.

QAGI: as QAGS, but handles integration over infinite integrals.

Full documentation is in Piessens *et al.*, 1983.

QPEPS

```
QPEPS(const epsabs, const epsrel);
```
  epsabs in: double, absolute accuracy requested (the default value is $\epsilon_a =$
        0)
  epsrel in: double, relative accuracy requested (the default value is $\epsilon_r =$
        10^{-10})

No return value.

Description

 Sets the accuracy which the integration routines should try to achieve. Let $\hat{I}$ be the approximation from the QuadPack routines to the integral:

$$I = \int_a^b f(x)\mathrm{d}x,$$

then the result will hopefully satisfy:

$$\left|I - \hat{I}\right| \leq \text{abserr} \leq \max\left\{\epsilon_a, \epsilon_r |I|\right\}.$$

Example

```
#include <oxstd.h>
#include <quadpack.h>

output(const sFunc, const result, const abserr)
{
    print(sFunc, result, " abserr=", abserr, "\n");
}
mydensn(const x)
{
    return densn(x);
}
main()
{
    decl result, abserr, pn = probn(1) - probn(0);

    QNG(densn, 0.0, 1.0, &result, &abserr);
    output("QNG: ", result, abserr);

    QAG(densn, 0.0, 1.0, 5, &result, &abserr);
    output("QAG: ", result, abserr);

    QAG(densn, 0.0, 1.0, 15, &result, &abserr);
    output("QAG: ", result, abserr);

    QAGS(densn, 0.0, 1.0, &result, &abserr);
    output("QAGS:", result, abserr);

    QAGP(densn, 0.0, 1.0, <0.1,0.9>, &result, &abserr);
    output("QAGP:", result, abserr);
```

```
QAGI(mydensn, 0, 1, &result, &abserr);
output("QAGI:", result, abserr);

print("using probn(): ", probn(1) - probn(0),
      " and ", probn(0), "\n");
}
```

produces

```
QNG: 0.341345 abserr=3.78969e-015
Quadpack warning 1
QAG: 0.330835 abserr=0.0101865
QAG: 0.341345 abserr=3.78969e-015
QAGS:0.341345 abserr=3.78969e-015
QAGP:0.341345 abserr=3.78969e-015
QAGI:0.5 abserr=1.24255e-011
using probn(): 0.341345 and 0.5
```

A1.3 SSFPack

SSFPack is a package for analysing Gaussian and non-Gaussian time series which can be placed in the state space form (SSF). Only a brief summary is given, together with some examples. SSFPack is fully documented in Koopman, Shephard and Doornik (1996); download information is presented in the next section.

A1.3.1 How to retrieve & install SSFPack

SSFPack can be downloaded from the World Wide Web at the site:
http://www.nuff.ox.ac.uk/shephard/ox/
In particular the four core files are zipped in SSFPack.zip:

sheppitt.h	header for sheppitt.ox;
sheppitt.ox	Ox code for SSFPack extended to non-Gaussian problems;
filter.dll	Dynamic Link Library for SSFPack;
ssf.h	header for SSFPack.

Some examples of their use and a postscript version of this paper are in ssfdocu.zip.

soft.ps	postscript version of the documentation;
ssfeg.ox	Ox code example of the use of time invariant algorithms;
ssfegnon.ox	Ox code example of estimating non-Gaussian likelihood;
ssfegtv.ox	Ox code example of the use of time varying algorithms;
ssffit.ox	Ox classes which allow the fitting of some familiar models;
ssfitarm.ox	Ox code example of fitting an ARMA$(2, 1)$ model;
ssfitnon.ox	Ox code example of non-Gaussian fitting.

To place all the files in the relevant directories, SSFPack.zip should be unzipped from the root directory on the drive where Ox has been installed. The instruction is pkunzip -d ssfpack.zip.

The filter.dll will be placed in the \ox\bin\ directory, along with the dlls from other packages such as QUADPACK. The same unzipping instruction should be followed for the ssfdocu.zip file. The result will be a directory \ox\packages\ssf\ which contains some Ox code, header files and a postscript version of this documentation. You will have to explicitly point to this directory when using OxRun, alternatively, add the directory to the PATH environment variable (using the system icon on the control panel or the autoexec.bat file).

A1.3.2 Overview

The statistical treatment of most linear time series is based on the state space form . We use a particular Gaussian SSF which is close to the setup in de Jong (1991). It joins a *measurement* equation

$$y_t = c_t + Z_t \alpha_t + G_t u_t, \quad t = 1, \cdots, n, \tag{A1.1}$$

with a *transition* equation for the *states* α_t

$$\alpha_{t+1} = d_t + T_t\alpha_t + H_t u_t. \tag{A1.2}$$

Throughout we will assume $G_t' H_t = 0$. All the algorithms developed here could have been set up to deal with the case where this is not true, but they become more complicated. Further, we will only deal with y_t being univariate. The transition equation is initialized at the first time point by setting

$$\alpha_0 = 0, \quad \text{implying} \quad \alpha_1 = H_0 u_0. \tag{A1.3}$$

The model is completed by assuming

$$u_t \sim \text{NID}(0,I) \quad \text{for} \quad t = 0, \ldots, n. \tag{A1.4}$$

This means we can write the initial condition about α_1 in terms of the mean $a_{1|0} = 0$ and variance $P_{1|0} = H_0 H_0'$.

A1.3.2.1 Kalman filter

The Kalman filter (denoted KF) is primarily a set of vector and matrix recursions. It has a variety of forms, but the one exploited here computes $a_{t|t-1} = \text{E}(\alpha_t|Y_{t-1})$ and $P_{t|t-1} = \text{MSE}\{(\alpha_t - a_{t|t-1})|Y_{t-1}\}$, the mean and mean square error (MSE) of the state, respectively, given the past information, $Y_{t-1} = (y_1, \ldots, y_{t-1})'$.

These expressions can be computed iteratively by using the KF which sets $t = 0$, $a_{1|0} = 0$, and $P_{1|0} = H_0 H_0'$ and then computes repeatedly for $t = 1, \ldots, n$,

$$
\begin{aligned}
v_t &= y_t - c_t - Z_t a_{t|t-1}, & F_t &= Z_t P_{t|t-1} Z_t' + G_t G_t', \\
& & K_t &= T_t P_{t|t-1} Z_t' F_t^{-1}, \\
a_{t+1|t} &= d_t + T_t a_{t|t-1} + K_t v_t, & P_{t+1|t} &= T_t P_{t|t-1} T_t' - K_t F_t K_t' + H_t H_t'.
\end{aligned}
\tag{A1.5}
$$

Here K_t is called the Kalman gain, while v_t and F_t are the one-step ahead prediction error (or innovation) and its mean square error, respectively.

A1.3.2.2 Likelihood evaluation

The KF outputs allows the computation of the log-likelihood function via the prediction decomposition, for, ignoring constants

$$
\begin{aligned}
\log f(y_1, \ldots, y_n; \varphi) &= \sum_{t=1}^{n} \log f(y_t|y_1, \ldots, y_{t-1}; \varphi) \\
&= -\tfrac{1}{2} \sum_{t=1}^{n} \log |F_t| - \tfrac{1}{2} \sum_{t=1}^{n} v_t' F_t^{-1} v_t.
\end{aligned}
\tag{A1.6}
$$

A1.3.2.3 Moment smoothing

We focus on estimating the disturbance vector u_t using the whole data set. This is called disturbance smoothing. Here the interest in u_t is limited to elements of $\varepsilon_t = G_t u_t$ and $\eta_t = H_t u_t$. We write

$$\tilde{\varepsilon}_t = \mathsf{E}(\varepsilon_t|y), \quad P^\varepsilon_{t|n} = \mathsf{MSE}(\tilde{\varepsilon}_t), \quad \text{and} \quad \tilde{\eta}_t = \mathsf{E}(\eta_t|y), \quad P^\eta_{t|n} = \mathsf{MSE}(\tilde{\eta}_t) \quad (A1.7)$$

respectively.

(1) Requires that F_t, v_t and K_t be stored from the KF.
(2) Set $t = n, r_n = 0$ and $N_n = 0$
(3) Compute

$$\begin{array}{llll}
e_t & = & F_t^{-1}v_t - K_t'r_t, & r_{t-1} & = & Z_t'F_t^{-1}v_t + L_t'r_t, \\
D_t & = & F_t^{-1} + K_t'N_tK_t, & N_{t-1} & = & Z_t'F_t^{-1}Z_t + L_t'N_tL_t, \quad (A1.8) \\
L_t & = & T_t - K_tZ_t.
\end{array}$$

(4) Record

$$\begin{array}{llll}
\tilde{\varepsilon}_t & = & G_tG_t'e_t, & P^\varepsilon_{t|n} & = & G_tG_t' - G_tG_t'D_tG_tG_t', \\
\tilde{\eta}_t & = & H_tH_t'r_t, & P^\eta_{t|n} & = & H_tH_t' - H_tH_t'N_tH_tH_t'.
\end{array} \quad (A1.9)$$

(5) Let $t = t - 1$. Goto 3 if $t \geq 1$.

Of course the disturbance sampler can be used to compute $\alpha_{t|n} = \mathsf{E}(\alpha_t|y_n)$ via a forward recursion of the form, for $t = 0, 1, \ldots, n - 1$,

$$a_{t+1|n} = d_t + T_t a_{t|n} + \tilde{\eta}_t. \quad (A1.10)$$

with $\alpha_{0|n} = 0$.

A1.3.2.4 Simulation signal smoothing

The de Jong and Shephard (1995) simulator draws from the smoothed signal $(c_1 + z_1\alpha_1, \ldots, c_n + z_n\alpha_n)' |y$. Again we write $\sigma_t^2 = G_tG_t'$ as this is a scalar.

(1) Requires that F_t, v_t and K_t be stored from the KF (A1.5).
(2) Set $t = n, r_n = 0$ and $N_n = 0$.
(3) Compute $e_t = F_t^{-1}v_t - K_t'r_t$ and $d_t = F_t^{-1} + K_t'N_tK_t$

$$\begin{array}{llll}
r_{t-1} & = & Z_t'F_t^{-1}v_t + L_t'r_t - V_t'\varsigma_t/c_t, & c_t & = & \sigma_t^2 - \sigma_t^4 d_t, \\
N_{t-1} & = & Z_t'F_t^{-1}Z_t + L_t'N_tL_t + V_t'V_t/c_t, & V_t & = & \sigma_t^2(d_tZ_t - K_t'N_tT_t),
\end{array} \quad (A1.11)$$

$L_t = T_t - K_tZ_t$. Simulate from $\varsigma_t \sim N(0, c_t)$.
(4) Record

$$\tilde{\omega}_t = \sigma_t^2 e_t + \varsigma_t. \quad (A1.12)$$

(5) Let $t = t - 1$. Goto 3 if $t \geq 1$.

Then $\tilde{\omega}_t$ is a draw from $G_t u_t | y$ or equivalently $y_t - \tilde{\omega}_t$ is a draw from the signal $(c_t + Z_t \alpha_t) | y$. This sampler involves only univariate simulations even when α_t is multivariate. Another feature of this sampler is that if many simulations are required then V_t and c_t can be computed once, allowing the simulations to be drawn by simply running repeatedly:

$$r_{t-1} = Z_t' F_t^{-1} v_t + L_t' r_t - V_t' \varsigma_t / c_t, \quad \varsigma_t \sim \mathsf{N}(0, c_t). \tag{A1.13}$$

A1.3.3 Function summary

The following are the SSFPack functions:

DisturbSmooth	sets up disturbance smoother
GaussLik	Gaussian log-likelihood
KalmanF	Kalman filter
SignalSmo	signal and state smoother
SimulSmoCov	set up the simulation smoother
SimulSmoSim	draws from the simulation smoother
SPApproxModel	Gaussian approximation model
SPTrueModel	true measurement log-density
SPMode	modal estimation
SPLikeEst	estimate of the log-likelihood
TVDisturbSmooth	DisturbSmooth for time varying SSF
TVKalmanF	KalmanF for time varying SSF
TVSignalSmo	SignalSmo for time varying SSF
TVSimulSmoCov	SimulSmoCov for time varying SSF
TVSimulSmoSim	SimulSmoSim for time varying SSF

The basic functions are for filtering, moment smoothing and simulation smoothing in time varying Gaussian state space forms. However, simplified functions are available if the SSF is time invariant. Examples are given below.

Various classes have been written which use these functions to allow easy estimation of some familiar time series models. These are documented in Koopman *et al.* (1996).

A1.3.4 Notation

Throughout the following consistent notation will be used for various model inputs:

vY	$1 \times n$ matrix of observations, $(y_1, \ldots, y_n)$.
mZT	$(s+1) \times s$ system matrix $\begin{pmatrix} Z \\ T \end{pmatrix}$.
mGH	$(s+1) \times (s+1)$ covariance matrix $\begin{pmatrix} GG' & 0 \\ 0 & HH' \end{pmatrix}$.
vCD	$1 \times (s+1)$ constants matrix $\begin{pmatrix} c \\ d \end{pmatrix}$
vIa	initial state $1 \times s$ vector $a_{1|0}$.
mIp	the $s \times s$ matrix of the $P_{1|0}$ initial MSE matrix of the state.
imZT	indexes mZT matrix. Elements are negative if time invariant. Else number corresponds to column of mTV.
imGH	indexes mGH matrix. Elements are negative if time invariant. Else number corresponds to column of mTV.
ivCD	indexes vCD matrix. Elements are negative if time invariant. Else number corresponds to column of mTV.
mTV	Values of the time varying elements of mZT and mGH.
sModel	string with model to approximate: "SV" or another string.

A1.3.5 Time invariant example

The first example deals with a local linear trend model, with

$$
\begin{aligned}
y_t &= \mu_t + \varepsilon_t, & \varepsilon_t &\sim \text{NID}(0, 1), \\
\mu_t &= \mu_{t-1} + \beta_{t-1} \\
\beta_t &= \beta_{t-1} + \xi_t, & \xi_t &\sim \text{NID}(0, 0.01).
\end{aligned}
$$

The file ssfeg.ox carries out a number of tasks: run a Kalman filter, compute the log-likelihood, run the disturbance smoother, signal extract, set up the simulation smoother, and finally, draw a single sample from the simulation smoother.

A1.3.6 Time varying example

The time invariant example is adjusted in ssfegtv.ox to allow the measurement error variance to change with each observation. In this example we set the variances equal to draw from $\chi_4^2/4$ random variables. The same calculations are performed on the data; however these are now based on the time varying functions. The code is in ssfegtv.ox.

A1.3.7 Examples for non-Gaussian SSF

Contained in the file ssfegnon.ox is an example of estimating the likelihood function for a non-Gaussian time series model. The particular model we focus on is the SV process.

Appendix A2

Extending Ox

Ox is an open system to which you can add functions written in other languages. Extending Ox requires an understanding of the innards of Ox, a decent knowledge of C, as well as the right tools. You also need a version of Ox with developer support. In addition, extending Ox is simpler on some platforms than others. Thus, it is unavoidable that writing Ox extensions is somewhat more complex than writing plain Ox code. However, there could be reasons for extending Ox, e.g. when you need the speed of raw C code (but make sure that the function takes up a significant part of the time it takes to run the program and that it actually will be a lot faster in C than in Ox!), or when code is already available in e.g. Fortran. This chapter gives many examples, which could provide a start for your coding effort.

When you write your own C functions to link to Ox, memory management inside the C code is your responsibility. So care is required: any errors can bring down the Ox program, or, worse, lead to erroneous outcomes.

Although this chapter is tailored towards producing Dynamic Link Libraries (DLL) for any Windows platform, most of it is pertinent to other platforms. It is just that working with DLLs is a lot simpler than statically linked libraries.

The penultimate section in this chapter documents the C function available to interface with Ox. The last section documents the C mathematical functions exported by the Ox DLL. Any program could use Ox as a function library by using direct calls to the Ox DLL. The remaining sections all give examples on extending Ox:

directory	purpose	section
ox/samples/threes	a simple example of linking C code	A2.1
	returning values in arguments	A2.3
ox/samples/callback	calling Ox functions from C	A2.4
ox/samples/ranapp	writing a C++ interface wrapper	A2.5
ox/samples/fortran	linking Fortran code	A2.6
ox/packages/quadpkd	linking a whole Fortran library	A2.6

In this chapter we link C code and Fortran code to Ox, but before we start, these are the requirements to link to the Ox DLL under Windows on the Intel platform:

- standard call (_stdcall) calling convention;
  this pushes parameters from right to left, and lets the function clean the stack;
- structure packing at 8 byte boundaries,
- flat 32-bit memory model.

A2.1 Linking C code: a simple example

In this section we shall write a function called Threes, which creates a matrix of threes (cf. the library function ones). The first argument is the number of rows, the second the number of columns. The C source code is in threes.c:

```
#include "/ox/dev/oxexport.h"

void OXCALL FnThrees(OxVALUE *rtn, OxVALUE *pv, int cArg)
{
    int i, j, c, r;

    OxLibCheckType(OX_INT, pv, 0, 1);

    r = OxInt(pv, 0);
    c = OxInt(pv, 1);
    OxLibValMatMalloc(rtn, r, c);

    for (i = 0; i < r; i++)
        for (j = 0; j < c; j++)
            OxMat(rtn, 0)[i][j] = 3;
}
```

- The oxexport.h header file defines all types and functions required to link to Ox.
- All functions have the same format:

  - OXCALL defines the calling convention;
  - rtn is the return value of the function. It is a pointer to an OxVALUE which is the container for any Ox variable. On input, it is an integer (OX_INT) of value 0. If the function returns a value, it should be stored in rtn.
  - pv is an array of cArg OxVALUEs, holding the actual arguments to the function.
  - cArg is the number of arguments used in the function call. Unless the function has a variable number of arguments, there is no need to reference this value.

- First, we check whether the arguments are of type OX_INT (we know that there are two arguments, which have index 0 and 1 in pv). The call to OxLibCheck-Type tests pv (the function arguments) from index 0 to index 1 for type OX_INT. *As a rule, arguments must be checked for type.* In this case, a double would also be valid, but automatically converted to an integer by the OxLibCheckType function. Any other argument type would result in a run-time error (checking for the number of arguments is done at compile time).

- For convenience, we put the first argument in r, and the second in c. OxInt accesses the integer in an OxVALUE. The first argument is the array of OxVALUEs, the second argument is the index in the array. This specifies the dimension of the requested matrix.
- The return type is a matrix, and that matrix has to be allocated in the rtn value, using the right dimensions. This is done with the OxLibValMatMalloc function. A run-time error is generated if there is not enough memory to allocate the matrix.
- Finally we have to set the matrix to the value 3. OxMat accesses the allocated matrix. The dimensions of that matrix are accessed by OxMatc, OxMatr, but here we already know the dimension of the matrix.

Note that the function arguments, as contained in pv, may only be changed if they are declared as const. *It is safest to never change the arguments in the function*, except from conversion from int to double and vice versa. Another exception is when the argument is a pointer in which the caller expects a return value. An example will follow shortly.

The threes.c file should compile without problems into a DLL file. Makefiles for the Microsoft, Watcom and Borland compilers have been provided; note the calling conventions mentioned above, and the need to link in the library files oxwin.lib (Visual C++), oxwin_bc (Borland C++), or the definition file oxwin.wc (Watcom C++).

Then the function can be used as follows:

```
#include <oxstd.h>

extern "/ox/samples/threes/msvc20/threes,FnThrees"
    Threes(const r, const c);

main()
{
    print(Threes(3,3));
}
```

The function is declared as extern, with the code in the DLL file /ox/samples/threes/msvc20/threes. The name of the function in threes.dll is FnThrees, but in our Ox code we wish to call it Threes. After this declaration, we can use the function Threes as any other standard library function.

Note that the operating system has to be able to find the DLL file. Here we give the complete path, but if it is moved to the /ox/bin directory, and that directory is in the path, then just the name would be sufficient. Also make sure that FnThrees is the exact name in the DLL files; some compilers could, for example, prefix an underscore (and C++ functions could be subject to name mangling).

A2.2 The threes example for Linux, SunOS and HP

The current versions of Ox for Linux (on Intel machines) and SunOS/HP-UX do not support dynamic linking. Instead, you need to recreate a new, statically linked, version of the executable. Examples for Linux are in ox/samples/threes/linux (Sun/HP examples are not given but work in the same way). For all platforms, the necessary library files (mtlib.a, jdlib.a, dblib.a and libox.a) are in ox/dev/linux, ox/dev/sun and ox/dev/hp. Makefiles are in those directories as well; run these as, e.g.: make -f oxlinux.mak.

The makefiles for the threes example relinks a slightly modified version of oxlinux.c with threes.c. This will produce the executable a.out, which you will have to rename to something else (*but not oxlinux!*).

Under Linux, the compiler used to create the libraries is *gcc* version 2.5.8; under SunOS 4.1 it is *gcc* version 2.7.0, under HP-UX *gcc* version 2.6.0.

A2.3 Linking C code: returning values in arguments

Returning a value in an argument only adds a minor complication. Remember that by default all arguments in Ox and C are passed by value, and assigments to arguments will be lost after the function returns. To return values in arguments, pass a pointer to a variable, so that the called function may change what the variable points to.

To refresh our memory, here is some simple Ox code:

```
#include <oxstd.h>

func1(a)
{    a = 1;
}
func2(const a)
{    a[0] = 1;
}
main()
{
    decl b;

    b = 0;   func1(b);    print(b);
    b = 0;   func2(&b);   print(b);
}
```

This will print 01. In func1 we cannot use the const qualifier because we are changing the argument. In func1 the argument is not changed, only what it points to.

The first serious example is the invert function from the standard library, which also illustrates the use of a variable argument list.

```
static void OXCALL
fnInvert(OxVALUE *rtn, OxVALUE *pv, int cArg)
{
```

```
    int   r;   double det;

    OxLibCheckSquareMatrix(pv, 0, 0);
    if (cArg == 2)
        OxLibCheckType(OX_ARRAY, pv, 1, 1);

    r = OxMatr(pv, 0);
    OxLibValMatDup(rtn, OxMat(pv, 0), r, r);

    if (IInvDet(OxMat(rtn, 0), r, &det) != 0)
    {
        MatFree(OxMat(rtn, 0), r, r);
        PopErrorMessage("invert(): inversion failed");
        OxZero(rtn, 0);
    }
    else if (cArg == 2)
        OxSetDbl( OxArray(pv,1), 0, det);
}
```

- OxLibCheckSquareMatrix(pv, 0, 0) is equivalent to a call to OxLibCheckType(OX_MATRIX, pv, 0, 0); followed by a check if the matrix is square.
- Only if there is a second argument, do we check if it is of type OX_ARRAY.
- OxMatr gets the number of rows in the first argument (we already know that it is a matrix, with the same number of rows as columns).
- Next, we duplicate (allocate a matrix and copy) the matrix in the first argument to the return value. We shall overwrite this with the actual inverse.
- If the matrix inversion fails, the matrix in rtn is freed, rtn is changed back to an integer with value 0.
- Otherwise, but only if the second argument was provided, do we put the determinant (det) in that argument. OxArray(pv, 1) accesses the array at element 1 in pv. This is then used in the same way as pv was used: accessing the first entry in the array (number 0).

A more complex example is that for the square root free Choleski decomposition decldl, again from the standard library. The first argument is the symmetric matrix to decompose, the next two are arrays in which we expect the function to return the lower triangular matrix and vector with diagonal elements.

```
static void OXCALL
fnDecldl(OxVALUE *rtn, OxVALUE *pv, int cArg)
{
    int   i, j, r;   MATRIX md, ml;

    OxLibCheckSquareMatrix(pv, 0, 0);
    OxLibCheckType(OX_ARRAY, pv, 1, 2);
    OxLibCheckArrayMatrix(pv, 1, 2, OxMat(pv, 0));

    r = OxMatr(pv, 0);
```

```
OxLibValMatDup(OxArray(pv, 1), OxMat(pv, 0), r, r);
OxLibValMatMalloc(OxArray(pv, 2), 1, r);
ml = OxMat( OxArray(pv, 1), 0);
md = OxMat( OxArray(pv, 2), 0);

if (!ml || !md)
    OxRunError(ER_OM, NULL);
if (ml == md)
    OxRunError(ER_ARGSAME, NULL);

if ( (OxInt(rtn, 0) = !ILDLdec(ml, md[0], r)) == 0)
    PopErrorMessage("decldl(): decomposition failed");

                    /* diagonal of ml is 1, upper is 0 */
for (i = 0; i < r; i++)
{    for (j = i + 1; j < r; j++)
        ml[i][j] = 0;
    ml[i][i] = 1;
}
}
```

The new functions here are:

- `OxLibCheckArrayMatrix` which checks that the arrays do not point to the matrix to decompose, as e.g. in `decldl(msym, &msym, &md);`.
- `OxLibValMatMalloc` allocates space for a matrix.
- `OxRunError` generates a run-time error message. The statement `if (ml == md)` checks if the arrays do not point to the same variable. If so, we have allocated a matrix twice, but end up with the last matrix for both arguments. This prevents code of the form `decldl(msym, &md, &md);`.

A2.4 Calling Ox functions from C

This section deals with reverse communication: inside the C code, we wish to call an Ox function. The example is a numerical differentiation routine written in C, used to differentiate a function defined in Ox code.

```
#include "/ox/dev/oxexport.h"
                    /* the Ox code function to call */
static OxVALUE *pvOxFunc;

static int myFunc(int cP, VECTOR vP, double *pdFunc,
    VECTOR vScore, MATRIX mHess)
{
    OxVALUE rtn, arg, *prtn, *parg;

    prtn = &rtn;  parg = &arg;
    OxSetMatPtr(parg, 0, &vP, 1, cP);

    if (!FOxCallBack(pvOxFunc, prtn, parg, 1))
```

```
                return 1;
        OxLibCheckType(OX_DOUBLE, prtn, 0, 0);
        *pdFunc = OxDbl(prtn, 0);

    return 0;
    }

    void OXCALL FnNumDer(OxVALUE *rtn,OxVALUE *pv,int cArg)
    {
        int c;

        OxLibCheckType(OX_FUNCTION, pv, 0, 0);
        pvOxFunc = pv;                    /* function pointer */
        OxLibCheckType(OX_MATRIX, pv, 1, 1);

        c = OxMatc(pv, 1);
        OxLibCheckMatrixSize(pv, 1, 1, 1, c);
        OxLibValMatMalloc(rtn, 1, c);

        if (!FNum1Derivative(
            myFunc, c, OxMat(pv, 1)[0], OxMat(rtn, 0)[0]))
        {
            OxFreeByValue(rtn);
            OxZero(rtn, 0);
        }
    }
```

First we discuss FnNumDer which preforms the actual numerical differentiation by calling FNum1Derivative:

- Argument 0 in pv must be a function, argument 1 a matrix, from which we only use the first row (expected to hold the parameter values at which to differentiate). The function argument is stored in the global variable pvOxFunc, so that it can be used later.
- OxLibCheckMatrixSize checks whether the matrix is $1 \times$ c (since the c value is from that matrix, only the number of rows is checked).
- Finally, the C function FNum1Derivative is called to compute the numerical derivative of myFunc. When successful, it will leave the result in the first row of the matrix in rtn (for which we have already allocated the space).

The myFunc function is a wrapper which calls the Ox function:

- Space for the arguments and the return value is required. There is always only one return value, and here we also have just one argument for the Ox function, resulting in the OxVALUE rtn and arg. We mainly work with pointers to OxVALUEs, stored here in prtn and parg for convenience. The argument is set to a $1 \times$ cP matrix. A VECTOR is defined as a double * and a MATRIX as a double **, so that the type of &vP is MATRIX, which is always the type used for the matrix in the OxVALUE.

- FOxCallBack calls the Ox function in the first argument. The next three arguments are the arguments to that Ox function: return type, function arguments, and
  number of arguments. FOxCallBack returns TRUE when successful, FALSE
  otherwise.
- After checking the returned value for type OX_DOUBLE, we can extract that double
  and return it in what pdFunc points to.

The following Ox code would call this function from the DLL. The dRosenbrock
function is the one written in Ox, and called from C.

```
#include <oxstd.h>

extern "/ox/samples/callback/dllrel/callback,FnNumDer"
    FnNumDer(const sFunc, vP);

dRosenbrock(const vPt)
{
    return -100 * (vPt[0][1] - vPt[0][0] ^ 2) ^ 2
            - (1 - vPt[0][0]) ^ 2;
}
main()
{
    decl vp = zeros(cp, 1);

    print( FnNumDer(dRosenbrock, vp') );
}
```

A2.5 Writing a C++ interface wrapper

Ox is limited in terms of output, and especially input. It is possible, however, to use
much more powerful tools, such as a modern C++ compiler, to add dialogs and menus.
In that way, a much better interface could be written than ever possible directly in
Ox. The knowledge from the previous section already suffices to write such a wrapper. There is, however, a second form of simplified callbacks (not allowing for arguments, and bypassing the main function), which we discuss here. The full example is
in ox/samples/ranapp. The code uses Microsoft Foundation Class (MFC) and Microsoft Visual C++, but similar code could be written using other compilers and application frameworks. Here we shall only treat Ox specific sections of the code.

The RanApp application reports all text and graphics output in *GiveWin*, through just
one function call. It does, however, require correctly installed copies of givewin.exe
and oxgwin.dll to work.

```
#include "/ox/dev/oxexport.h"
#include "/ox/dev/oxgwin.h"

int iMainIP;
```

```
static int iDoOxRun(const char *sExePath)
{
    iMainIP = 0;

    // Must startup GiveWin and install linking functions
    if (!FOxGiveWinStart())
        return 0;                                    // fail

    char *argv[10];  int argc;
    char *sapp = strdup((char *)sExePath);

    if (sapp)
    {   char *s;
        if ( (s = strstr(strlwr(sapp), ".exe")) != NULL)
            strcpy(s, ".ox");
        else
            free(sapp), sapp = NULL;
    }

    argv[0] = "RanApp";
    argv[1] = sapp ? sapp : "ranapp";
    argv[2] = "-r-";   // do not run, just compile and link
    argv[3] = "-ic:/ox/include";
    argc = 4;
    argv[argc] = NULL;

    iMainIP = OxMain(argc, argv);

    free(sapp);

return iMainIP;
}

void CRanAppDlg::OnGenerate()
{
    m_variance.EnableWindow();
    m_draw.EnableWindow();

    FOxRun(iMainIP, "OnGenerate");
}
void CRanAppDlg::OnDraw()
{
    FOxRun(iMainIP, "OnDraw");
}
void CRanAppDlg::OnVariance()
{
    FOxRun(iMainIP, "OnVariance");
}
```

- iDoOxRun simulates a call to Ox with command line arguments comparable to running Ox from the command line.
- FOxGiveWinStart starts *GiveWin* for Ole automation communication. When

successful, Ox calls to `print` and graphics functions will appear in *GiveWin*.

- Next, we set up the command line. The first argument is always the name of the program, so is not really important. The second argument, argument 1, is the name of the Ox code to compile; that code is in `ranapp.ox`, and here the full path name is obtained from the `sExePath` string. The third argument prevents the Ox program from running, restricting to a compile and link. The fourth argument sets the include path (so this program will not work if Ox has been installed on the D drive; an alternative would be to extract the path from `sExePath`).

- `OxMain` compiles the code and returns a value > 1 when successful. That value is stored in `iMainIP` and used in subsequent calls to specific Ox functions.

- We shall not discuss the interface code. But note that when we compile the Ox program successfully, the Generate button lights up. Then, when Generate is pressed, the `OnGenerate` function from `ranapp.ox` (given below) is called, and the Draw and Variance buttons become active. These buttons also lead to a call to underlying Ox code.

Below is a listing of `ranapp.ox`, the program behind this application. It is a simple Ox program which draws random numbers in `OnGenerate`, prints their variance matrix in `OnVariance`, and draws the correlogram and spectrum in `OnDraw`.

```
#include <oxstd.h>
#include <oxdraw.h>

decl mX;

OnGenerate()
{
    mX = rann(30,2);
}
OnVariance()
{
    print( variance(mX) );
}
OnDraw()
{
    DrawCorrelogram(0, mX[][0]', "ran1", 4);
    DrawSpectrum(1, mX[][0]', "ran1", 4);
    ShowDrawWindow();
}
```

A2.6 Linking Fortran code

Linking Fortran code to Ox does not pose any new problems, apart from needing to know how function calls work in Fortran. The simplest solution is to write C wrappers around the Fortran code, and use a Fortran and C compiler from the same vendor (here: Watcom).

Arguments in Fortran functions are always by reference: change an argument in a function, and it will be changed outside the function. For this reason, well-written Fortran code copies arguments to local variables when the change need not be global.

Two examples are provided. The directory ox/samples/fortran contains a simple test function in Fortran, and a C wrapper which also provides a function which is called from Fortran. The second example is in ox/packages/quadpkd. There, we provide wrappers for five QuadPack (see §A1) functions, thus adding univariate numerical integration routines to Ox.

A2.7 Ox function summary

All functions which interface with Ox use the OXCALL specifier. This, in turn, is just a relabelling of JDCALL, defined in ox/dev/jdsystem.h. Currently, this declares the calling convention for the Microsoft, Borland and Watcom compilers on the Intel platform. For other compilers on this platform, and on other platforms, it defaults to nothing. So, to add support for a new compiler, you could:

(1) leave jdsystem.h unchanged, and set the right compiler options when compiling (this is the preferred approach);
(2) add support for the new compiler in jdsystem.h.

Ox extension function syntax

```
void OXCALL FnFunction(OxVALUE *rtn, OxVALUE *pv,
    int cArg);
```

rtn	in:	pointer to an OxVALUE of type OX_INT and value 0
	out:	receives the return value of pvFunc
pv	in:	the arguments of the function call; *they must be checked for type before being accessed.*
	out:	unchanged, apart from possible conversion from OX_INT to OX_DOUBLE or vice versa
cArg	in:	number of elements in pv; unless the function has a variable number of arguments, there is no need to reference this value.

No return value.

Description

This is the syntax required to make a function callable from Ox. FnFunction should be replaced by an appropriate name, but is not the name under which the function is known inside an Ox program.

FOxCallBack

```
bool FOxCallBack(OxVALUE *pvFunc, OxVALUE *rtn,
    OxVALUE *pv, int cArg);
```

pvFunc	in:	the function to call, must be of type OX_FUNCTION or OX_INTFUNC
rtn	out:	receives the return value of pvFunc
pv	in:	the arguments of pvFunc
cArg	in:	number of elements in pv

Return value

TRUE if the function is called successfully, FALSE otherwise.

Description

Calls an Ox function from C.

FOxLibAddFunction

```
bool FOxLibAddFunction(char *sFunc, OxFUNCP pFunc,
    bool fVarArg);
```

sFunc	in:	string describing function
pFunc	in:	pointer to C function to install
fVarArg	in:	TRUE: has variable argument list

Return value
> TRUE if function installed successfully, FALSE otherwise.

Description
> OxFUNCP is a pointer to a function declared as:

```
void OXCALL Func(OxVALUE *rtn, OxVALUE *pv, int cArg);
```

> The syntax of sFunc is:
> *arg_types$function_name*\0
> *arg_types* is a c (indicating a const argument) or a space, with one entry for each declared argument.
> This function links in C library functions statically, e.g. for part of the drawing library:

```
FOxLibAddFunction("cccc$Draw",        fnDraw,        0);
FOxLibAddFunction("ccccc$DrawT",       fnDrawT,       0);
FOxLibAddFunction("ccc$DrawX",         fnDrawX,       0);
FOxLibAddFunction("ccccc$DrawMatrix",  fnDrawMatrix,  1);
FOxLibAddFunction("cccccc$DrawTMatrix",fnDrawTMatrix, 1);
FOxLibAddFunction("ccccc$DrawXMatrix", fnDrawXMatrix, 1);
```

> This function is not required when using the extern specifier for external linking, as used in all examples in this chapter.

FOxRun

```
bool FOxRun(int iMainIP, char *sFunc);
```

iMainIP	in:	return value from OxMain
sFunc	in:	name in Ox code of function to call

Return value
> TRUE if the function is run successfully, FALSE otherwise.

Description
> Calls a function by name, bypasses main().

IOxRunInit

```
int  IOxRunInit(void);
```

Return value

Zero for success, or the number of link errors.

Description

Links the compiled code and initializes to prepare for running the code.

IOxVersion

```
int   IOxVersion(void);
```

Return value

Returns 100 times the version number, so 100 for version 1.00.

OxFnDouble,OxFnDouble2,OxFnDouble3,OxFnDoubleInt

```
void OxFnDouble(OxVALUE *rtn, OxVALUE *pv,
    double (OXCALL * fn1)(double) );
void OxFnDouble2(OxVALUE *rtn, OxVALUE *pv,
    double (OXCALL * fn2)(double,double) );
void OxFnDouble3(OxVALUE *rtn, OxVALUE *pv,
    double (OXCALL * fn3)(double,double,double) );
void OXCALL OxFnDoubleInt(OxVALUE *rtn, OxVALUE *pv,
    double (OXCALL * fndi)(double,int) )
```

rtn	out:	return value of function
pv	in:	arguments for function fn
fn1	in:	function of one double, returning a double
fn2	in:	function of two doubles, returning a double
fn3	in:	function of three doubles, returning a double
fndi	in:	function of a double and an int, returning a double

No return value.

Description

These functions are to simplify calling C functions, as for example in:

```
static void OXCALL
    fnProbgamma(OxVALUE *rtn, OxVALUE *pv, int cArg)
    {   OxFnDouble3(rtn, pv, DProbGamma);
    }
static void OXCALL
    fnProbchi(OxVALUE *rtn, OxVALUE *pv, int cArg)
    {   OxFnDouble2(rtn, pv, DProbChi);
    }
static void OXCALL
    fnProbnormal(OxVALUE *rtn, OxVALUE *pv, int cArg)
    {   OxFnDouble(rtn, pv, DProbNormal);
    }
```

OxFreeByValue

```
void OxFreeByValue(OxVALUE *pv);
```
      pv   in: pointer to value to free

                     out: freed value

No return value.

Description

    Frees the matrix/string/array (i.e. pv is OX_MATRIX, OX_ARRAY, or OX_STRING) if it has property OX_VALUE.

OxLibArgError

```
void OxLibArgError(int iArg);
```
      iArg   in: argument index

No return value.

Description

    Reports an error in argument iArg, and generates a run-time error.

OxLibArgTypeError

```
void OxLibArgTypeError(int iArg, int iExpect,
    int iFound);
```
      iArg   in: argument index

      iExpect   in: expected type, one of OX_INT, OX_DOUBLE, OX_MATRIX, etc.

      iFound   in: found type

No return value.

Description

    Reports a type error in argument iArg, and generates a run-time error.

OxLibCheckArrayMatrix

```
void OxLibCheckArrayMatrix(OxVALUE *pv, int iFirst,
    int iLast, MATRIX m);
```
      pv   in: array of values of type OX_ARRAY

      iFirst   in: first in array to check

      iLast   in: last in array to check

      m   in: matrix

No return value.

Description

    Checks if any of the values in pv[iFirst]...pv[iLast] (these must be of type OX_ARRAY) coincide with the matrix m.

OxLibCheckMatrixSize

```
void OxLibCheckMatrixSize(OxVALUE *pv, int iFirst,
    int iLast, int r, int c);
```

pv	in:	array of values of any type
iFirst	in:	first in array to check
iLast	in:	last in array to check
r	in:	required row dimension
c	in:	required column dimension

No return value.

Description

Checks whether all the values in pv[iFirst]...pv[iLast] are of type OX_MATRIX, and whether they have the required dimension.

OxLibCheckSquareMatrix

```
void OxLibCheckSquareMatrix(OxVALUE *pv, int iFirst,
    int iLast);
```

pv	in:	array of values of any type
iFirst	in:	first in array to check
iLast	in:	last in array to check

No return value.

Description

Checks whether all the values in pv[iFirst]...pv[iLast] are of type OX_MATRIX, and whether the matrices are square.

OxLibCheckType

```
void OxLibCheckType(int iType, OxVALUE *pv, int iFirst,
    int iLast);
```

iType	in:	required type, one of OX_INT, OX_DOUBLE, OX_MATRIX, etc.
pv	in:	array of values of any type
	out:	OX_INT changed to OX_DOUBLE or vice versa
iFirst	in:	first in array to check
iLast	in:	last in array to check

No return value.

Description

Checks whether all the values in pv[iFirst]...pv[iLast] are of type iType.

OxLibValArrayCalloc

```
void OxLibValArrayCalloc(OxVALUE *pv, int c);
```
    pv   in: value
                out: allocated to type array
    c   in: number of elements
No return value.

Description

Makes pv of type OX_ARRAY and allocates an array of c OxVALUEs in that OX_ARRAY.

OxLibValMatDup

```
void OxLibValMatDup(OxVALUE *pv, MATRIX mSrc,
    int r, int c);
```
    pv   in: value
                out: allocated to type matrix
    mSrc   in: source matrix
    r,c   in: number of rows, columns of source matrix
No return value.

Description

Makes pv of type OX_MATRIX, allocates an $r \times c$ matrix for it, and duplicates mSrc in that matrix. You could use OxFreeByValue to free the matrix, but normally that would be left to the Ox run-time system.

OxLibValMatMalloc

```
void OxLibValMatMalloc(OxVALUE *pv, int r, int c);
```
    pv   in: value
                out: allocated to type matrix
    r,c   in: number of rows, columns of source matrix
No return value.

Description

Makes pv of type OX_MATRIX and allocates an $r \times c$ matrix for it. You could use OxFreeByValue to free the matrix, but normally that would be left to the Ox run-time system.

OxLibValZero

```
void OxLibValZero(OxVALUE *pv);
```
    pv   in: value
                out: set to zero and OX_NULL
No return value.

Description

Sets pv to an integer of value zero with property OX_NULL. Using such a value in an expression in Ox leads to a run-time error (variable has no value).

OxMain

```
int   OxMain(int argc, char *argv[]);
```
argc   in: number of command line arguments
argv   in: command line argument list (first is program name)

Return value

The entry point for main() if successful, or a value ≤ 1 if there was a compilation or link error.

Description

Processes the Ox command line, including compilation, linking and running.

OxMainInit

```
void OxMainInit(void);
```

No return value.

Description

Sets output destination to stdout, and links the standard run-time and drawing library.

OxMessage

```
void OxMessage(char *s);
```
s   in: text to print

No return value.

Description

Prints a message.

OxRunError

```
void OxRunError(int iErno, char *sToken);
```
iErno   in: error number
sToken   in: NULL or offending token

No return value.

Description

Reports a run-time error message using OxRunErrorMessage.

OxRunErrorMessage

```
void OxRunErrorMessage(char *s);
    s           in:   message text
```
No return value.

Description
>   Reports a run-time error message and exits the program.

OxRunExit
```
void OxRunExit(void);
```
No return value.

Description
>   Cleans up after running a program.

OxRunMessage
```
void OxRunMessage(char *s);
    s           in:   message text
```
No return value.

Description
>   Reports a run-time error message.

SetOxMessage
```
void SetOxMessage(
    void (OXCALL * pfnNewOxMessage)(char *) );
    pfnNewOxMessage   in:   new message handler function
```
No return value.

Description
>   Installs a message handler function which is used by OxMessage.

SetOxPipe
```
void SetOxPipe(int cPipe);
    cPipe      in:   > 0: sets pipe buffer size, else uses default buffer size
```
No return value.

Description
>   Activates piping of output to another destination than stdout. The output from
>   the print function will from now on be handled by the OxPuts function.

SetOxPuts
```
void SetOxPuts(void (OXCALL * pfnNewOxPuts)(char *) );
```

pfnNewOxPuts   in: new OxPuts function

No return value.

Description

Replaces the OxPuts function by pfnNewOxPuts. Is used together with SetOxPipe to redirect the output from print.

SetOxRunMessage

```
void SetOxRunMessage(
    void (OXCALL * pfnNewOxRunMessage)(char *) );
```

pfnNewOx-   in: new message handler function
RunMessage

No return value.

Description

Installs a message handler function which is used by OxRunMessage and OxRunErrorMessage.

SOxGetTypeName

```
char * SOxGetTypeName(int iType);
```

iType   in: type, one of OX_INT, OX_DOUBLE, OX_MATRIX, etc.

Return value

A pointer to the text of the type name.

SOxIntFunc

```
char * SOxIntFunc(void);
```

Return value

A pointer to the name of the currently active internal function.

A2.8 Macros to access OxVALUEs

macro	purpose	input type
OxInt(pv, i)	accesses the integer value in pv[i]	OX_INT
OxDbl(pv, i)	accesses the double value in pv[i]	OX_DOUBLE
OxMat(pv, i)	accesses the matrix value in pv[i]	OX_MATRIX
OxMatc(pv, i)	accesses the no of columns in pv[i]	OX_MATRIX
OxMatr(pv, i)	accesses the no of rows in pv[i]	OX_MATRIX
OxStr(pv, i)	accesses the string value in pv[i]	OX_STRING
OxStrLen(pv, i)	accesses the string length in pv[i]	OX_STRING
OxArray(pv, i)	accesses the array value in pv[i]	OX_ARRAY
OxZero(pv, i)	sets pv[i] to OX_INT of value 0	—
OxSetInt(pv, i, j)	sets pv[i] to OX_INT of value j	—
OxSetDbl(pv, i, d)	sets pv[i] to OX_DOUBLE of value d	—
OxSetMatPtr(pv, i, m, cr, cc)	sets pv[i] to OX_MATRIX pointing to the cr × cc matrix m	—

A2.9 Ox exported mathematics functions

A2.9.1 MATRIX and VECTOR types

This section documents the C functions exported from the OxWin DLL to perform mathematical tasks. With the DLL installed, any C or C++ function could call these functions to perform a mathematical task. The primary purpose is, if you, for example, wish to use some random numbers in your C extension to Ox. It is also possible to just use these functions without using Ox at all.

To use any of the functions in this section, you need to include both jdtypes.h and jdmath.h (in this order), e.g.

```
#include "/ox/dev/jdtypes.h"
#include "/ox/dev/jdmath.h"
```

Or, if you have set up the information for your compiler such that /ox/dev is in the include search path:

```
#include "jdtypes.h"
#include "jdmath.h"
```

Several types are defined in ox/dev/jdtypes.h, of which the most important are MATRIX, VECTOR and bool.

The MATRIX type used in this library is a pointer to a column of pointers, each pointing to a row of doubles. A VECTOR is just a pointer to an array of doubles. In a MATRIX, consecutive rows (the VECTORs) do not necessarily occupy contiguous memory space. Suppose m is a 3 by 3 matrix, then the memory layout can be visualized as:

```
m    ⟶ m[0]
     m[0] ⟶   m[0][0],m[0][1],m[0][2]    first row
     m[1] ⟶   m[1][0],m[1][1],m[1][2]    second row
     m[2] ⟶   m[2][0],m[2][1],m[2][2]    third row
```

Matrices can be manipulated as follows, using the 3×3 matrix m:

- m[0] is a VECTOR, the first row of m;
- &m[1] is a MATRIX, the last two rows of m;
- &m[1][1] is a VECTOR, the last two elements of the second row.
- &(&m[1])[1] is a MATRIX, the last two elements of the second row (this is only a 1 row matrix, since there is no pointer to the third row).

A MATRIX is allocated by a call to MatAlloc and deallocated with MatFree. For a VECTOR the functions are VecAlloc and free, e.g.:

```
MATRIX m;   VECTOR v;   int i, j;

m = MatAlloc(3, 3);
v = VecAlloc(3);

if (!m || !v)              /* yes: error exit */
    printf("error: allocation failed!");

MatZero(m, 3, 3);               /* set m to 0 */
MatZero(&v, 1, 3);              /* set v to 0 */

for (i = 0; i < 3; ++i)  /* set both to 1 */
{   for (j = 0; j < 3; ++j)
        m[i][j] = 1;
    v[i] = 1;
}

/* ... do more work                         */

MatFree(m2, 3, 3);    /* done: free memory */
free(v);
```

Note that the memory of a matrix is owned by the original matrix. It is safe to exchange rows by swapping pointers, e.g.:

```
VECTOR t = m2[0]; m2[0] = m2[1]; m2[1] = t;
```

Rows cannot be exchanged between different matrices this way; instead the elements must be copied from one row to the other. Columns have to be done element by element as well.

As a final example, we show how to define a matrix which points to part of another matrix. For example, to set up a matrix which points to the 2 by 2 lower right block in m, allocate the pointers to rows:

```
MATRIX m2 = MatAlloc(2, 0);
m2[0] = &m[1][1];
```

```
m2[1] = &m[2][1];
// do work with m and m2, then free m2:

MatFree(m2, 2, 0);
```

Again note that the memory of the elements is still owned by m; deallocating m deletes what m2 tries to point to.

A2.9.2 Exported matrix functions

The following list gives the exported C functions, with their Ox equivalent.

c_abs	cabs
c_div	cdiv
c_mul	cmul
c_sqrt	csqrt
DBetaFunc	betafunc
DDensBeta	densbeta
DDensChi	denschi
DDensF	densf
DDensNormal	densn
DDensT	denst
DGammaFunc	gammafunc
DGetInvertEps	inverteps
DLogGamma	loggamma
DPolyGamma	polygamma
DProbBeta	probbeta
DProbChi	probchi
DProbF	probf
DProbGamma	probgamma
DProbNormal	probn
DProbT	probt
DQuanChi	quanchi
DQuanF	quanf
DQuanNormal	quann
DQuanT	quant
DRanBeta	ranbeta
DRanChi	ranchi
DRanExp	ranexp
DRanF	ranf
DRanGamma	rangamma
DRanNormalPM	rann
DRanPM	ranu

DRanT	rant
DTailProbChi	tailchi
DTailProbF	tailf
DTailProbNormal	tailn
DTailProbT	tailt
DTrace	trace
DTraceAB	trace(AB)
DVecsum	sumr(A)
FArmaVar	armavar
FGetAcf	acf
FGetPartAcf	pacf
INullSpace	nullspace
FPeriodogram	periodogram
FPPtDec	choleski
IEigValPoly	polyroots
IEigValReal	eigen
IEigValSym	eigen
IEigVecReal	eigensym
IEigVecSym	eigensym
IGenEigVecSym	eigensymgen
IInvDet	invert
IInvert	invert
ILDLbandDec	decldlband
ILDLdec	decldl
ILUPdec	declu
IntMatAlloc	
IntVecAlloc	
IntMatFree	
IOlsNorm	ols2c,ols2r
IOlsQR	ols2,ols2
IRanBinomial	ranbinomial
IRanPoisson	ranpoisson
ISVDdec	decsvd
ISymInv	invert
LDLbandSolve	solveldlband
LDLInv	solveldl
LDLsolve	solveldl
LRanPMSeed	ranseed
LUPsolve	solvelu
MatAcf	acf
MatAdd	A+c*B

MatAB	A*B
MatABt	A*B'
MatAtB	A'B
MatBSBt	BSB'
MatBtSB	B'SB
MatBtB	B'B
MatBtBVec	A=B-y; A'A
MatAlloc	
MatCpy	
MatDup	A = B
MatFree	
MatI	unit
MatNaN	
MatZero	zeros
MatGenInvert	1 / A, decsvd
MatPartAcf	pacf
MatRan	ranu
MatRanNormal	rann
MatReflect	reflect
MatStandardize	standardize
MatTranspose	transpose operator: '
MatVariance	variance
MatZero	zeros
SetFastMath	use command line switch to turn off
SetInvertEps	inverteps
ToeplitzSolve	solvetoeplitz
VecAlloc	
VecDup	

A2.9.3 Matrix function reference

c_abs, c_div, c_mul, c_sqrt

```
double c_abs(double xr, double xi)
bool c_div(double xr, double xi, double yr, double yi,
    double *zr, double *zi);
void c_mul(double xr, double xi, double yr, double yi,
    double *zr, double *zi);
void c_sqrt(double xr, double xi, double *yr,double *yi);
```

Return value

c_abs returns the result. c_div returns FALSE in an attempt to divide by 0,

TRUE otherwise. The other functions have no return value.

DBetaFunc

```
double DBetaFunc(double dX, double dA, double dB);
```

Return value

Returns the incomplete beta function $B_x(a, b)$.

DDensChi, DDensF, DDensNormal, DDensT

```
double DDensBeta(double x, double a, double b);
double DDensChi(double x, double dDf);
double DDensF(double x, double dDf1, double dDf2);
double DDensNormal(double x);
double DDensT(double x, int iDf);
```

Return value

Value of density at x.

DGammaFunc

```
double DGammaFunc(double dX, double dR);
```

Return value

Returns the incomplete gamma function $G_x(r)$.

DLogGamma

```
double DLogGamma(double dA);
```

Return value

Returns the logarithm of the gamma function.

DPolyGamma

```
double DPolyGamma(double dA, int n);
```

Return value

Returns the derivatives of the loggamma function; $n = 0$ is first derivative: digamma function, and so on.

DProbBeta, DProbChi, DProbF, DProbGamma, DProbNormal, DProbT

```
double DProbBeta(double x, double a, double b);
double DProbChi(double x, double dDf);
double DProbF(double x, double dDf1, double dDf2);
double DProbGamma(double x, double dR, double dA);
double DProbNormal(double x);
double DProbT(double x, int iDf);
```

Return value

Probabilities of value less than or equal to x.

DQuanChi, DQuanF, DQuanNormal, DQuanT

```
double DQuanChi(double p, double dDf);
double DQuanF(double p, double dDf1, double dDf2);
double DQuanNormal(double p);
double DQuanT(double p, int iDf);
```

Return value

Quantiles at p.

DGetInvertEps

```
double DGetInvertEps(void);
```

Return value

Returns inversion epsilon, ϵ_{inv}, see SetInvertEps.

DRanBeta, DRanChi, DRanExp, DRanF, DRanGamma, DRanNormalPM, DRanPM, DRanT

```
double DRanBeta(double a, double b);
double DRanChi(double dDf);
double DRanExp(double dLambda);
double DRanF(double dDf1, double dDf2);
double DRanGamma(double dR, double dA);
double DRanNormalPM(void);
double DRanPM(void);
double DRanT(int iDf);
```

Return value

Returns random numbers from various distributions.

DRanPM generates uniform random numbers (PM = Park & Miller),
DRanNormalPM standard normals (PM = Polar-Marsaglia).

DTailProbChi, DTailProbF, DTailProbGamma, DTailProbNormal, DTailProbT

```
double DTailProbChi(double x, double dDf);
double DTailProbF(double x, double dDf1, double dDf2);
double DTailProbGamma(double x, double dR, double dA);
double DTailProbNormal(double x);
double DTailProbT(double x, int iDf);
```

Return value

Probabilities of values greater than x.

DTrace, DTraceAB
```
double DTrace(MATRIX mat, int cA);
double DTraceAB(MATRIX mA, MATRIX mB, int cM, int cN);
    mA[cM][cN]          in:  matrix
    mB[cN][cM]          in:  matrix
```
Return value
> DTrace returns the trace of A.
> DTraceAB returns the trace of AB.

DVecsum
```
double DVecsum(VECTOR vA, int cA);
    vA[cA]              in:  vector
```
Return value
> DVecsum returns the sum of the elements in the vector.

FArmaVar
```
bool FArmaVar(VECTOR vP, int p, int q, double dVar,
    VECTOR vSigma, int cT);
    vP[s]               in:  ARMA coefficients vP[0:p-1] AR coeffs,
                             vP[p:p+q-1] MA coeffs, $s \geq p + q$
    p                   in:  no of AR coefficients
    q                   in:  no of MA coefficients
    dVar                in:  variance of disturbance
    vSigma[cT]          in:  vector
                        out: autocovariance function of ARMA($p, q$) process
```
Return value
> Returns TRUE if successful.

FGetAcf, FGetAcfRun
```
bool FGetAcf(VECTOR vX, int cT, int cLag, VECTOR vAcf);
bool FGetAcfRun(VECTOR vX, int cT, int cLag,VECTOR vAcf);
    vX[cT]              in:  variable of which to compute correlogram
    cT                  in:  number of observations
    cLag                in:  required no of correlation coeffs
    vAcf[cLag]          out: correlation coeffs 1...cLag (0. if failed); unlike
                             acf(), the autocorrelation at lag 0 (which is 1)
                             is not included.
```
Return value
> FGetAcf uses the full sample means (the standard textbook correlogram),
> whereas FGetAcfRun uses the running means (leading to the proper correlation
> between the variable and its lag). Also see under acf and DrawCorrelogram.

FGetPartAcf

```
bool FGetPartAcf(VECTOR vAcf, int cAcf, VECTOR vPartAcf);
    vAcf[cAcf]              in:   autocovariance function
    vPartAcf[cAcf-1]  in:   matrix
                           out:  partial autocorrelation function
```

Return value

Returns TRUE if successful, FALSE for non-stationary acf.

FPeriodogram

```
bool FPeriodogram(VECTOR vX, int cT, int iTrunc, int cS,
    VECTOR vS, int iMode);
    vX[cT]      in:   variable of which to compute correlogram
    cT          in:   number of observations
    iTrunc      in:   truncation parameter $m$
    cS          in:   no of points at which to evaluate spectrum
    vS[cS]      out:  periodogram
    iMode       in:   0: (truncated) periodogram,
                      1: smoothed periodogram using Parzen window,
                      2: estimated spectral density using Parzen window (as option
                      1, but divided by $c(0)$).
```

Return value

Returns TRUE if successful, FALSE if out of memory.

FPPtDec

```
bool FPPtDec(MATRIX mA, int cA)
    mA[cA][cA]            in:   symmetric p.d. matrix to be decomposed
                         out:  contains $P$
```

Return value

TRUE: no error;

FALSE: Choleski decomposition failed.

Description

Computes the Choleski decomposition of a symmetric pd matrix A: $A = PP'$.
P has zeros above the diagonal.

INullSpace

```
int INullSpace(MATRIX mA, int cM, int cN, bool fAppend);
    mA[cM][cM]            in:   cM by cN matrix of rank cN, cM > cN (allocated
                               size must be cM by cM)
                         out:  null space of $A$ is appended (fAppend==TRUE)
                               or mA is overwritten by null space.
```

Return value

> −1: failure: couldn't find all singular values, or out of memory;
> ≥ 0: rank of null space.

Description

> Uses ISVDdec to find the orthogonal complement A^*, $m \times m - n$, of an $m \times n$ matrix A of rank n, $n < m$, such that $A^{*\prime}A^* = I$, $A^{*\prime}A = 0$.
>
> Note that the append option requires that A has full column ranks (if not the last $m - n$ columns of U are appended).

IEigValPoly, IEigValReal, IEigVecReal

```
int IEigValPoly(VECTOR vPoly, VECTOR vEr, VECTOR vEi,
    int cA);
int IEigValReal(MATRIX mA, VECTOR vEr,VECTOR vEi,int cA);
int IEigVecReal(MATRIX mA, VECTOR vEr,VECTOR vEi,int cA);
```
vPoly[cA]	in: coefficients of polynomial (as in polyroots()).
	out: unchanged.
mA[cA][cA]	in: unsymmetric matrix.
	out: used as working space. IEigVecReal: holds eigenvecs in columns.
vEr[cA]	out: real part of eigenvalues
vEi[cA]	out: imaginary part of eigenvalues

Return value

> 0   success
> 1   maximum no of iterations (50) reached
> 2   NULL pointer arguments or memory allocation not succeeded.

Description

> IEigValPoly computes the roots of a polynomial.
>
> IEigValReal computes the eigenvalues of a double unsymmetric matrix.
>
> IEigVecReal computes the eigenvalues and vectors of a double unsymmetric matrix.

IEigValSym, IEigVecSym

```
int  IEigValSym(MATRIX mA, VECTOR vEv, int cA);
int  IEigVecSym(MATRIX mA, VECTOR vEv, int cA);
```
mA[cA][cA]	in: symmetric matrix.
	out: IEigValSym: strict upper diagonal has been used as working space. IEigVecSym: the rows contain the normalized eigenvectors (ordered).
vEv[cA]	out: ordered eigenvalues (smallest first)

Return value

See `IEigValReal`.

Description

`IEigValSym` computes the eigenvalues of a symmetric matrix. `IEigVecSym` computes the eigenvalues and (normalized) eigenvectors of a symmetric matrix.

IGenEigVecSym

```
int   IGenEigVecSym(MATRIX mA, MATRIX mB, VECTOR vEval,
      VECTOR vSubd, int cA);
```

`mA[cA][cA]`	in:	symmetric matrix.
	out:	the rows contain the normalized eigenvectors (sorted according to eigenvals, largest first)
`mB[cA][cA]`	in:	symmetric pd. matrix.
	out:	work
`vEval[cA]`	out:	ordered eigenvalues (smallest first)
`vSubd[cA]`	out:	index of ordered eigenvalues
`cA`	in:	dimension of matrix;

Return value

0,1,2: see `IEigValReal`; -1: Choleski decomposition failed.

Description

Solves the general eigenproblem $Ax = \lambda Bx$, where A and B are symmetric, B also positive definite.

IInvert, IInvDet

```
int   IInvert(MATRIX mA, int cA);
int   IInvDet(MATRIX mA, int cA, double pdDet);
```

`mA[cA][cA]`	in:	ptr to matrix to be inverted
	out:	contains the inverse, if successful
`pdDet`	out:	determinant of matrix

Return value

0: success; 1,2,3: see `ILDLdec`.

Description

Computes inverse of a matrix using LU decomposition.

ILDLbandDec

```
int ILDLbandDec(MATRIX mA, VECTOR vD, int cB, int cA);
```

mA[cB][cA]	in:	ptr to sym. pd. band matrix to be decomposed
	out:	contains the L matrix (except for the 1's on the diagonal)
vD[cA]	out:	the reciprocal of D (not the square root!)
cB	in:	1+bandwidth

Return value

See ILDLdec.

Description

Computes the Choleski decomposition of a symmetric positive band matrix. The matrix is stored as in decldlband.

ILDLdec

int ILDLdec(MATRIX mA, VECTOR vD, int cA);

mA[cA][cA]	in:	ptr to sym. pd. matrix to be decomposed only the lower diagonal is referenced;
	out:	the strict lower diagonal of A contains the L matrix (except for the 1's on the diagonal)
vD[cA]	out:	the reciprocal of D (not the square root!)

Return value

0	no error;
1	the matrix is negative definite;
2	the matrix is (numerically) singular;
3	NULL pointer argument

Description

Computes the Choleski decomposition of a symmetric positive definite matrix.

ILUPdec

int ILUPdec(MATRIX mA, int cA, int *piPiv,
    double *pdLogDet, int *piSignDet, MATRIX mUt);

mA[cA][cA]	in:	ptr to matrix to be decomposed
	out:	the strict lower diagonal of A contains the L matrix (except for the 1's on the diagonal) the upper diagonal contains U.
piPiv[cA]	out:	the pivot information
pdLogDet	out:	the *logarithm* of the absolute value of the determinant of A
piSignDet	out:	the sign of the determinant of A; 0: singular; $-1, -2$: negative determinant; $+1, +2$: positive determinant; $-2, +2$: result is unreliable
mUt[cA][cA]	in:	NULL or matrix
	out:	used as workspace

Return value

0	no error;
-1	out of memory;
≥ 1	the matrix is (numerically) singular;
	the return value is one plus the singular pivot.

Description

Computes the LU decomposition of a matrix A as: $PA = LU$.

IntMatAlloc, IntMatFree, IntVecAlloc

```
INTMAT IntMatAlloc(int cM, int cN);
void IntMatFree(INTMAT im, int cM, int cN);
INTVEC IntVecAlloc(int cM);
```

cM, cN   in: required matrix dimensions

Return value

IntMatAlloc returns a pointer to the newly allocated cM × cN matrix of integers (INTMAT corresponds to int **), or NULL if the allocation failed, or if cM was 0. Use IntMatFree to free such a matrix.

IntVecAlloc returns a pointer to the newly allocated cM vector of integers (INTVEC corresponds to int *), or NULL if the allocation failed, or if cM was 0. Use the standard C function free to free such a matrix.

The allocated types are a matrix or vector of *integers*; there is no corresponding type in Ox, and the allocated matrix cannot be passed directly to Ox code.

IOlsNorm,IOlsQR

```
int IOlsNorm(MATRIX mXt, int cX, int cT, MATRIX mYt,
    int cY, MATRIX mB, MATRIX mXtXinv, MATRIX mXtX,
    bool fInRows);
```

mXt[cX][cT]	in:	X data matrix
	out:	unchanged
mYt[cY][cT]	in:	Y data matrix
	out:	unchanged
mB[cY][cX]	in:	allocated matrix
	out:	coefficients
mXtXinv[cX][cX]	in:	allocated matrix or NULL
	out:	$(X'X)^{-1}$ if !NULL
mXtX[cX][cX]	in:	allocated matrix or NULL
	out:	$X'X$ if !NULL
fInRows	in:	if FALSE, input is mXt[cT][cX], mYt[cT][cY]

```
int IOlsQR(MATRIX mXt, int cX, int cT, MATRIX mYt,
    int cY, MATRIX mB, MATRIX mXtXinv, MATRIX mXtX);
```

mXt[cX][cT]	in:	X data matrix
	out:	QR decomposition of X, but only if all three return arguments mB, mXtXinv, mXtX are NULL
mYt[cY][cT]	in:	Y data matrix
	out:	$Q'Y$
mB[cY][cX]	in:	allocated matrix or NULL
	out:	coefficients if !NULL
mXtXinv[cX][cX]	in:	allocated matrix or NULL
	out:	$(X'X)^{-1}$ if !NULL
mXtX[cX][cX]	in:	allocated matrix or NULL
	out:	$X'X$ if !NULL

Return value
- 0: out of memory,
- 1: success,
- 2: ratio of diagonal elements of $(X'X)$ is large, rescaling is adviced,
- −1: $(X'X)$ is (numerically) singular,
- −2: combines 2 and -1.

Description
    performs ordinary least squares (OLS).

IRanBinomial, IRanPoisson

```
int IRanBinomial(int n, double p);
int IRanPoisson(double dMu);
```

Return value
    Returns random numbers from Binomial/Poisson distributions.

ISVDdec

```
int ISVDdec(MATRIX mA, int cM, int cN, VECTOR vW,
    bool fDoU, MATRIX mU, bool fDoV, MATRIX mV,
    VECTOR v_1, bool fSort);
```

mA[cM][cN]	in:	matrix to decompose, cM $\geq$ cN
	out:	unchanged
vW[cN]	in:	vector
	out:	the n (non-negative) singular values of A
fDoU	in:	TRUE: U matrix of decomposition required
mU[cM][cN]	in:	matrix
	out:	the matrix U (orth column vectors) of the decomposition if fDoU == TRUE. Otherwise used as workspace. mU may coincide with mA.
fDoV	in:	TRUE: V matrix required
mV[cM][cN]	in:	matrix
mV[cN][cN]	out:	the matrix V of the decomposition if fDoV == TRUE. Otherwise not referenced. mV may coincide with mU if mU is not needed.
v_1[cN]	out:	workspace
fSort	in:	if TRUE the singular values are sorted in decreasing order with U, V accordingly.

Return value

0: success

k: if the k-th singular value (with index k - 1) has not been determined after 50 iterations. The singular values and corresponding U, V should be correct for indices $\geq$ k.

Description

Computes the singular value decomposition.

ISymInv

```
int    ISymInv(MATRIX mA, int cA);
```

| mA[cA][cA] | in: | ptr to sym. pd. matrix to be inverted |
| | out: | contains the inverse, if successful |

Return value

0: success; 1,2,3: see ILDLdec.

LDLbandSolve

```
void LDLbandSolve(MATRIX mL, VECTOR vD, VECTOR vX,
    VECTOR vB, int cB, int cA);
```

mL[cB][cA]	in:	L from calling ILDLbandDec
vD[cA]	in:	the reciprocal of D
vX[cA]	out:	the solution vX (if (vX == vB) then vB is overwritten by the solution)
vB[cA]	in:	pointer containing the r.h.s. of $Lx = b$
cB	in:	1+bandwidth

No return value.

Description
Solves $Ax = b$, with $A = LDL'$ a symmetric positive definite band matrix.

LDLinv
```
void  LDLInv( MATRIX mL,  VECTOR vD,  int cA );
    mL[cA][cA]          in:  ptr to a matrix of which the strict lower diagonal
                             must contain L from the Choleski decomposi-
                             tion. (the upper diagonal is not referenced);
                        out: the lower diagonal contains the inverse
    vD[cA]              in:  contains the reciprocal of D
```
No return value.

Description
Computes the inverse of a symmetric matrix L, L, D must be the Choleski decomposition.

LDLsolve
```
void LDLsolve(MATRIX mL,  VECTOR vD,  VECTOR vX,
    VECTOR vB,  int cA);
    mL[cA][cA]          in:  ptr to a matrix of which the strict lower diagonal
                             must contain L from the Choleski decomposition
                             computed using ILDLdec. (the upper diagonal
                             is not referenced);
    vD[cA]              in:  contains the reciprocal of D
    vX[cA]              in:  pointer containing the r.h.s. of Lx = b;
    vB[cA]              out: contains the solution x (if (vX == vB) then vB
                             is overwritten by the solution)
```
No return value.

Description
Solves $Ax = b$, with $A = LDL'$ a symmetric positive definite matrix.

LRanPMSeed
```
long  LRanPMSeed(long lSeed);
    lSeed     in:  -1: reset seed, 0: only return seet, > 0: new seed
```
Return value
Returns the (new) seed.

LUPsolve

```
void LUPsolve(MATRIX mL, MATRIX mU, int *piPiv, VEC-
TOR vB, int cA);
```

mL[cA][cA]	in:	the strict lower diagonal contains the L matrix (except for the 1's on diag)
mU[cA][cA]	in:	the upper diagonal contains U: $PA = LU$ output from ILUPdec.
piPiv[cA]	in:	the pivot information (P)
vB[cA]	in:	rhs vector of system to be solved: $Ax = b$.
	out:	contains x.

No return value.

Description

Solves $AX = B$, with $A = LU$ a square matrix. Normally, this will be preceded by a call to ILUPdec. That function returns LU stored in one matrix, which can then be used for both mL and mU.

MatAcf

```
MATRIX MatAcf(MATRIX mAcf, MATRIX mX, int cT, int cX,
    int mxLag);
```

mAcf[mxLag+1][cX]	out:	correlation coefficients (0. if failed)
mX[cT][cX]	in:	variable of which to compute correlogram
cT	in:	number of observations
mxLag	in:	required no of correlation coeffs

Return value

Returns mAcf if successful, NULL if not enough observations.

MatAdd

```
MATRIX MatAdd(MATRIX mA, int cM, int cN, MATRIX mB,
    double dFac, MATRIX mAplusB);
```

mA[cM][cN]	in:	matrix A
mB[cM][cN]	in:	matrix B
dFac	in:	scalar c
mAplusB[cM][cN]	out:	$A + cB$

Return value

returns mAplusB $= A + cB$.

MatAB, MatABt, MatAtB, MatBSBt, MatBtSB, MatBtB, MatBtB-Vec

```
MATRIX MatAB(MATRIX mA, int cA, int cC, MATRIX mB,
    int cB, mat mAB);
```

```
mA[cA][cC]          in:  matrix A
mB[cC][cB]          in:  matrix B
mAB[cA][cB]         out: AB
```

MATRIX MatABt(MATRIX mA, int cA, int cC, MATRIX mB,
    int cB, mat mABt);

```
mA[cA][cC]          in:  matrix A
mB[cB][cC]          in:  matrix B
mABt[cA][cB]        out: AB'
```

MATRIX MatAtB(MATRIX mA, int cA, int cC, MATRIX mB,
    int cB, mat mAtB);

```
mA[cA][cC]          in:  matrix A
mB[cA][cB]          in:  matrix B
mAtB[cC][cB]        out: A'B
```

MATRIX MatBSBt(MATRIX mB, int cB, MATRIX mS,
    int cS, MATRIX mBSBt);

```
mB[cB][cS]          in:  matrix B
mS[cS][cS]          in:  symm.matrix S or NULL (equivalent to S = I)
mBSBt[cB][cB]       out: matrix containing BSB'
```

MATRIX MatBtSB(MATRIX mB, int cB, MATRIX mS,
    int cS, MATRIX mBtSB);

MATRIX MatBtB(MATRIX mB, int cB, int cS, MATRIX mBtB);

```
mB[cB][cS]          in:  matrix B
mBtB[cS][cS]        out: matrix containing B'B
```

MATRIX MatBtBVec(MATRIX mB, int cB, int cS, VECTOR vY, MAT-
RIX mBtB);

```
mB[cB][cS]          in:  matrix B
vY[cS]              in:  vector y
mBtB[cS][cS]        out: matrix containing (B − y)'(B − y)
```

Return value

MatAB returns mAB $=AB$.
MatABt returns mABt $=AB'$.
MatAtB returns mAtB $=A'B$.
MatBSBt returns mBSBt $=BSB'$.
MatBtSB returns mBtSB $=B'SB$.
MatBtB returns mBtB $=B'B$.
MatBtBVec returns mBtB $=(B − y)'(B − y)$.

MatAlloc

MATRIX MatAlloc(int cM, int cN);

```
cM, cN              in:  required matrix dimensions
```

Return value

Returns a pointer to the newly allocated cM × cN matrix, or NULL if the allocation failed, or if cM was 0. Use MatFree to free the matrix.

MatCpy, MatDup

```
MATRIX MatCpy(MATRIX mDest, MATRIX mSrc, int cM, int cN);
MATRIX MatDup(MATRIX mSrc, int cM, int cN);
    mSrc[cM][cN]        in:  m × n matrix A to copy/duplicate
    mDest[cM][cN]       in:  allocated matrix
                        out: copy of mSrc
```

Return value

Both return a pointer to the destination matrix which holds a copy of the source matrix. In the case of MatDup this is a newly allocated matrix (a return value of NULL indicates allocation failure), which must be deallocated with MatFree.

MatCpyTranspose

```
MATRIX MatCpyTranspose(MATRIX mDest, MATRIX mSrc, int cM,
    int cN);
    mSrc[cM][cN]        in:  m × n matrix A to copy
    mDest[cN][cM]       in:  allocated matrix
                        out: copy of the transpose of mSrc
```

Return value

A pointer to mDest.

MatFree

```
void MatFree(MATRIX mA, int cM, int cN);
    mA[cM][cN]          in:  matrix to free, previously allocated using
                             MatAlloc or MatDup
```

No return value.

MatGenInvert

```
MATRIX MatGenInvert(MATRIX mA, int cM, int cN,
    MATRIX mRes, VECTOR vSval);
    mA[cM][cN]          in:  m × n matrix A to invert
    mRes[cN][cM]        in:  allocated matrix
                        out: generalized inverse of A using SVD
    vSval[              in:  NULL or allocated vector
    min(cM,cN)]
                        out: sing.vals of A (if m ≥ n) or A' (if m < n);
```

Return value

    !NULL: pointer to mRes indicating success;

    NULL: failure: not enough memory or couldn't find all singular values.

Description

    Uses ISVDdec to find the generalized inverse.

MatI

```
MATRIX MatI(MATRIX mDest, int cM);
    mDest[cM][cM]    in:  allocated matrix
                     out: identity matrix
```

Return value

    Returns a pointer to mDest.

MatNaN

```
MATRIX MatNaN(MATRIX mDest, int cM, int cN);
    mDest[cM][cN]    in:  allocated matrix
                     out: matrix filled with the NaN value (Not a
                          Number)
```

Return value

    Returns a pointer to mDest.

MatPartAcf

```
MATRIX MatPartAcf(MATRIX mPartAcf, MATRIX mAcf,
    int mxLag, int cX);
    mPartAcf[cAcf-   in:  matrix
    1][cX]
                     out: partial autocorrelation function
    mAcf[cAcf][cX]   in:  autocovariance function
```

Return value

    Returns mPartAcf if successful, NULL if not enough observations.

MatRan, MatRanNormal

```
MATRIX MatRan(MATRIX mA, int cR, int cC)
MATRIX MatRanNormal(MATRIX mA, int cR, int cC)
    mA[cR][cC]       in:  allocated matrix
                     out: filled with random numbers
```

Return value

    Both functions return mA

    MatRan generates uniform random numbers, MatRanNormal standard normals.

MatReflect, MatTranspose

```
MATRIX MatReflect(MATRIX mA, int cA);
MATRIX MatTranspose(MATRIX mA, int cA);
     mA[cA][cA]          in:  matrix
                         out: transposed matrix.
```

Return value

Both return a pointer to mA.

Description

MatTranspose transposes a matrix. MatReflect reflects a matrix around its secondary diagonal.

MatVariance

```
MATRIX MatStandardize(MATRIX mXdest, MATRIX mX, int cT,
     int cX);
     mXdest[cT][cX]      out: standardized mX matrix
     mX[cT][cX]          in:  data which to standardize
     cT                  in:  number of observations
```

Return value

Returns mXdest if successful, NULL if not enough observations.

MatVariance

```
MATRIX MatVariance(MATRIX mXtX, MATRIX mX, int cT,
     int cX, bool fCorr);
     mXtX[cX][cX]        out: variance matrix (fCorr is FALSE) or correlation
                              matrix (fCorr is TRUE)
     mX[cT][cX]          in:  variable of which to compute correlogram
     cT                  in:  number of observations
```

Return value

Returns mXtX if successful, NULL if not enough observations.

MatZero

```
MATRIX MatZero(MATRIX mDest, int cM, int cN);
     MatZero[cM][cN]   in:  allocated matrix
                       out: matrix of zeros
```

Return value

Returns a pointer to mDest.

SetFastMath

```
void    SetFastMath(bool fYes);
```

fYes   in: TRUE: switches *Fastmath* mode on, else switches it off

Description

When *FastMath* is active, memory is used to optimize some matrix operations. *FastMath* mode uses memory to achieve the speed improvements. The following function are *FastMath* enhanced: `MatBtB`, `MatBtBVec`

SetInvertEps

```
void    SetInvertEps(double dEps);
```
dEps   in: sets inversion epsilon ϵ_{inv} to dEps if dEps $\geq$ 0, else to the default.

Description

The following functions return singular status if the pivoting element is less than or equal to ϵ_{inv}: `ILDLdec`, `ILUPdec`, `ILDLbandDec`, `IOrthMGS`. Less than $10\epsilon_{inv}$ is used by `IO1sQR`.

A singular value is considered zero when less than $\|A\|_\infty 10\epsilon_{inv}$ in `MatGenInvert`.

The default value for ϵ_{inv} is $1000 \times$ DBL_EPSILON.

ToeplitzSolve

```
void ToeplitzSolve(VECTOR vR, int cR, int cM, MATRIX mB,
    int cB, VECTOR v_1);
```
vR[cR]	in:	vector specifying Toeplitz matrix
cM	in:	dimension of Toeplitz matrix, cM $\geq$ cR, remainder of vR is assumed zero.
mB[cM][cB]	in:	cM $\times$ cB rhs of system to be solved
	out:	contains X, the solution to $AX = B$
v_1[cM]	in:	work vector
	out:	changed, v_1[0] is the logarithm of the determinant

Return value

0: success; 1: singular matrix or v_1 is NULL.

Description

Solves $AX = B$ when A is symmetric Toeplitz.

VecAlloc

```
VECTOR VecAlloc(int cM);
```
cM   in: required size of vector

Return value

Returns a pointer to the newly allocated vector, or NULL if the allocation failed, or if cM was 0.

Description

A vector allocated with `VecAlloc` may be freed by using the standard C function `free`.

VecDup

```
VECTOR VecDup(VECTOR vSrc, int cM);
```

vSrc[cM]   in: m vector to duplicate

Return value

Return a pointer to the newly allocated destination vector, which holds a copy of the source vector. A return value of `NULL` indicates allocation failure.

Appendix A3

Comparing Gauss and Ox syntax

A3.1 Introduction

This chapter compares Gauss syntax with Ox. In the two column format, Gauss is discussed on the left, and Ox in the right-hand column. The aim is to aid Gauss users in understanding Ox. Elements of Ox syntax which are not needed for that purpose (such as classes) are not discussed here.

A3.2 Comparison

A3.2.1 Comment

The @ ... @ style of comment does not exist in Ox.

Ox comment style is /* ... */ (as in Gauss) or // which indicates a comment up to the end of the line.

A3.2.2 Program entry

A Gauss program starts execution at the first executable statement (which is not a procedure/function/keyword etc.).

An Ox program starts execution at the function main.

A3.2.3 Case and symbol names

Gauss is not case sensitive, except inside strings. Symbol names may be up to 32 characters.

Ox is case sensitive. Symbol names may be up to 60 and strings up to 1024 characters.

A3.2.4 Types

Gauss primarily has a matrix type.

Ox is implicitly typed, and has the following types: integer, double, matrix, string, array, file, function, class. Type is determined at run time (and can change at run time). E.g. `a=1;` creates an integer, `a=1.0;` a double and `a=<1>;` a matrix.

A3.2.5 Matrix indexing

Indexing starts at 1, so `m[1,1]` is the first element in a matrix. Vectors only need one index. A matrix can be indexed by a single index, a list of numbers, or an expression evaluating to a vector or matrix (in which case no spaces are allowed). A dot indicates all elements, for example:

```
w[1,1]
w[2:5,3:6]
w[1 3:4,.]
w[a+b,c]
```

Indexing starts at 0, so `m[0][0]` is the first element in a matrix. Ox can be made to start indexing at 1, see §12.8.3; this will lead to a somewhat slower program. Vectors are matrices with one row or one column, and need two indices.

A matrix can be indexed by a single index, a list of numbers, or an expression evaluating to a vector or matrix (including matrix constants) or a range. The upper or lower index in a range may be omitted. A empty index indicates all elements, for example:

```
w[0][0]
w[1:4][2:5]
w[<0,2:3>][]
w[a + b][c]
w[:4][2:]
```

A3.2.6 Arrays

Gauss implements arrays using the varput and varget function.

The array is a type in Ox, e.g. `{"one", "two", <1,2>}` is an array constant, where the first two elements are a string, and the last a matrix. To print these: `print(a[0], a[1], a[2]);`. A new array is created with the new operator.

A3.2.7 Declaration and constants

In Gauss, a variable can be assigned a value with a `let` or implicit `let` statement. If the variable doesn't exist yet, it is declared, otherwise it is redeclared. A variable can be declared explicitly with the `declare` statement. Assignment in a let statement may consist of a number, a sequence of numbers (or strings) separated by spaces, or numbers in closed in curly brackets. The latter specifies a matrix, with a comma separating rows, and a space between elements in a row (these are not proper matrix constants, because they cannot be used in expressions). A variable outside a function is also created if a value is assigned to it (and it doesn't exist yet).

```
let w = { 1 1 1 };
let y0 = 1 2;
let y1[2,2] = 1 1 2 2;
y2[2,2] = {1 1, 2 2}; /*(1)*/
let w[2,2] = 1;
let w[2,2];
w = zeros(2,2);
```

The line labelled (1) is an implicit let which creates a 2×2 matrix. A statement like `y2[2,2] = 1;` on the other hand puts the value one in the 2,2 position of y, which therefore must already exist.

Ox has explicit declaration of variables. A value can be assigned to a variable at the same time as it is declared. If the variable has external scope (i.e. is assigned outside any function), you can use constants only, (matrix or other constants). Such constants can also be used in expressions.

```
decl w  = < 1,1,1 >;
decl y0 = <1,2>;
decl y1 = <1,1; 2,2>;
decl y2 = <1,1; 2,2>;
decl w[2][2] = 1;
decl w[2][2];
decl w = zeros(2, 2);
        /* only inside func-
tion */
```

If all statements would be used together, the compiler would complain about the last three declarations: w was already declared earlier (no redeclaration is possible, but re-assignment is, of course). The last declaration involves code, and can only be made inside a function.

A3.2.8 Expressions

Assignment statements are quite similar, e.g. `y = a .* b + 3 - d;` works in both Gauss and Ox, whether the variables are matrices or scalars.

Ox allows multiple assigments, e.g. `i = j = 0;`. In addition there are conditional and dot-conditional expressions (§12.7.14).

A3.2.9 Operators

The following have a different symbol:

Gauss	Ox
.*.	**
/=	!=
not	!
and	&
or	|

The following Gauss operators are not supported in Ox: % (Ox has the `idiv` function) ! *~ .'.

For $x!$ use `exp(loggamma(x+1))` in Ox.

The text form of the relational operators are not available in Ox, so e.g. use .< instead of .LT.

There are no special string versions of operators in Ox.

The ^ operator is matrix power, not element by element power.

And finally, x=A/b (with A and b conformable) does not solve a linear system, but is executed as x=A*(1/b). This fails, because intended is x=(1/A)*b. The 1/A part in Ox computes the generalized inverse if the normal inverse does not work, see §12.7.5.

A3.2.10 Loop statements

Gauss has the `do while` and `do until` loop:

```
i = 1;
do while (i <= 10);
    /* something */
    i = i + 1;
endo;

i = 10;
do until (i < 1);
    /* something */
    i = i - 1;
endo;
```

Ox has the for, while and do while loop statements (note the difference in the use of the semi-colon).

```
for (i = 0; i < 10; ++i)
{
    /* something */
}

i = 10;
while (i >= 1)
{
    /* something */
    --i;
}

i = 1;
do
{   /* something */
    ++i;
} while (i <= 10);
```

A3.2.11 Conditional statements

```
if i == 1;
    /* statements */
elseif i = 2;
    /* statements */
else;
    /* statements */
endif;
```

```
if (i == 1)
{    /* statements */
}
else if (i = 2)
{    /* statements */
}
else
{    /* statements */
}
```

Again notice the difference in usage of parenthesis and semi-colons.

A3.2.12 Printing

In Gauss, a `print` statement consists of a list of items to print. A space separates the items, unless they are in parenthesis. An expression without an equal sign is also treated as a print statement.

Ox has a `print` function, which gives the expressions to print, separated by a comma. Strings which contain a format are not printed but apply to the next expression.

A3.2.13 Functions

Gauss has procedures (`proc`), keywords and single-line functions (`fn`). Procedures may return many values; no values can be returned in arguments. Local variables are declared with the `local` statement.

Ox only has functions which may return zero or one value. Values can be returned in arguments. Variables are declared using `decl`. Variables have a lifetime restricted to the brace level at which they are declared.

```
proc(2) = foo(x, y);
    local a,b;
    /* code */
    retp (a,b);
endp;

{c, d} = foo(1, 2);
```

```
foo(const x, const y,
                const retb)
{    decl a,b;
    /* code */
    retb[0] = b;
    return a;
}
c = foo(1, 2, &d);
```

A3.2.14 Input and Output

Gauss .fmt files are different between the MS-DOS/Windows versions (little endian) and the Unix versions (big endian).

Ox can read and write .fmt files, and read .dht/.dat files. These are always written/read in little-endian mode (the Windows/MS-DOS way of storing doubles on disk; Unix systems use big-endian mode). So a .fmt file can be written on a PC, transferred (binary mode!) to a Sun, and read there. Ox can also read Excel files, see under loadmat.

A3.2.15 String manipulation

Gauss allows storing of strings in a matrix, and provides special operators to manipulate matrices which consists of strings.

A string is an inbuilt data type in Ox and arrays of strings can be created. It is possible to store a string which is 8 characters or shorter in a matrix or double as e.g. d = double("aap");, and extract the string as string(d);

A3.3 G2Ox

G2Ox is a program that translates Gauss code into Ox. It is fairly rudimentary, and can certainly not be relied upon to translate all Gauss programs correctly. But it is a useful starting point. The command line syntax is.

```
g2ox Gaussfilename[.prg] Oxfilename[.ox]
```

Assuming that a program test.prg needs be translated to test.ox, type:

```
g2ox test test
```

This will produce three files:

    test.ox   – the produced source code;
    test.h   – the corresponding header file;
    test.log   – the translation log.

G2Ox uses the input file g2ox.cvt to find out which functions are supported, which functions need renaming and which are not supported. When running test.ox, the file g2ox.ox is automatically included. This file provides the translation layer for many functions (note that a lot of functions do not yet have a translation), and sets array indexing to start at one. Array indexing from one, and the fact that many functions are wrapped in a thin layer means that there is a speed penalty.

G2Ox does not support the following constructs: dataloop, gosub, keyword.

Appendix A4

Some matrix algebra

This chapter summarizes the matrix algebra necessary to understand the matrix capabilities of Ox. For a more thorough overview consult Magnus and Neudecker (1988), Dhrymes (1984), Rao (1973, Chapter 1) or Anderson (1984, Appendix A), among many others.

To define the elementary operators on matrices we shall write $(a_{ij})_{m,n}$ for the $m \times n$ matrix $\mathbf{A}$ when this is convenient:

$$\mathbf{A} = (a_{ij})_{m,n} = \begin{pmatrix} a_{11} & \cdots & a_{1n} \\ \vdots & & \vdots \\ a_{m1} & \cdots & a_{mn} \end{pmatrix}.$$

So, for example the 3×2 matrix of ones is:

$$\begin{pmatrix} 1 & 1 & 1 \\ 1 & 1 & 1 \end{pmatrix}.$$

- *addition,* $\mathbf{A}$ is $m \times n$, $\mathbf{B}$ is $m \times n$:

$$\mathbf{A} + \mathbf{B} = (a_{ij} + b_{ij})_{m,n}.$$

- *multiplication,* $\mathbf{A}$ is $m \times n$, $\mathbf{B}$ is $n \times p$, c is a scalar:

$$\mathbf{AB} = \left(\sum_{k=1}^{n} a_{ik} b_{kj} \right)_{m,p}, \quad c\mathbf{A} = (ca_{ij})_{m,n}.$$

- *dot-multiplication* (hadamard product), $\mathbf{A}$ is $m \times n$, $\mathbf{B}$ is $m \times n$:

$$\mathbf{A} \odot \mathbf{B} = (a_{ij} b_{ij})_{m,n}.$$

For example:

$$\boldsymbol{\Omega} \odot \mathbf{S} = \begin{pmatrix} \omega_{11} s_{11} & \omega_{12} s_{12} \\ \omega_{21} s_{21} & \omega_{22} s_{22} \end{pmatrix}.$$

- *kronecker product,* $\mathbf{A}$ is $m \times n$, $\mathbf{B}$ is $p \times q$:

$$\mathbf{A} \otimes \mathbf{B} = (a_{ij}\mathbf{B})_{mp,nq} \,.$$

For example, with $\mathbf{\Omega} = (\omega_{ij})_{2,2}$, $\mathbf{S} = (s_{ij})_{2,2}$:

$$\mathbf{\Omega} \otimes \mathbf{S} = \begin{pmatrix} \omega_{11}s_{11} & \omega_{11}s_{12} & \omega_{12}s_{11} & \omega_{12}s_{12} \\ \omega_{11}s_{21} & \omega_{11}s_{22} & \omega_{12}s_{21} & \omega_{12}s_{22} \\ \omega_{21}s_{11} & \omega_{21}s_{12} & \omega_{22}s_{11} & \omega_{22}s_{12} \\ \omega_{21}s_{21} & \omega_{21}s_{22} & \omega_{22}s_{21} & \omega_{22}s_{22} \end{pmatrix}.$$

- *transpose,* $\mathbf{A}$ is $m \times n$:

$$\mathbf{A}' = (a_{ji})_{n,m} \,.$$

- *determinant,* $\mathbf{A}$ is $n \times n$:

$$|\mathbf{A}| = \sum (-1)^{c(j_1,\ldots,j_n)} \prod_{i=1}^{n} a_{ij_i}$$

where the summation is over all permutations $(j_1, \ldots, j_n)$ of the set of integers $(1, \ldots, n)$, and $c(j_1, \ldots, j_n)$ is the number of transpositions required to change $(1, \ldots, n)$ into $(j_1, \ldots, j_n)$. In the 2×2 case the set $(1, 2)$ can be transposed once into $(2, 1)$, so $|\mathbf{\Omega}| = (-1)^0 \omega_{11}\omega_{22} + (-1)^1 \omega_{12}\omega_{21}$.

- *trace,* $\mathbf{A}$ is $n \times n$:

$$\mathrm{tr}\mathbf{A} = \sum_{i=1}^{n} a_{ii}.$$

- *rank,* $\mathbf{A}$ is $m \times n$: the rank of $\mathbf{A}$ is the number of linearly independent columns (or rows, row rank always equals column rank) in $\mathbf{A}$, $\mathrm{r}(\mathbf{A}) \leq \min(m, n)$. If $\mathbf{A}$ is $n \times n$ and of full rank then:

$$\mathrm{r}(\mathbf{A}) = n.$$

- *symmetric matrix,* $\mathbf{A}$ is $n \times n$: $\mathbf{A}$ is symmetric if:

$$\mathbf{A}' = \mathbf{A}.$$

- *matrix inverse,* $\mathbf{A}$ is $n \times n$ and of full rank (non-singular, which is equivalent to $|\mathbf{A}| \neq 0$) then $\mathbf{A}^{-1}$ is the unique $n \times n$ matrix such that:

$$\mathbf{A}\mathbf{A}^{-1} = \mathbf{I}.$$

This implies that $\mathbf{A}^{-1}\mathbf{A} = \mathbf{I}$; $\mathbf{I}$ is the $n \times n$ identity matrix:

$$\begin{pmatrix} 1 & 0 & \cdots & 0 \\ 0 & 1 & \cdots & 0 \\ \vdots & \vdots & & \vdots \\ 0 & 0 & \cdots & 1 \end{pmatrix}.$$

- *orthogonal matrix*, $\mathbf{A}$ is $n \times n$: $\mathbf{A}$ is orthogonal if:

$$\mathbf{A}'\mathbf{A} = \mathbf{I}.$$

Then also $\mathbf{A}\mathbf{A}' = \mathbf{I}$; further: $\mathrm{r}(\mathbf{A}) = n$, $\mathbf{A}' = \mathbf{A}^{-1}$.
- *orthogonal complement*, $\mathbf{A}$ is $m \times n$, $m > n$ and $\mathrm{r}(\mathbf{A}) = n$, define the orthogonal complement $\mathbf{A}_\perp$ as the $m \times (m-n)$ matrix such that: $\mathbf{A}'\mathbf{A}_\perp = \mathbf{0}$ with $\mathrm{r}(\mathbf{A}_\perp) = m - n$ and $\mathrm{r}(\mathbf{A} : \mathbf{A}_\perp) = m$. $\mathbf{A}_\perp$ spans the *null space* of $\mathbf{A}$; $\mathrm{r}(\mathbf{A}_\perp)$ is called the *nullity* of $\mathbf{A}$.
- *idempotent matrix*, $\mathbf{A}$ is $n \times n$: $\mathbf{A}$ is idempotent if:

$$\mathbf{A}\mathbf{A} = \mathbf{A}.$$

An example is the projection matrix $\mathbf{M}_X = \mathbf{I} - \mathbf{X}(\mathbf{X}'\mathbf{X})^{-1}\mathbf{X}'$.
- *vectorization*, $\mathbf{A}$ is $m \times n$:

$$\mathrm{vec}\mathbf{A} = \begin{pmatrix} a_{11} \\ \vdots \\ a_{m1} \\ \vdots \\ a_{1n} \\ \vdots \\ a_{mn} \end{pmatrix},$$

which is an $mn \times 1$ vector consisting of the stacked columns of $\mathbf{A}$.
If $\mathbf{A}$ is $n \times n$ and symmetric, we can use the vech operator to vectorize the unique elements, thus ignoring the elements above the diagonal:

$$\mathrm{vech}\mathbf{A} = \begin{pmatrix} a_{11} \\ \vdots \\ a_{n1} \\ a_{22} \\ \vdots \\ a_{n2} \\ \vdots \\ a_{nn} \end{pmatrix},$$

which is a $\frac{1}{2}n(n+1) \times 1$ vector.

- *diagonalization*, $\mathbf{A}$ is $n \times n$:

$$\mathrm{dg}\mathbf{A} = \begin{pmatrix} a_{11} & 0 & \cdots & 0 \\ 0 & a_{22} & \cdots & 0 \\ \vdots & \vdots & & \vdots \\ 0 & 0 & \cdots & a_{nn} \end{pmatrix} = \mathrm{diag}\,(a_{11}, a_{22}, \ldots, a_{nn}).$$

- *positive definite*, $\mathbf{A}$ is $n \times n$ and symmetric: $\mathbf{A}$ is positive definite if $\mathbf{x}'\mathbf{A}\mathbf{x} > 0$ for all $n \times 1$ vectors $\mathbf{x} \neq \mathbf{0}$, positive semi-definite if $\mathbf{x}'\mathbf{A}\mathbf{x} \geq 0$ for all $\mathbf{x} \neq \mathbf{0}$, and negative definite if $\mathbf{x}'\mathbf{A}\mathbf{x} < 0$ for all $\mathbf{x} \neq \mathbf{0}$.
- *eigenvalues and eigenvectors*, $\mathbf{A}$ is $n \times n$: the eigenvalues of $\mathbf{A}$ are the roots of the characteristic equation:

$$|\mathbf{A} - \lambda\mathbf{I}| = 0.$$

If λ_i is an eigenvalue of $\mathbf{A}$, then $\mathbf{x}_i \neq \mathbf{0}$ is an eigenvector of $\mathbf{A}$ if it satisfies:

$$(\mathbf{A} - \lambda_i\mathbf{I})\,\mathbf{x}_i = \mathbf{0}.$$

- *Choleski decomposition*, $\mathbf{A}$ is $n \times n$ summetric and positive definite, then:

$$\mathbf{A} = \mathbf{P}\mathbf{P}',$$

where $\mathbf{P}$ is a unique lower triangular matrix with positive diagonal elements.
- *LU decomposition*, $\mathbf{A}$ is $n \times n$, then:

$$\mathbf{A} = \mathbf{L}\mathbf{U}',$$

where $\mathbf{L}$ is a lower triangular matrix with ones on the diagonal and $\mathbf{U}$ is upper diagonal.
- *singular value decomposition*, decomposes an $m \times n$ matrix $\mathbf{A}$, $m \geq n$, into:

$$\mathbf{A} = \mathbf{U}\mathbf{W}\mathbf{V}',$$

with:

$\mathbf{U}$ is $m \times n$ and $\mathbf{U}'\mathbf{U} = \mathbf{I}_n$,
$\mathbf{W}$ is $n \times n$ and diagonal, with non-negative diagonal elements,
$\mathbf{V}$ is $n \times n$ and $\mathbf{V}'\mathbf{V} = \mathbf{I}_n$.

The diagonal of $\mathbf{W}$ holds the singular values. The number of non-zero singular values is the rank of $\mathbf{A}$, also see §12.7.5.1.

The SVD can be used to find the orthogonal complement of $\mathbf{A}$. Assume $\mathrm{r}(\mathbf{A}) = n$ and compute the singular value decomposition of the $(m \times m)$ matrix $\mathbf{B} = (\mathbf{A} : \mathbf{0})$. The last $m - n$ diagonal elements of $\mathbf{W}$ will be zero. Corresponding to that are the last $m - n$ columns of $\mathbf{U}$ which form $\mathbf{A}_\perp$:

$$\mathbf{B} = (\mathbf{A} : \mathbf{0}) = \mathbf{U}\mathbf{W}\mathbf{V}' = (\mathbf{U}_1 : \mathbf{U}_2) \begin{pmatrix} \mathbf{W}_1 & \mathbf{0} \\ \mathbf{0} & \mathbf{0} \end{pmatrix} \begin{pmatrix} \mathbf{V}_1' \\ \mathbf{V}_2' \end{pmatrix}.$$

Here $\mathbf{U}$, $\mathbf{V}$ and $\mathbf{W}$ are $(m \times m)$ matrices; $\mathbf{U}_2'\mathbf{U}_1 = \mathbf{0}$ so that $\mathbf{U}_2'\mathbf{A} = \mathbf{U}_2'\mathbf{U}_1\mathbf{W}_1\mathbf{V}_1' = 0$ and $\mathrm{r}(\mathbf{A} : \mathbf{U}_2) = m$ as $\mathbf{U}_2'\mathbf{U}_2 = \mathbf{I}$.

- *differentiation*, define $f(\cdot) : \mathbb{R}^m \mapsto \mathbb{R}$ then:

$$\nabla f = \frac{\partial f(\mathbf{a})}{\partial \mathbf{a}} = \begin{pmatrix} \frac{\partial f(\mathbf{a})}{\partial a_1} \\ \vdots \\ \frac{\partial f(\mathbf{a})}{\partial a_m} \end{pmatrix}, \quad \nabla^2 f = \frac{\partial^2 f(\mathbf{a})}{\partial \mathbf{a}\partial \mathbf{a}'} = \left(\frac{\partial^2 f(\mathbf{a})}{\partial a_i \partial a_j} \right)_{m,m}.$$

If $f(\cdot)$ is a log-likelihood function we shall write $\mathbf{q}(\cdot)$ for the first derivative (or score), and $\mathbf{H}(\cdot)$ for the second derivative (or Hessian) matrix.
For $f(\cdot) : \mathbb{R}^{m \times n} \mapsto \mathbb{R}$ we define:

$$\frac{\partial f(\mathbf{A})}{\partial \mathbf{A}} = \left(\frac{\partial f(\mathbf{A})}{\partial a_{ij}} \right)_{m,n}.$$

- *Jacobian matrix*, for a vector function $\mathbf{f}(\cdot) : \mathbb{R}^m \mapsto \mathbb{R}^n$ we define the $n \times m$ Jacobian matrix $\mathbf{J}$:

$$\frac{\partial \mathbf{f}(\mathbf{a})}{\partial \mathbf{a}'} = \begin{pmatrix} \frac{\partial f_1(\mathbf{a})}{\partial a_1} & \cdots & \frac{\partial f_1(\mathbf{a})}{\partial a_m} \\ \vdots & & \vdots \\ \frac{\partial f_n(\mathbf{a})}{\partial a_1} & \cdots & \frac{\partial f_n(\mathbf{a})}{\partial a_m} \end{pmatrix} = \begin{pmatrix} (\nabla f_1)' \\ \vdots \\ (\nabla f_m)' \end{pmatrix} = (\nabla \mathbf{f})'.$$

The transpose of the Jacobian is called the gradient, and corresponds to the $\mathbf{q}(\cdot)$ above for $n = 1$ (so in that case the Jacobian is $1 \times m$ and the score $n \times 1$). The Jacobian is the absolute value of the determinant of $\mathbf{J}$ when $m = n$: $\|\mathbf{J}\|$.
Normally we wish to compute the Jacobian matrix for a transformation of a coefficient matrix: $\mathbf{\Psi} = \mathbf{F}(\mathbf{\Pi}')$ where $\mathbf{F}$ is a matrix function $\mathbf{F}(\cdot) : \mathbb{R}^{m \times n} \mapsto \mathbb{R}^{p \times q}$:

$$\mathbf{J} = \frac{\partial \mathrm{vec}\mathbf{\Psi}}{\partial (\mathrm{vec}\mathbf{\Pi}')'},$$

with $\mathbf{\Pi}$ $n \times m$ and $\mathbf{\Psi}$ $p \times q$ so that $\mathbf{J}$ is $pq \times mn$.

References

Abramowitz, M. and Stegun, I. A. (1984). *Pocketbook of Mathematical Functions.* Frankfurt/Main: Verlag Harri Deutsch.

Anderson, T. W. (1984). *An Introduction to Multivariate Statistical Analysis* 2nd edition. New York: John Wiley & Sons.

Barnett, S. (1990). *Matrices – Methods and Applications.* Oxford: Clarendon Press.

Berry, K. J., Mielke Jr, P. W. and Cran, G. W. (1977). Remark AS R83: A remark on algorithm AS 109: Inverse of the incomplete beta function ratio, *Applied Statistics*, **39**, 309–310.

Best, D. J. and Roberts, D. E. (1975). Algorithm AS 91: The percentage points of the χ^2 distribution, *Applied Statistics*, **24**, 385–389.

Cooper, B. E. (1968). Algorithm AS 3: The integral of student's t-distribution, *Applied Statistics*, **17**, 189–190.

Cran, G. W., Martin, K. J. and Thomas, G. E. (1977). Remark AS R19 and algorithm AS 109: A remark on algorithms AS 63: The incomplete beta integral; AS 64: Inverse of the incomplete beta function ratio, *Applied Statistics*, **26**, 111–114.

de Jong, P. (1991). The diffuse Kalman filter, *Ann. Statist.*, **19**, 1073–1083.

de Jong, P. and Shephard, N. (1995). The simulation smoother for time series models, *Biometrika*, **82**, 339–50.

Devroye, L. (1986). *Non-Uniform Random Variate Generation.* New York: Springer-Verlag.

Dhrymes, P. J. (1984). *Mathematics for Econometrics* 2nd edition. New York: Springer-Verlag.

Dobbe, J. G. G. (1995). Algorithm alley: Faster FFTs, *Dr. Dobb's Journal*, **February**, 125–133.

Doornik, J. A. and Hendry, D. F. (1994). *PcFiml 8: An Interactive Program for Modelling Econometric Systems.* London: International Thomson Publishing.

Dubrulle, A. (1970). A short note on the implicit ql algorithm for symmetric tridiagonal matrices, *Numerische Mathematik*, **15**, 450.

Fletcher, R. (1987). *Practical Methods of Optimization* 2nd edition. New York: John Wiley & Sons.

Golub, G. H. and Van Loan, C. F. (1989). *Matrix Computations.* Baltimore: The Johns Hopkins University Press.

Granger, C. W. J. and Newbold, P. (1986). *Forecasting Economic Time Series* 2nd edition. New York: Academic Press.

Green, P. J. and Silverman, B. W. (1994). *Nonparametric Regression and Generalized Linear Models. A Roughness Penalty Approach.* London: Chapman and Hall.

Harvey, A. C. (1993). *Time Series Models* 2nd edition. Hemel Hempstead: Harvester Wheatsheaf.

Hastie, T. J. and Tibshirani, R. J. (1994). *Generalized Additive Models.* London: Chapman and Hall.

Hendry, D. F., Neale, A. J. and Ericsson, N. R. (1991). *PC-NAIVE, An Interactive Program for Monte Carlo Experimentation in Econometrics. Version 6.0*. Oxford: Institute of Economics and Statistics, University of Oxford.

Hill, I. D. (1973). Algorithm AS 66: The normal integral, *Applied Statistics*, **22**, 424–427.

Kernighan, B. W. and Ritchie, D. M. (1988). *The C Programming Language* 2nd edition. Englewood Cliffs, NJ: Prentice Hall.

Kiefer, N. M. (1989). The ET interview: Arthur S. Goldberger, *Econometric Theory*, **5**, 133–160.

Koopman, S. J., Shephard, N. and Doornik, J. A. (1996). SSFPack 1.0: Filtering, smoothing and simulation algorithms for state space models in Ox, Nuffield College, Oxford, available at at http://hicks.nuff.ox.ac.uk/shephard/ox.htm.

Lacey, S. and Box, R. (1991). A fast, easy sort, *Byte*, **April**.

Longley, G. M. (1967). An appraisal of least-squares for the electronic computer from the point of view of the user, *Journal of the American Statistical Association*, **62**, 819–841.

Magnus, J. R. and Neudecker, H. (1988). *Matrix Differential Calculus with Applications in Statistics and Econometrics*. New York: John Wiley & Sons.

Majunder, K. L. and Bhattacharjee, G. P. (1973). Algorithm AS 64. Inverse of the incomplete beta function ratio, *Applied Statistics*, **22**, 411–414.

Martin, R. S., Reinsch, C. and Wilkinson, J. H. (1968). Householder's tridiagonalization of a symmetric matrix, *Numerische Mathematik*, **11**, 181–195.

Martin, R. S. and Wilkinson, J. H. (1968a). The implicit *ql* algorithm, *Numerische Mathematik*, **12**, 377–383.

Martin, R. S. and Wilkinson, J. H. (1968b). Similarity reduction of a general matrix to Hessenberg form, *Numerische Mathematik*, **12**, 349–368.

McLeod, I. (1975). Derivation of the theoretical autocovariance function of autoregressive-moving average time series, *Applied Statistics*, **24**, 255–256. Correction in *Applied Statistics*, **26**, 194.

O'Neil, R. (1970). Algorithm AS 47: Function minimization using a simplex procedure, *Applied Statistics*, **20**, 338–345. Improved version in Griffiths, P. and Hill, I. D. (eds) (1985), *Applied Statistics Algorithms*. Chichester: Horwood.

Park, S. and Miller, K. (1988). Random number generators: Good ones are hard to find, *Communications of the ACM*, **31**, 1192–.

Parlett, B. N. and Reinsch, C. (1969). Balancing a matrix for calculation of eigenvalues and eigenvectors, *Numerische Mathematik*, **13**, 293–304.

Peters and Wilkinson, J. H. (1970). Eigenvectors of real and complex matrices by *lr* and *qr* triangulazations, *Numerische Mathematik*, **16**, 181–204.

Petzold, C. (1992). *Programming Windows 3.1*. Redmond: Microsoft Press.

Piessens, R., de Donker-Kapenga, E., Überhuber, C. W. and Kahaner, D. K. (1983). *QUADPACK, A Subroutine Package for Automatic Integration*. Heidelberg: Springer-Verlag.

Press, W. H., Flannery, B. P., Teukolsky, S. A. and Vetterling, W. T. (1988). *Numerical Recipes in C*. New York: Cambridge University Press.

Priestley, M. B. (1981). *Spectral Analysis and Time Series*. London: Academic Press.

Rao, C. R. (1973). *Linear Statistical Inference and its Applications* 2nd edition. New York: John Wiley & Sons.

Ripley, B. D. (1987). *Stochastic Simulation*. New York: John Wiley & Sons.

Shea, B. L. (1988). Algorithm AS 239: Chi-squared and incomplete gamma integral, *Applied Statistics*, **37**, 466–473.

Shea, B. L. (1991). Algorithm AS R85: A remark on algorithm AS 91: The percentage points of the χ^2 distribution, *Applied Statistics*, **40**, 233–235.

Silverman, B. W. (1986). *Density Estimation for Statistics and Data Analysis*. London: Chapman and Hall.

Stroustrup, B. (1988). *The C++ Programming Language* 2nd edition. Reading, MA: Addison Wesley.

Wichura, M. J. (1988). Algorithm AS 241: The percentage points of the normal distribution, *Applied Statistics*, **37**, 477–484.

Wilkinson, J. H. (1965). *The Algebraic Eigenvalue Problem*. Oxford: Oxford University Press.

Wirth, N. (1987). *Compilerbouw*. Schoonhoven, The Netherlands: Academic Service. Dutch version. Original German version published in 1986 by B.G. Teubner Verlag, Stuttgart.

Subject Index